Active Investment Management

Wiley Finance Series

Active Investment Management

Finding and Harnessing Investment Skill

Charles Jackson

WILEY

Other Wiley Editorial Offices

John Wiley & Sons Inc., 111 River Street, Hoboken, NJ 07030, USA

Jossey-Bass, 989 Market Street, San Francisco, CA 94103-1741, USA

Wiley-VCH Verlag GmbH, Boschstr. 12, D-69469 Weinheim, Germany

John Wiley & Sons Australia Ltd, 33 Park Road, Milton, Queensland 4064, Australia

John Wiley & Sons (Asia) Pte Ltd, 2 Clementi Loop #02-01, Jin Xing Distripark, Singapore 129809

John Wiley & Sons Canada Ltd, 22 Worcester Road, Etobicoke, Ontario, Canada M9W 1L1

Wiley also publishes its books in a variety of electronic formats. Some content that appears
in print may not be available in electronic books.

British Library Cataloguing in Publication Data

A catalogue record for this book is available from the British Library

ISBN 0-470-85886-9

Typeset in 10/12pt Times by TechBooks, New Delhi, India
Printed and bound in Great Britain by TJ International Ltd, Padstow, Cornwall, UK
This book is printed on acid-free paper responsibly manufactured from sustainable forestry
in which at least two trees are planted for each one used for paper production.

For Frances, Rebecca and David

Contents

Preface

Active investment management emerged as a term in the 1970s to distinguish it from passive investment management. Before the passive form was invented, all investment management was what we now call active management. The story of active management therefore starts with the story of investment management and the industry that has grown up to provide it.

There is an anecdote about three sages who are ushered into a darkened room and asked to report on what they find. The first one calls out: "It is a sheet of leather." The second one says: "No, it is a hosepipe." The third one says: "You are both wrong. It is a flywhisk." The object is an elephant, and one is holding an ear, one the trunk and one the tail.

Publications about active management, investment skill and the investment industry usually have equally diverse perspectives. No one appears to have looked at the whole beast. Rather, they tend to cover very different types of material.

Books and articles by commentators and journalists about memorable episodes and investors concentrate on what happened and what they did. Papers and books by financial economists study financial markets and corporate finance.[1] Practical guides by investment experts describe how successful practitioners approach specialised areas such as equities, bonds, risk management, pension funds, hedge funds and technical analysis. Financial historians tell the stories of financial markets, centres or institutions.

In developing the story of where active management has come from, where it is today and where it is heading, I have become convinced that all four approaches are relevant. In other words, one needs to combine specific experiences, economic and financial theory, currently accepted industry best practice and knowledge of the way the past has shaped the present.

I have included accounts of episodes that took place around me not only because they played a major role in shaping my own experience but also because they are representative of what was going on at the time. I have used Mercury Asset Management (MAM) as shorthand for the business that started as the Investment Department or Division of SG Warburg & Co. and then became in turn: Warburg Investment Management (WIM), Mercury Warburg Investment Management (MWIM), MAM and finally Merrill Lynch Investment Management (MLIM). Between 1985 and 1998 I was the team leader of the part of the business that specialised in fixed interest and currencies.

I have not written a separate chapter on derivatives because they can be viewed as special forms of ownership of the underlying securities. This is obvious with contracts such as forwards or futures, but it is also true of options. Financial economic theory shows, by making certain assumptions, that a dynamically managed portfolio comprising the correct weights of cash and the security can duplicate an option. Option prices feature in Chapter 6 because the premium the buyer of an option pays the seller or writer is essentially compensation for taking on extra risk. The market price of an option therefore also provides a market price for risk.

The book distinguishes between traditional products, such as mutual funds, and alternative products, such as hedge funds. Traditional products are more heavily regulated, more constrained on investment strategy and more constrained on the form and amount of charges to investors. There is a fundamental problem with actively managed traditional products that is sapping investor confidence and causing a drift towards passively managed and alternative products. This is that, on average, traditional products underperform the benchmarks they are set. Many investors and advisors consider that alternative products do a better job than traditional products of creating value from active management. As they are lightly regulated, they are less constrained on investment strategy and pricing. In particular, they have more freedom to go short of securities, to leverage and to charge performance fees.

The book focuses on three key groups in the industry together with the investors they serve and the financial economists who develop theories about investors and markets. They are: advisors, the management teams of investment firms and investment professionals. Each has a distinct agenda and each has well-established philosophical differences as to what constitutes the best way of going about their tasks.

Advisors work for investors. They form views on setting investment policy, selecting investment managers and formulating discretionary investment mandates. There is a philosophical difference between those advisors who seek discretionary mandates of their own and those advisors who present their views as recommendations. The former group are sometimes called managers of managers. The latter group are usually called either investment consultants, if the investor is an institution, or financial advisors, if the investor is a private individual.

Investment management firms provide investment products to investors. Their investment professionals perform their normal functions but their managers have to make decisions that are business rather than investment in nature. These decisions include fee decisions, operating expense levels, hire–fire and compensation decisions on investment professionals and product structuring decisions. There is a philosophical difference between those firms believing that investment products are bought, or sought out by investors and advisors, and those firms believing that investment products have to be sold, or brought to investors' attention. The former are organised around investment while the latter are organised around distribution.

Investment professionals take decisions on buying and selling securities for the actively managed products with which they are involved. Investment professionals are usually called portfolio managers but, depending on the product's performance-generating process, their main role could be as traders, security analysts, quantitative researchers or economists. There is a philosophical difference between those investment professionals who believe that successful active investment management is an art requiring individual flair and those who believe that it is a science requiring disciplined teamwork.

Investors come in all shapes and sizes but are usually classified geographically: North America, Europe, Far East, etc.; by type: mass market, high net worth, institutional, etc.; and by characteristics such as: attitude to risk and liabilities. Institutional investors include pension funds, insurance companies and endowments while private investors range from owners of pools of capital larger than those of most institutions to individuals who can only afford to invest small amounts. There is a philosophical difference between the investment objectives of institutional investors, who seek to match liabilities and those of private investors, who seek to maximise return after taking account of risk.

Financial economists create theoretical hypotheses and test them empirically. These are designed to predict market and investor behaviour. Over the past 50 years they have developed an interrelated set of ideas, which is sometimes known as Modern Portfolio Theory (MPT). MPT has mounted a radical challenge to conventional thinking about investment. Its main proposition is that investors organise their investments both to maximise expected portfolio return and to minimise expected dispersion of portfolio return. You therefore only have to know the effect an investment opportunity will have on an investor's expected return and dispersion of return to be able to predict what weight he will assign to it in his portfolio.

A key part of MPT is the Efficient Market Hypothesis (EMH). This is that, if dispersion truly reflects risk, then capital markets are perfectly efficient. A simple but powerful conclusion of the EMH is that the best possible portfolio of risky assets an investor can hold is the market portfolio. As the closest possible proxy for the market portfolio is an index fund, the EMH leads directly to passive investing. Some proponents of the EMH reject the possibility of successful active investment management with a quasi-religious fervour. Similarly, some believers in active management reject the EMH and other propositions of MPT with similar zeal.

This is both a pity and unnecessary. MPT is a model that reflects reality. It does so to a reasonable degree of accuracy, but not perfectly. As such, it provides many powerful conceptual insights into the behaviour of investment industry participants. Chapters 6–10, 13 and 14 include examples of such insights.

However, as also described in the text, the evidence of successful active management and my own experience of bond and currency market anomalies lead me to believe that there are a number of commercially exploitable market inefficiencies. These provide a self-correcting mechanism that maintains the overall efficiency of the market. If efficiency falls off, more loopholes appear for longer to attract the enterprising. Their profits draw in more market operators, causing loopholes to close up faster, sometimes crushing the unwary. The existence of these inefficiencies reduces the accuracy of models based on MPT. This is a particular problem for those models dealing with risk.

While financial economists and investment professionals adopting a quantitative approach make extensive use of mathematics, investment professionals adopting a more intuitive approach usually do not. Skilled practitioners of the latter type are still able to do very well for their investors and themselves.

There is a story of a student who was thrown out of business school because he could not perform the simplest calculations. Some years later, he returned as a successful businessman to his alma mater. His professors asked him how he had done it. His reply was: "Well it's simple really. I was experimenting in my garage and I found a way to make something for a hundred dollars. Then I found I could sell it for three hundred dollars. Then I found I could sell a lot more. Boy, those three per cents sure do add up."

Although statistics and calculus are optional extras for investment professionals, both are essential tools for other players: investors and advisors use statistics to assess the chance that an actively managed product has done well through skill rather than through luck; financial economists and advisors use calculus to model market behaviour. Some mathematics is therefore necessary in a book like this and I have used verbal descriptions of a number of mathematical relationships to illustrate points in the main text. For those interested in where these relationships come from, I have cross-referenced them to a Technical Appendix that sets out derivations using equations and mathematical symbols.

ENDNOTE

1. During 1999, 88.8% of the 937 articles submitted to and 88.1% of the 59 articles published in the *Journal of Finance*, the leading journal in this field, were in the two categories "General Financial Markets" and "Corporate Finance and Governance". Report of the Editor, *Journal of Finance*, vol. 55, August 2000.

Acknowledgements

My largest debt of gratitude is owed to the investment professionals, investors, consultants, advisors and brokers, whose wisdom and ingenuity I have tapped through their words or, more often, their deeds. From them and from their activities, I have learnt most of what I know about active management, the investment industry and the behaviour of industry participants.

Any account of active management leads rapidly to the unresolved problems and paradoxes that form such a large part of the landscape of the investment industry. While content for many years to accept these features of the professional environment and work around them, I have always been curious as to why they have come into existence and to what extent they are interrelated. Part of the book is an attempt to indicate possible resolutions of some of these questions, one of the most important of which is the philosophical challenge to active management that comes from financial economics.

I therefore owe a special debt of gratitude to Jack McDonald and the finance faculty of the Stanford Business School, who awakened my interest in the why of investment as well as the how. I would also like to thank James Dow and the finance faculty of the London Business School, who gave me the opportunity to get up to speed on current financial economic thinking by spending two terms as a visiting student attached to their PhD programme.

My warmest thanks are due to Rachael Wilkie and the rest of the editorial team at John Wiley & Sons. Among them, I would especially like to thank Sam Hartley and Chris Swain for all their help and patience. Finally, I am deeply grateful to my wife Frances for her love, support and readiness to tolerate my, at times total, absorption in the project over the past two years.

Part I
Asset Classes and Products

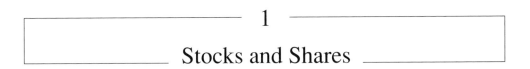

1
Stocks and Shares

Risky assets providing returns to investors have been with us ever since man domesticated animals* and established the first pastoral societies. Assets in the form of herds of cattle and flocks of sheep and goats provided yields in the form of milk and wool. Capital gains came from kids, calves and lambs, while capital could be liquidated to provide meat, tallow and hides. The risk came from the chance that the animals could be stolen or die of disease, drought or starvation.

1.1 THREE KEY PRECONDITIONS

To move from this pastoral world to a modern capitalist society investing in stocks, shares and other equity-related instruments has required three key preconditions.

1.1.1 Property rights

The first precondition was the establishment of a legal framework that defined and protected rights to property. While citizens of the USA, the UK and other advanced capitalist economies take this protection for granted, it does not exist in much of the Third World and the former Soviet bloc, as the following topical examples illustrate:

> After about 50 years of farming in Zimbabwe, Guy Cartwright and his wife, Rosalind, are left with a rented flat in Harare, two vehicles, furniture and a pension worth $5.77 a month after the government seized their property . . . Since the flawed presidential elections last month, 150 white farmers have been evicted illegally from their properties and the pace is gathering. Among the new occupants of the properties are Cabinet ministers, MPs and senior officers of the army, police, secret police and the prisons department.[1]

> An Oxfordshire farmer who set up a business in Romania, tempted by cheap labour and big profits, has seen his £35,000 grain crop stolen from under his nose by the mafia. Tony Sabin, 45, was told "your land is in England" as burly men with guns barred him from fields he had spent three years seeding and fertilising, while the gangland combine harvesters roared into action. What Sabin, and many of his contemporaries who have ventured into the rich alluvial lowlands of Eastern Europe, failed to realise is that although the region has vast tracts of premium soil, their rights may be poorly protected.[2]

Without such protection, a property owner is restricted to what he can physically hold or induce others to hold on his behalf. Transferable securities, or pieces of paper setting out economic rights that can be pledged or sold, are of limited use in such a system. Even with legal backing, it is still sometimes hard to persuade people to accept that a piece of paper is on a par with possessions you can get your arms around.†

Bearer securities were introduced from an early stage that, like banknotes, gave the holder the unconditional right to the underlying assets. An obvious advantage is that they can be shifted

---

* Farmers in the English-speaking world still call their animals stock.
† This perhaps explains the efforts made to ensure that such documents look and feel impressive.

across borders without paperwork.* The bearer form was also used for Eurodollar certificates of deposit (short-dated money market instruments denominated in dollars). When the market for these got going in the 1970s, bearer securities were not familiar in city back offices.

A former colleague was sitting at his desk one day when a clerk appeared before him. The following dialogue ensued.

Clerk: You have just bought $1 m of this.

Colleague: Yes, for the YYY portfolio.

Clerk: Well, it was delivered to us this morning and no one knows what to do with it, so here it is.

Dumps it on desk and withdraws, leaving over 50 years' salary in bearer form. Pause for visions of a life of leisure to clear before said colleague sends the tempting piece of paper to safe custody.

1.1.2   Limited liability

The second key development was the establishment of limited liability. This took some time to happen. Creditors were reluctant to let debtors off the hook in this way. The dominant form of business organisation until the middle of the nineteenth century remained the partnership or its close relative the common law company[†] where, in addition to sharing in the profits, investors were liable to the company's creditors for any losses without limit.

The first step away from unlimited liability was the creation of a special form of enterprise to pursue business objectives considered to be of national importance. Chartered companies were granted the special privilege of limited liability so their securities were easily transferable.[‡]

The most successful English chartered companies were the East India Company and the Bank of England. The East India Company was chartered by Elizabeth I in 1600, with a monopoly on all English trade to the east of the Cape of Good Hope and to the west of the Straights of Magellan. Initially, shareholders only had the right to venture, or invest in trade goods for a specific voyage. Each voyage was separately accounted for. This was quickly changed so that shareholders participated in all voyages pro rata, or in proportion to their shareholdings. William III chartered the Bank of England in 1694 with a monopoly of joint stock, or limited liability, banking in England.

The Bank of England's monopoly of limited liability banking continued until the passage of the Companies Act 1862, which made limited liability a standard corporate feature. The US equivalent of a limited company, a state chartered corporation, also emerged in the nineteenth century.[3] At first, corporations were handled as exceptions, which had to be justified by reference to the public good. Until 1846, those wishing to form a corporation in New York State had to get special laws enacted by the legislature.[4] By the end of the Civil War in 1865, most of the impediments to forming a corporation had been removed. By the end of the century, the limited liability company in the UK and the state chartered corporation in the USA had become the

---

* One former colleague, like most male Swiss nationals, was a member of the army reserve. His job in time of war was to occupy an office at one of the border posts and check, for authenticity, the bearer securities of refugees seeking to enter Switzerland.

† A partnership with transferable interests.

‡ In return for their charters and charter renewals these companies provided large loans on easy terms to the government. This method of raising government finance was known, in a return to the pastoral metaphor, as milking.

dominant legal form for any large business enterprise. There were, of course, exceptions. One of the largest enterprises in America, Carnegie Steel, remained a private partnership until its acquisition in 1901 by US Steel for the then unprecedented consideration of US$447 million.[5]

The problem with unlimited liability as a business structure is that diversification, far from reducing risk, multiplies the chance of being exposed to unlimited loss. A wealthy investor would therefore minimise the number of his investments and ownership of business assets would, and did, remain highly concentrated. Unlimited liability still continues, most notably in partnerships of lawyers and accountants and in Lloyds of London. But even there it is in decline. US courts' interpretations of liabilities resulting from asbestosis and environmental pollution have resulted in claims that have bankrupted many individual underwriters and forced Lloyds to accept limited liability corporate underwriters. The growth in professional indemnity claims is one of the main factors driving lawyers and accountants to incorporate.

1.1.3   Public financial markets

The third key development has been the creation of liquidity and market prices through the establishment of public markets* in financial securities. Liquidity makes investment in long-term assets or claims more attractive as they can be converted into cash provided buyers can be found.

Stocks without a public quotation are known as private, or unquoted, equity. Without market prices, valuations have to rely on historic prices (book value, amortised book value, etc.) or appraisal. As appraisal also relies on the average historic prices of similar assets, valuations that do not use market prices tend both to lag market prices and to be more stable than valuations based on market prices. This can affect behaviour, as John Maynard Keynes commented. Keynes was not only a very influential economist but also a highly successful investor, who made a lot of money for himself and his college.

> Some bursars will buy without a tremor unquoted and unmarketable investments in real estate which, if they had a selling quotation for immediate cash available at each audit, would turn their hair grey. The fact that you do not know how much its ready money quotation fluctuates does not, as is commonly supposed, make an investment a safe one.[6]

By the same token, using market prices for valuations can also affect behaviour. One of MAM's clients in the 1990s was the provident fund of the employees of an agency of a major supranational organisation. Beneficiaries of the fund were given monthly performance reports. A minus sign created a storm of negative feedback for the treasurer. Unsurprisingly, the risk part of the portfolio's objectives boiled down to avoiding negative months. This led to a very conservative investment policy that concentrated on short-dated bonds.

1.2   MARKET PERFORMANCE

While the investors in an enterprise were originally also the businessmen who ran it, the emergence of legal title, limited liability and liquidity in turn led to the emergence of a distinct group of investors owning diversified portfolios of stocks. These investors needed to know how their portfolios were doing in the context of the market.

---

* So called to distinguish them from private trading arrangements. The key feature of a public market such as a stock exchange is that it provides a publicly available quote, or price, for all securities listed, or traded on it. These quotes make it easy to value portfolios of listed securities. The existence of a quote does not necessarily mean that you can sell your position at the quoted level in one transaction. I remember taking over a month in 1980 to sell a million Swiss francs of a Eurobond through the exchange where it was listed. I got my price but had to dribble the position out in over 20 transactions to do it.

1.2.1   Stock indices and performance measurement

Performance measurement originally focused on the average annualised yield achieved. This is known as the money-weighted return (A2.5) and is the best measure of how well or badly a portfolio has done its job of creating wealth for its owner. It is still used for measuring the performance of private equity investments. Its flaw is that two different portfolios with identical asset weights but different cash flows into and out of them will have different money-weighted returns. Thus it does a poor job of measuring whether the asset weights have been successful or not.

The growth of professional investment management and the need to evaluate its results created a demand for a measure that was independent of the effect of cash flows. This measure is known as the time-weighted return (A2.6). As can be seen by comparing the two formulae, the same investment results can produce quite different time-weighted and money-weighted returns.

The increasing popularity of time-weighted returns as a way of measuring the performance of a stock portfolio raised the issue of what these returns should be compared with in order to assess whether the portfolio weights were successful or not. Money invested in stocks could have been invested in cash, so the test of whether a year has been good for stocks is not whether they have had a positive return but whether they have done better than cash. Private equity performance is still compared with cash.

But the availability of market prices allowed analysts to construct hypothetical portfolios of publicly quoted stocks against which actual portfolios of publicly quoted stocks could be compared. As the purpose of the comparison was to assess manager skill, time-weighted performance was measured. If the manager constructed his own benchmark, there was always the risk that he would create one that made him look good. There was thus a need for benchmarks provided by independent third parties.

Time series of price data on individual stock prices and market averages began to be collected. The Dow Jones average was first published in the USA in 1885 and, as the name suggests, is an average of the prices of 30 leading shares. It is designed to be simple to calculate and to answer the question: are stock prices going up or down?

An average like the Dow Jones gives the same weight to each price, irrespective of the value of the underlying company. It does not necessarily tell you whether the value of the market is going up or down. An average that provides a better answer to the market question is one that is weighted by value of company, or market capitalisation. Products known as capitalisation-weighted indices* were introduced: the Standard & Poor's (S&P) index family was started in 1957 in the USA and what is now called the Financial Times Stock Exchange (FTSE) index family was started in 1962 in the UK. Predictably, the S&P 500 tracks the top 500 US companies while the FTSE 100 tracks the top 100 UK companies. As we will see later, the market return has an important place in modern thinking about investment.

1.2.2   Twentieth century performance

Researchers have now reconstructed index data going back to the beginning of the last century. There are thus estimates available of price movements that span generations of financial market participants. The annual equity gilt study published by Barclays Capital provides one such

---

* An early attempt at a capitalisation-weighted metric was prepared in the UK by *The Bankers Magazine* from January 1907 onwards. It tracked the value of 387 representative securities traded on the stock exchange made up of 108 fixed interest securities and 279 shares, which were then described as "speculative securities". Subsequent indices monitored the two classes of security separately.

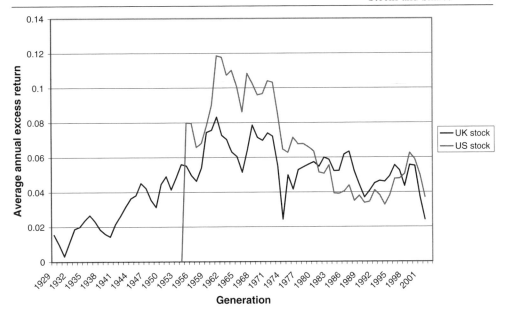

Figure 1.1   Stock returns for different generations
(Raw data sourced from Barclays Capital)

database[7] (Barcap). This tracks the returns on stocks, bonds and cash in the UK since 1900 and in the USA since 1926.

Stocks have beaten cash in more than half the years covered by the study. Over the period since 1926, the US stock market beat cash in 51 years out of 77. Its worst year was 1931 when the market underperformed cash by 46.6%, while its best year was 1933 when the market beat cash by 60.6%.

Over the full period since 1900, the UK stock market beat cash in 61 years out of 103. Over the period since 1926, it beat cash in 47 years out of 77. Its worst year was 1974 when the market underperformed cash by 55.7%, and its best year was 1975 when the market beat cash by 125%. The chance of cash beating the market is therefore approximately one in three in the USA and two in five in the UK.

It is a well known mathematical fact that averaging the performance stocks achieve against cash for each year always exaggerates the long-term annualised average return.* Using the standard correction for this, the annualised average extra return on stocks relative to cash was 5.8% in the USA and 3.9% in the UK. The experience of investing in stocks over the full period was thus very positive in both the USA and the UK.

But both capital markets and capital market participants have undergone several cycles of change since 1926, let alone 1900. It is possible that people tend to attach more importance to market movements they or a colleague have actually experienced than to market movements experienced by previous generations, which they might view as irrelevant ancient history. Figure 1.1 plots the average return relative to cash for different 30-year periods. Thus, for

---

* Thus in the UK, the performance of stocks relative to cash over the two years 1974 and 1975 is −0.3%, or an annualised average of −0.15%. But the arithmetic average of the two relative returns of −55.7% and 125% is 34.7%, which is clearly misleading. Following standard practice, I will correct for this going forward by using natural logarithms [(A1.5)–(A1.7)], which have the effect of creating geometric averages. A further advantage of logarithms is that they are consistent with limited liability as no return that can be expressed as a logarithm can ever take a stock price into negative territory.

example, the period between 1931 and 1960 inclusive could be taken to represent the collective experience of market participants in 1960.

Different generations of market participants have seen things rather differently. The figure shows that generational experience of equity excess returns has varied between nearly 12% and below 4% in the USA and between 8% and nearly zero in the UK.* Despite this discrepancy, the US experience has not consistently bettered the UK experience. For those investors who were active in the markets between the early 1980s and the mid-1990s, the UK stock market experience was actually better than the US stock market experience. Because the current generation has experienced both the 2000–2 and the 1973–4 bear markets, its experience is at the low end of the range in both countries.

Although equity excess returns have been positive for every generation so far, the wide variation in results experienced by different generations means that the past is a rather imperfect guide to the future. Both the UK and the USA have just experienced three consecutive years of negative excess returns between 2000 and 2002. The last time both countries experienced a simultaneous three-year bear market was the period, starting with the year of the great US stock market crash, between 1929 and 1931. Individual bear markets of this longevity are also ancient history. The last time the USA experienced a three-year bear market was between 1930 and 1932, while the last time the UK experienced a three-year bear market was a generation later between 1960 and 1962. These bear phases have therefore proved the exception rather than the rule. The critical question for long-term equity investors is to what extent this will continue to be the case.

This question also has a bearing on active investment management. For if one can reliably expect that a passive investment in stocks will beat cash by a substantial margin over long periods of time, successful active management is not an essential prerequisite for achieving excess returns. Indeed, active management itself becomes an optional extra. But if this margin becomes slender or unreliable, successful active management becomes essential for investors seeking to beat cash and prepared to take some risk to do it.

1.3   ACTIVE EQUITY MANAGEMENT

The emergence of a separate group of investors and a specialised discipline of performance measurement led in turn to an investment management industry specialising in actively managing the delegated assets of investors. Investment professionals, who are organised into investment firms,[†] select portfolios of stocks for investors. Investment banks provide execution, or help in buying and selling stocks, and research services. A peculiarity of the industry, which will be discussed further in Chapter 13, is that research is generally paid for by a margin added to the cost of execution.

At the same time, the availability of price and accounting data has fuelled the growth of academic financial research by providing ready means to test theoretical propositions empirically. The US led the way in this and the historical databases on US stocks such as CRSP and COMPUSTAT are unparalleled elsewhere in the world for breadth, depth and accessibility.

All investment professionals involved in active management show skill by successfully predicting which financial asset prices are going up, on a relative or absolute basis, and which

---

* The two ranges are not directly comparable because of the shorter US data series.
† Some of these firms have become very large enterprises. In the UK, two leading specialist investment management companies demerged from their associated investment banking businesses (MAM in 1995 and Schroder in 2001). Both (Schroder immediately and MAM after a year) joined the FTSE 100, or index of the UK's largest 100 companies.

are going down. Many active equity managers follow the discipline of trying both to forecast cash flows and to estimate the present value of these cash flows relative to market price. The most popular active equity strategies are to invest either in growth stocks or in small stocks. Chapter 11 presents evidence that both these strategies do particularly well in equity bull markets. This chapter also provides a much more detailed account of how active managers go about their task.

1.3.1   Dividend valuation models

The only payments companies make to their shareholders and therefore the only corporate information that is automatically disclosed is the level of dividends.* It was therefore natural for analysts to project dividends forward, discount projected dividends back to the present at a suitable rate and treat the result as an estimate of the stock's value. If this value was higher than the price, the stock was cheap. If lower, the stock was expensive.

The constant growth model illustrates the relationship between price, yield, expected return and dividend growth rate in the simplest possible case where the dividend growth rate is constant. The price is equal to the prospective dividend divided by the return less the growth rate (A2.21). The annual return that can be expected is equal to the prospective dividend yield plus the dividend growth rate (A2.22).

The model gives some simple insights into the relationship of the stock market with the economy. Thus, if the share of the economy represented by dividends is constant, the growth in dividends will equal the growth in the economy. If the growth rate falls and the expected return on stocks is constant, equation (A2.21) tells us that the value of the market has to fall. Similarly, if a historical bull market, or period of high returns, drives equity yields down then equation (A2.22) tells us that one of three things has to happen to preserve excess return. The real growth rate has to go up or the share of dividends in the economy has to go up or the real risk-free rate has to go down.

What dividend valuation models fail to take into account is that, if companies reinvest earnings profitably, they will grow and dividend yields lower than bond yields are possible, as long as the equity risk premium, or required extra return from equities relative to bonds, is lower than the dividend growth rate. A UK broker's recommendation[8] from 50 years ago illustrates that the UK stock market was taking its time to adjust its thinking to incorporate the information on retained earnings made available by the 1948 Companies Act.

> Peninsular and Oriental Steam Navigation Company stood at £2.9375 to yield 5.25%. The dividend was covered 9.5 times by earnings for a historic price to earnings ratio of 2. The estimated asset value per share was £9 [February 1953].

UK active managers in the 1950s thus had an excellent opportunity to take advantage of information that companies were required to publish but which the market was not incorporating into prices. When the adjustment eventually took place, the shift in emphasis from dividends to profits resulted in an important development. In 1958 in the USA and 1959 in the UK, equity yields fell below bond yields. Since then, the yield gap has always been negative in both countries, although it is now (February 2003) very close to zero in the UK, suggesting that the UK market currently equates the dividend growth rate with the equity risk premium.

---

* Until the UK Companies Act 1948 required companies to publish accounts consolidating the profits and balance sheets of their subsidiaries, they only had to report the dividends paid by subsidiaries. Dividends were thus the only publicly available information that reflected subsidiary performance.

1.3.2   Growth stocks

The availability of good quality public earnings information meant that the price to earnings ratio replaced dividend yield as the key tool used by investment professionals for assessing the attractiveness of a given share. Self-financed growth prospects were recognised as different for companies in businesses with high earnings growth potential, or growth stocks, from those for companies in businesses with low earnings growth potential, or value stocks.*

The earnings growth rate is the correct growth rate to use in equations (A2.21) and (A2.22) provided that the payout ratio, or ratio of dividends to earnings, is constant. Equation (A2.22) shows how high earnings growth rates equate to high returns for stocks with constant payout ratios. This explains why growth stocks are so attractive to investors.

Equation (A2.21) shows that, as the expected growth rate approaches the expected return, anything up to an infinite share price can be justified. This gives some insight into why even much more sophisticated models than the constant growth model were able to justify very full valuations of new economy stocks in the 1990s, which subsequently joined the "90% club" or the "99% club".†

1.3.3   Small stocks

Many practitioners believe that small capitalisation stocks do better than large capitalisation stocks. From 1926 to 1997, one study showed that small stocks outperformed large stocks in the USA by 1.5% per annum.[9] This message finds a receptive audience among both investment professionals and investors. The intuitive argument in favour of concentrating on small stock investment is that some small stocks become large ones so that a portfolio containing enough exposure to successful small stocks will beat the broad market average.

Another attraction of specialist small stock investment is that small capitalisation stocks are less intensively researched and therefore may offer more opportunity for superior stock selection. However, the outperformance has not been consistent. In the USA, most of the historical outperformance of small stocks was concentrated in the years between 1975 and 1983.[10]

1.3.4   Sorting active approaches

In addition to growth and small stocks, investment professionals specialise in many other groups of stocks. Investors and their advisors have taken to sorting them accordingly. There are two purposes to this.

First, comparing the performance of investment professionals adopting similar approaches is likely to prove a better test of active management skill than comparing the performance of investment professionals adopting different approaches. This is because the market sector favoured by one approach may perform better than that favoured by another approach, resulting in relative performance that has little to do with active management skill. For example, an investment professional concentrating on small stocks may select small stocks very unskilfully but still outperform the broad market index because small stocks on average have outperformed

---

* So called because they tended to have more assets per share, or higher book to market asset ratios, and higher dividend yields than growth stocks.
† The percentages refer to the decline in stock price from the peak.

Table 1.1

	Growth	Blend	Value
Large capitalisation	X	X	X
Intermediate	X	X	X
Small capitalisation	X	X	X

the index by more than his choices have underperformed the small stock average. Second, it gives investors the opportunity to diversify their share portfolios by dividing them between approaches favouring different kinds of stocks.

The US mutual fund tracking firms Morningstar Inc. and Lipper Inc. adopt a classification scheme with the 3×3 matrix of Table 1.1 at its centre, which captures the two key dimensions of growth and size.

In addition to this scheme for general equity funds, there is a special group of sector fund categories, which cover products investing in one industry or group of industries. The Lipper sector fund categories are: Science and Technology, Health and Biotechnology, Utilities, Natural Resources and Gold-Orientated.

1.4   INSTITUTIONAL INVESTORS

In 1945, individuals owned between 60 and 70% of quoted equities in the UK.[11] By the end of 1999, this had fallen to 15.3%. Three types of investor benefited: foreigners now owned 29.3 %, pension funds now owned 19.3% and insurance companies now owned 21.6%.[12] Pension funds and life insurance companies are collectively known as institutional investors. At the end of 1999, the total assets of UK life insurers were £977 billion while the total assets of UK pension funds were £824 billion.[13]

Institutional investors handle long-term savings for individuals and thus form part of the investment industry. Annual premiums or contributions are invested in a life fund or pension fund, which generates a lump sum on retirement that is then used to buy a fixed retirement income. In order to encourage this activity, the government exempts such premiums and contributions from tax. What is distinctive about them is that they attempt to reduce investors' exposure to unexpected market losses. This gives them an added appeal to investors over that of investment firms who merely pass on the risks and returns (less fees) of the portfolios they manage to the investors who own them.

The dominant form of life insurance retirement product is the with-profits policy while the dominant form of pension fund is the defined benefit fund. The past strength and present weakness of both is their flexibility. In neither case is the final payment equal to the cumulative annual payments plus investment returns minus expenses.

1.4.1   Life insurance

The final payout on a with-profits policy is largely at the discretion of the life insurer, who can smooth returns or profits to shield the policyholder from the effects of stock market volatility by protecting him from the adverse effects of retiring in the middle of a stock market downturn. The disadvantage is that policyholders' payments can be affected by factors other than the return on the investments made on their behalf. Two recent episodes in the UK, involving mis-selling and guaranteed annuity rates, have highlighted this weakness and accelerated a move towards products that segregate investors' assets.

In the first episode, many UK investors were able to claim compensation from insurance companies unable to prove to their regulator's satisfaction that they had made the required disclosures when the policies were initiated. 68 out of 72 companies paid the compensation out of their life funds, thus transferring wealth from those investors who had not claimed compensation to those who had. The remaining four passed the costs to their shareholders.[14]

In the second episode, UK insurance companies guaranteed the rate at which they converted their final payouts into annuities for certain investors. Falling annuity rates made it likely that these guarantees would be expensive to meet. As at December 2002, UK life insurers had provided in excess of £12 billion against their anticipated costs.[15] At the time of writing, it seems likely that the bulk of these costs will be borne by the life funds, i.e. the unguaranteed investors.*

1.4.2   Pension funds

The final payout on a defined benefits pension scheme is a function of final salary and years of service. Annual payments† are made to the scheme designed to be sufficient to provide the expected final payout for each beneficiary provided security returns meet expectations. Once again, beneficiaries are protected from the effects of unexpected falls in the stock market. In this case, the employer or sponsor guarantees the benefits. The sponsor originally had two great advantages. First, attrition meant that very few employees remained until retirement. Those who left early were only able to transfer a fraction of the savings made on their behalf to the funds of their new employers.‡ This reduced costs. Second, the sponsor had a large measure of discretion over the timing and size of payments into and out of the fund. He was thus able to use it as a tax advantaged corporate savings scheme.

Regulation has eroded both advantages over time at the same time as increased life expectancy has increased the sponsor's financial exposure. In response to this, the recent trend in both the UK and the USA has been for sponsors to close§ or close to new entrants schemes offering defined benefits and replace them with defined contribution schemes where the beneficiary has segregated assets but no sponsor guarantee.

1.5   CONCLUSION

Since the general introduction of limited liability in the late nineteenth century, diversified portfolios of stocks and shares have become the principal form in which investors commit risk

---

* The UK mutual insurer Equitable Life sought to protect its unguaranteed investors by reducing its final payouts to its guaranteed investors by the cost of their guarantees. In 2000, this was ruled illegal in a surprise decision by the House of Lords (the UK supreme court). As Equitable was a mutual with no shareholders to pick up the tab, this ruling put all the different classes of policyholders at each other's throats.

† These payments are sometimes made by the employer alone and sometimes by the employees and employer together. The former is known as a non-contributory scheme. The distinction is more apparent than real as the employer treats contributions on the employee's behalf as another form of employee compensation.

‡ My first three jobs lasted two, three and four years. Each employer had a non-contributory defined benefit scheme with delayed vesting. By leaving each firm early, I lost all nine years' accrued benefit.

§ As members of recently closed schemes in the UK have discovered, adequate funding for regulatory purposes is not necessarily sufficient to hedge all a closed scheme's accrued liabilities with an insurer. In such a case, because retired members have priority over active members, their pensions are honoured in full if funds are sufficient. This leaves a much reduced pot for active members who consequently have significantly to reduce their expectations of benefits. The public rightly perceives this as unfair but action to correct it will increase the burden on sponsoring firms and accelerate the rate of closure.

capital to business enterprise. Stocks, shares and all other forms of financial asset also rely on legally protected property rights and liquid security markets. During the twentieth century, the return on stocks in the USA and the UK has exceeded the return on cash and other forms of financial investment by a wide margin. This has not been without risk. In any single year, the probability of stocks underperforming cash has been one-third in the USA and two-fifths in the UK.

The increase over the twentieth century in the value of holdings of stocks and shares has resulted in the emergence of equity investors, as distinct from the businessmen who run the underlying enterprises. This in turn has led to demand for the services of the specialists who collectively form the investment industry. Investment professionals seeking to beat the broad market averages have tended to concentrate either on stocks with a shared characteristic such as growth potential or small size or on stocks within a specific industry or market sector. These distinctions form the basis of schemes to classify different approaches to active management. The twentieth century also saw a shift in the pattern of ownership from individuals to intermediaries, or institutional investors, who specialise in transforming risk and reward. The disadvantages of indirect ownership are beginning to cause this trend to reverse.

ENDNOTES

1. *Times*, 22 April 2002.
2. *Sunday Times*, 9 September 2001.
3. "In 1814, Francis Cabot Lowell, a Boston merchant, founded the first (US) public company, when he built a textile factory on the banks of the Charles River in Waltham, Massachusetts, and called it the Boston Manufacturing Company." *The New Yorker*, 23 September 2002.
4. Paul Johnson, *A history of the American People*. London: Weidenfeld, 1997, p. 466.
5. Johnson, p. 461.
6. J. Maynard Keynes, Memo for the Estates Committee, King's College, 8 May 1938 [quoted in J.J. Siegel, *Stocks for the Long Run*. New York: McGraw-Hill, 1998, p. 232].
7. Available on www.equity-giltstudy@barcap.com. The US data comes from the Centre for Research in Security Prices (CRSP) at the Chicago University GSB.
8. Quoted in J. Littlewood, *The Stock Market*. London: Financial Times Management, 1998, p. 85.
9. Siegel, p. 94. Siegel uses the performance of the bottom quintile by size of the stocks quoted on the New York Stock Exchange as a proxy for small stocks from 1926 to 1981.
10. Siegel, p. 95. All the outperformance of these stocks came between 1975 and 1983, when small stocks outperformed large stocks by 19.6% per annum. Excluding these nine years, small stocks underperformed large stocks in the study by 0.7% per annum.
11. Littlewood, p. 6.
12. ONS: Share ownership. A report on the ownership of shares at 31/12/99, p. 8.
13. Institutional investment in the UK, a review. HM Treasury report, chaired by P. Myners, March 2001, p. 127 and *Pension Fund Indicators*, UBS Global Asset Management 2000, p. 16.
14. Letter in the *Times*, 18 December 2002.
15. *Times*, 16 December 2002.

2
Investment Products

When an investor delegates the management of part or all of his wealth to an investment firm, it is important that both firm and investor have the same understanding of what the firm is going to do with the money. This understanding, or investment agreement, covers topics such as investor objectives, investor policy, performance measurement, fees and guidelines, or the degree of discretion the investor is prepared to give. All these are discussed in greater detail in later chapters.

An investment firm can have an investment agreement with either an individual investor or a group of investors. The former gives rise to a segregated portfolio while the latter, where all the investors accept the same terms, gives rise to a pooled product. A pooled product is clearly attractive to an investment firm, as it allows the firm to capture economies of scale by managing all the investors' portfolios as a single portfolio. Where segregated portfolios are managed on similar terms, the investment firm can group them together and manage them as (almost) a single portfolio. Such groups of segregated portfolios are also often referred to as a product.

2.1   TRADITIONAL PRODUCTS

Products can be classified according to how their guidelines deal with three factors, which are generally reckoned to have a major influence on portfolio uncertainty: illiquidity, as the investor risks not being able to realise his portfolio when he needs it; short selling and leverage,* as both can cause portfolio bankruptcy if stock prices go too far in the wrong direction. Traditional open-ended products proscribe all three, or severely limit them. Traditional pooled products divide into two kinds.

2.1.1   Closed-end products

The widespread availability of limited liability in the UK from 1862 led rapidly[†] to the introduction of investment companies which invested in portfolios of publicly traded financial securities and financed themselves by issuing other securities. No new legal framework had to be introduced as the agreements between investors in such companies and the investment firms that managed them were exactly the same as the agreements between any investor and the management of a company he invests in. However, the prospectus usually set out what kinds of assets the company would acquire and what restrictions it would have on leverage and short selling. Many investment firms trace their origins to the role of managing investment companies of this type.[‡]

---

* Short selling is selling stock you have not got, while leverage is buying stock with borrowed money. As the possible rise in the share you have shorted is unlimited, the loss is also unlimited. As the stock you buy on credit may go to zero, the loss from leverage is only limited by the borrowings themselves.

[†] One of the first, Foreign & Colonial Investment Trust, was launched in 1868.

[‡] Such products are called "closed-end" because the portfolio is unaffected by investor transactions. Performance measurement is simple and unambiguous. With no investor cash flows, time-weighted returns equal money-weighted returns.

The problem with securities issued by such companies was and is that their price does not need to bear any fixed relationship to the value of their share of the underlying assets of the company. Depending on supply, demand and market perception, it can be higher (at a premium) or lower (at a discount). The volatility of this relationship adds another layer of risk for the investor. Worse, the management of an investment company trading at a premium will always be tempted to try to grow revenues by issuing more securities, investing the proceeds in the market and hoping that the expanded portfolio continues to trade at a premium. The possibility of this tends to keep market prices at a discount to asset values. When prices are at a discount, the process can be reversed and value created by liquidating assets and using the proceeds to buy back shares in the investment company (essentially the same assets at a discount). Unfortunately, the interests of the investor and management now conflict as the lost assets result in lower management compensation as these products usually charge fees as a percentage of assets under management.

The tendency to go to a discount makes it hard to raise capital for investment companies of this type and investors tend to insist on management committing to buy-back* programmes and open-ending provisions.[†]

Closed-end products can be arranged into schemes with interlocking ownership, which have the effect of leveraging control and, if debt is introduced, performance. This activity is known as financial engineering. To illustrate the effect on control of such schemes, I will define control as owning at least 50% of the equity.

Such a scheme might comprise a series of companies: A, B and C. Company A has capital of two dollars. The scheme promoter subscribes one dollar to A and sells the other dollar to the public. He then floats B with capital of four dollars. A invests its entire capital in B and the other two dollars of B's securities are sold to the public. He then floats C with capital of eight dollars in which B invests its four dollars and the other four dollars is sold to the public. Thus a three-tiered scheme allows one dollar to control eight. Clearly, the more tiers there are, the less needs to be put up to control a given amount in the bottom tier.

To illustrate the effect on performance of such schemes, once debt is introduced, consider a series of companies: X, Y and Z. Each can borrow up to 50% of assets. Company X has capital of four dollars of which two dollars is equity and two dollars is debt. The scheme promoter buys one dollar of the equity and sells the other to the public as before. He then floats Y with capital of $16 again evenly divided between debt and equity. X uses its entire capital to buy half the equity. By the time Z has been floated on the same terms, the original dollar will be controlling 64. Because of the leverage, movements in the value of the assets of the company in the bottom tier have a geared effect on movements in the value of the equity in the higher tiers. In the example, a drop of 12.5% in the value of the assets of company Z reduces the value of Z's equity by 25%, which results in a drop of 50% in the value of company Y's equity, which in turn wipes out company X's equity.

Schemes to lever performance and control were commonplace in investment company promotions during the run up to the great crash in October 1929. One such scheme[1] involved the launch of three companies in quick succession: the Goldman Sachs Trading Corporation (launched December 1928), the Shenandoah Corporation (launched July 1929) and the Blue Ridge Corporation (launched August 1929). Each was a substantial investor in the company in the tier below and the bottom two companies were highly leveraged. In addition, the top

---

* As the term suggests, programmes where cash generated by the company is committed to buying the company's securities.
† Open-ending provisions give investors the right to vote periodically on whether to convert the company to an open-ended structure.

company bought back about two-thirds of the stock it sold to the public. The result was that stock in the top company was issued at US$104, touched US$222.5 after the buy-backs and by 1932 had fallen to US$1.75.

In 1972, Sir Denys Lowson, a former Lord Mayor of London, together with members of his family and business associates, bought 80% of the shares in the National Group of Unit Trusts from 10 investment companies. These 10 companies formed part of a wider group of 32 investment companies that were either unquoted or publicly quoted in the UK and with which Lowson was closely involved. The Lowson private interests then sold the National shares in early 1973, at a multiple of nearly 14 times what they paid, to generate a profit for themselves of £4.8 million. The subsequent outcry was such that Lowson issued the following statement in July 1973:

> The transaction has been criticised, and I have felt obliged to consider very carefully whether, irrespective of the strict legal position, it would be right to retain the benefits arising from it. I have come to the conclusion that it would be wrong for me to do so, and that it would be in accordance with the best traditions of the City of London, which I have served for some 45 years, for me to restore the position.

The findings of the subsequent enquiry[2] shed some light on why Lowson felt impelled to give the money back and why his references to best traditions and service were felt by some to contain more than a hint of irony. It painstakingly analysed the cross-holdings of the Lowson group and found an interlocking web of control where all but two companies had more than 50% of their shares owned by other Lowson companies or interests.

More recently, UK Split Capital Investment Trusts (SCITs) have provided a contemporary example of the performance effect of leverage. A SCIT issues two forms of security: zero coupon instruments,* which are secured by the capital of the trust, and shares, which entitle the owner to the trust's income and the residual capital value after the zeros have been paid off. These shares are by definition leveraged because of the zeros. But the practice grew up of investing in the shares of other SCITs. The more shares a SCIT buys in other SCITs, the more performance leverage it acquires. The leverage comes both from its own zero coupons and from the leverage of the SCIT shares it owns. Figure 2.1 shows the average performance and number in each group of groups of SCITs with different levels of ownership in other SCIT shares over the two years from end March 1999, as calculated by the FSA.[3] Because of limited liability, the performance could not be less than minus 100%. Over the same period, the FTSE 100 returned −16.2%.

2.1.2 Open-ended products

Open-ended structures rely on market prices for their operation. Portfolios are valued at market price and this value is divided by the number of units outstanding to give the net asset value per unit (NAV). New investors can buy units at NAV while investors taking money out can exchange units for cash at NAV. There is no discount problem. This simple but powerful advantage has, over time, established the open-ended structure as the product structure of choice.[†]

---

* These are bonds that pay no income but promise to pay a fixed capital sum on maturity. They are priced at a discount to this and their yield is given by setting C to zero in (A2.7).

[†] As the cash flows take place at NAV, the return on a constant number of units equals the time-weighted return. For this reason, time-weighted return is sometimes called unitised return.

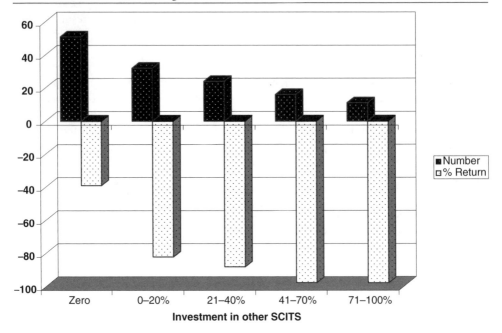

Figure 2.1   Effect of leverage on performance

The first US open-ended product, Massachusetts Investment Trust, was launched in 1924,[4] while the first UK open-ended product was launched in 1931 by Municipal and General Securities.* By 1944,[5] the volume of assets in US open-ended products such as mutual funds had overtaken the volume of assets in US closed-end products. This only happened in the UK in 1985.[6]

One reason for the relatively slow advance of the open-ended structure was that unlike closed-end products, which were able to fit into company law, the investment industry and its regulators have needed to develop new procedures, rules and regulations for open-ended products. These have resulted in slightly different treatment of the two key areas of product bankruptcy and equity between investors.

When a closed-end product goes bankrupt, the normal rules of corporate bankruptcy apply. When an open-ended product goes bankrupt, responsibility for any shortfall in assets is much less clear-cut. Regulators and investment firms consequently assign a high priority to preventing open-ended products from going bust. With regulators, this response takes the form of banning, or severely restricting, leverage and short positions in those open-ended products that fall into their jurisdictions.

Although traditional open-ended products rarely need to make use of it, there is a simple alternative way to avoid product bankruptcy. This is for the product manager to monitor NAV against the worst case cost of liquidating the product's positions and to liquidate if NAV falls to this level. "Most [commodity trading] fund prospectuses contain a clause that calls for the fund to dissolve if ... the net asset value per share falls below a predetermined level (most often 25 to 30 per cent of the initial capital an investor pays in)."[7]

---

* The present-day M&G.

With a closed-end product, while some shareholders may be more equal than others in terms of control, all are equitably treated to the extent that they have the same proportionate claim on the assets of the product. Things are not so straightforward with an open-ended product, where the mechanism is biased towards benefiting investors who buy or sell units at the expense of those who stay put.

To illustrate this, let us assume that the product manager does not want subscriptions and redemptions to affect product policy or active strategy. A subscription therefore has to be invested in a miniature version of the existing portfolio. For equity to be maintained between the new investor and the existing investor, the prices paid have to be the same as the prices used to calculate the NAV. But they are likely to be higher as net investment tends to take place in times of rising prices and buying pushes prices up in any case. The subscription therefore increases the size of the portfolio by a smaller fraction than the increase in the number of units. The new investor consequently gains at the expense of the existing investors.

Similarly, if an investor withdraws money, a miniature version of the existing portfolio has to be sold. If the prices achieved in the actual sale are lower than the prices used to calculate NAV, which is likely as net disinvestment tends to take place in times of falling prices and selling pushes prices down in any case, the exiting investor gains at the expense of the investors who stay.

The key to equity between investors in open-ended products is therefore the accuracy with which the prices used to calculate NAV reflect the actual prices obtained in the market. The more liquid and diversified the securities in the underlying portfolio are, the more accurate the match and the more equitable the product. Not surprisingly, regulations emphasise liquidity and diversification.

Although traditional products make limited use of them, other mechanisms are available to maintain equity. First, the product manager can charge subscribers more than he pays redeemers. The difference between the two prices, or spread, should reflect the bid to offer spread of the underlying securities. Second, the manager can demand a notice period for subscriptions and redemptions. Third, he can restrict subscriptions and redemptions by, say, setting a limit on the size of transactions within a set period. The less liquid the securities in the underlying portfolio are, the wider the spread, the longer the notice period and the more onerous the restrictions have to be.

2.1.3 Index products

Index products are well adapted to the open-ended structure as the securities in their underlying portfolios are well diversified and, in the case of large capitalisation indices, highly liquid. Chapter 1 introduced the concept of capitalisation-weighted indices. We will see in Chapter 6 that these form a good proxy for the market portfolio, which is the best possible portfolio to hold if markets are efficient. Index funds were introduced over 30 years ago, shortly after financial economists developed efficient market theory.

At first sponsors were worried about replicating indices fully. Wells Fargo introduced one of the earliest index funds in 1970. "It chose to replicate the S&P 500 except for a few issues that seemed to be in danger of bankruptcy. The latter were omitted out of some concern about liability exposure relating to the prudent man rule."[8] Fortunately, the emphasis on portfolio rather than individual security risk in the 1974 US Employee Retirement Income Security Act (ERISA) soon laid these fears to rest.

Because decisions about what proportions of which stocks to own are taken out of the product managers' hands, index funds are also known as passive products. Passive products are the logical investment for those who believe either that markets are efficient or that it is impossible in practice to find superior active managers. They are also attractive to investors because they are low cost.

The share of such products has been growing. Over 25% of US institutional assets and 20% of UK institutional assets were already indexed by 2000.

As the index designer sets the rules that determine portfolio construction, there is no need for the index fund provider to have expensive investment decision makers. Turnover is only generated by corporate events and by securities entering and leaving the index. Transactions costs are consequently lower than those of the typical active fund.

By sponsoring firm revenue, indexed products are still tiny compared to active products. The reason for this discrepancy is that index funds based on standard indices such as the S&P 500 are a commodity and compete on price. Competitive pressures have driven the fees down to less than one basis point, or one-hundredth of 1% of assets, for large institutional investors. For small private investors, the Barclays Global Investors (BGI) Exchange Traded S&P 500 Index Fund charges nine basis points while index, or tracker, equity mutual funds charge 20 basis points in the USA and 50 basis points in the UK.

A general problem with capitalisation-weighted indices is that some investors are more willing to trade their shares than others. Shares held by such investors are described as the free float, while shares held by investors who are unwilling to trade are described as tightly held. Two specific issues for index funds arising from this problem are corporate cross-holdings and initial public offerings (IPOs). Both problems get more acute as the proportion of the market owned by index funds rises.

The corporate cross-holding problem can be seen by considering what happens when a component company A of the index owns, as a strategic stake, a proportion $(1 - p)$ of another component company B of the index. In effect the index is double counting this part of B as it appears once in A's capitalisation and once in B's capitalisation.

The distortions this causes can be seen by remembering that if index funds own a proportion p of the capitalisation of the companies in the index, then by definition they have to own all the proportion p of the securities of B that are not owned by A. Thus the shares of B are bid up, in this case until the last share not owned by A is forthcoming. In addition, the shares of A will also rise to reflect the enhanced value of its asset.

A large-scale example of the cross-holding effect can be seen in the Japanese stock market, where the capitalisation of the index is greatly inflated by cross-holdings. It was then pumped up further in the 1980s by a domestic asset price bubble. For a while, the capitalisation of the Japanese stock market was higher than that of the US stock market.

Similarly, if privately held company C has an IPO of a proportion p of its shares and its capitalisation is such that it enters the index immediately, the index funds have to buy the entire IPO in order to get the right weight of C in their portfolios.

The IPO effect probably contributed to the late 1990s technology stock price bubble in the USA and UK, as IPOs of 10–15% of capitalisation (compare with the 20–25% owned by index funds) went straight into large capitalisation indices.

Index designers and index fund providers are already addressing these issues through changes[9] in index design and transparency. Changes in capital market mechanisms could help here too. For example index funds, which have to acquire stock, could be granted special privileges in primary issues such as the right to bid non-competitively.* Whether this happens or not, it is likely that cross-holdings, IPOs, corporate actions and index additions and deletions will create far fewer anomalies in the future.

2.2   ALTERNATIVE PRODUCTS

Alternative products are products, predominantly open-ended, whose guidelines allow more investment in illiquid securities, more leverage and more short selling than traditional product guidelines allow. The cases described in this section are partly chosen to illustrate the problems that can arise for open-ended products in the areas of performance measurement, product bankruptcy and equity between investors who withdraw and those who remain.

Because investment products that are publicly available in major financial centres such as the USA and UK are required by regulation to conform to traditional lines, alternative products issued in such centres have to accept restricted availability to investors in return for increased investment flexibility. Many investment firms issue alternative products in offshore centres, where the regulation is less onerous.

2.2.1   Illiquid assets

The main illiquid assets are private equity and property, or real estate. In the USA, these products are organised as partnerships, where the investor preserves his limited liability through being a limited partner, whose losses are limited to his investment. The investment firm is called the general partner, and takes on unlimited liability.

In the UK, there is a special form of unit trust that is unauthorised for public sale, which provides strategies to pension funds that are not allowed by the regulations applying to publicly offered products. The most common type of strategy provided has been property investment, when the vehicles are known as Pension Fund Property Unit Trusts (PFPUTs). The measured performance of these vehicles has very attractive characteristics. Their volatility is lower than the volatility of pension funds as a whole and their correlation with other pension fund assets is also low.

The allocation of UK pension funds to property rose steadily during the 1960s and early 1970s, reaching a peak of 18% in 1981. Its intuitive appeal was that it was thought to be inflation-proof[†] and exempt from labour disputes.

However, because property is an illiquid asset, the measured performance comes from appraised rather than market prices. For the same reason, there are many restrictions that prevent investors from selling at the appraised price.

Advisors began to question whether a performance series based on appraised prices truly reflected property's performance relative to the market price performance of competing assets. Evidence to support these misgivings came from the quoted property share sector, which had average returns nearly 2% below PFPUTs. Of equal concern, volatility and correlations with other pension fund assets were much higher than those of PFPUTs. Between 1973 and 2001, while PFPUT return volatility was 10%, with a correlation of 0.5, property share return volatility

---

was three times that of PFPUTs, with a correlation of 0.8.[10] UK pension fund allocations drifted down during the 1980s and 1990s to a low of 4% in 1999 before recovering to 6% in 2001.[11]

2.2.2   Liquid assets

The common name for an alternative product investing in liquid assets is a hedge fund. Alfred Winslow Jones, an Australian journalist who wrote for *Fortune Magazine*, introduced hedge funds. He launched a partnership in 1949, which balanced its long positions in stock against its short positions.*

Long Term Capital Management (LTCM) had its origins in the very successful Domestic Fixed Income Arbitrage Group at Salomon Brothers. This averaged profits of US$0.5 billion a year.[12] Its leader, John Meriwether, had been forced to leave Salomon in 1991 after a scandal involving US Treasury auctions, which is discussed in more detail in Chapter 4.

The senior traders in the Arbitrage Group joined Meriwether in setting up LTCM, which was designed to reproduce the success they had enjoyed at Salomon. LTCM started trading in March 1994 with US$1.25 billion of capital, 12% of which was subscribed by the partners themselves. Other recruits included two leading financial economists, Robert Merton and Myron Scholes.[13]

The investment process followed that developed at Salomon and many of the successful positions at Salomon were reproduced in the new fund. True to its name, the fund locked initial investors in for three years.[14] Risk for the whole portfolio was controlled by proprietary technology known as a risk aggregator.[15] This summarised risk as volatility, or the expected daily standard deviation of portfolio return. Consistent with their strategy of maintaining constant risk, the volatility measured by the risk aggregator remained remarkably constant throughout the life of the fund.[16] LTCM's total commitments were a multiple of its capital. However, its positions were not confined to futures and forwards but included swaps, option writing and long and short positions in virtually any financial instrument. LTCM was extremely successful at minimising its borrowing costs by playing off potential lenders against each other.

At first, things went very well. At the end of 1997, the return to investors after fees was a cumulative 182%, while partners' capital had grown to US$1.9 billion. Volatility had been much lower than predicted, suggesting that the risk aggregator was overly conservative in measuring risk. The partners were concerned that the fund had too much capital to generate adequate returns and elected to return US$2.7 billion to investors, leaving remaining capital of US$4.7 billion. Interestingly, in view of what followed, LTCM estimated that the cost to its counterparties of liquidating its positions was US$2.8 billion.[17]

In 1998, it went wrong. Poor market conditions drove the value of the fund down so that by close of business on 21 August, it was only worth US$2.9 billion, perilously close to its liquidation threshold, if its cost of liquidation equated to its counterparties' cost of liquidation. Ironically,† one of the largest losing positions was in options, which eventually cost US$1.3 billion.[18]

Strenuous efforts to raise new capital proved unavailing, and by early September it was clear to LTCM and its counterparties that it would have to liquidate, which meant transferring

---

* This investment strategy corresponds to a class of hedge funds now called market neutral.
† Merton and Scholes had been awarded the Nobel Prize for Economics in 1997 for their work on the Black–Scholes equity option valuation formula, which could be used to deduce the expected volatility of the underlying equity price from the option price.

ownership of its positions back to them. As by that time the fund's value was well below estimated liquidation cost, dumping the positions on the market was no longer an option. The counterparties collectively prepared for the inevitable by aggressively marking the prices of LTCM's positions down relative to the market.[19]

When the net worth of the fund fell to US$400 million[20] at the end of September, the Federal Reserve brokered a solution whereby 13 of the counterparties collectively injected US$3.65 billion into the fund in return for 90%, thus acquiring the same proportion of the positions.*

2.2.3   Offshore products

The principal offshore investment centres are Bermuda, various Caribbean and Pacific Islands, the UK Channel Islands and special EU zones in Luxembourg and Dublin. They compete in providing a lightly regulated environment that minimises constraints on investment strategy and fee structure. While more difficult for domestic investors to access, offshore products have the added benefit that large pools of capital have migrated to these centres for tax and other reasons and are thus available for investment. Many hedge funds offer the same investment strategy in the form of either a limited partnership or an offshore fund.

Investors Overseas Services (IOS) flourished during the 1960s. IOS had two main products, the International Investment Trust (IIT), organised in Luxembourg, and the Fund of Funds, organised in Ontario. The registrations outside the USA were because the US Investment Company Act 1940, passed in response to the fall out from the great crash, made it illegal for one US registered company to own more than 3% of any other.[21]

The Fund of Funds was an early form of "manager of manager" investment product. It started life investing in mainstream US mutual funds. It then shifted to proprietary funds in each of which it was the sole investor. The first proprietary fund was effectively a hedge fund run by two former apprentices of Winslow Jones. Fees charged on these funds were, at 0.5% flat and 10% of the upside, rather low by modern standards.[22] The 1% flat charge at the total fund level was in line with modern practice.

The underlying investment problem was that there was neither expertise, nor clear responsibility, nor process for manager selection and portfolio construction. The founders of IOS, Bernie Cornfeld and Ed Cowett, were heavily involved but neither Cornfeld, a salesman, nor Cowett, a lawyer, had any real investment expertise.

Initial policy was to select, fund and disfund managers based on very short-term investment performance. This naïve strategy of effectively buying high and selling low resulted in mediocre investment performance.

In their search for better performance they then moved into illiquid assets by setting up a natural resources proprietary fund in March 1968. Investors' money began to flow into such assets as Arctic oil leases without any changes to the terms upon which investors could withdraw. When investors began to redeem,[23] only the liquid asset managers could be fired or disfunded fast enough, so the percentage of illiquid assets climbed inexorably. By August 1970, they comprised 60% of the Fund of Funds at appraised value. At that point, IOS management

---

* Coincidentally, this left the investors in the fund in the same position as the one they would have been in if LTCM had behaved like a fund reaching its liquidation threshold on August 21. For then, it would have sold 90% of its positions at an estimated cost of 90% of US$2.8 billion, or US$2.5 billion, leaving 10% of its positions and a net worth of US$400 million. Effectively, during September, the counterparties made the fund pay the liquidation costs by marking its positions down relative to the market, which was otherwise relatively stable.

placed them in a separate closed-end vehicle. The fund price plummeted 60% to a level 25% below the original issue price of eight years before.[24]

2.3 ACTIVE OVERLAYS

A useful way of looking at an actively managed investment product is to isolate the actively managed part of it as an overlay. An overlay is a portfolio of financial securities, or forward commitments to buy financial securities, matched in value by a portfolio of sales of, or forward commitments to sell, different financial securities. The active strategy is based on the expectation that what is bought, usually known as the overlay's long position, will show more price appreciation than what is sold, usually known as the overlay's short position. If the active strategy is successful, the overlay will show a profit. If it is unsuccessful, the overlay will show a loss. These profits and losses will affect the overlay's capital, which is consumed or generated as market prices move against the overlay or in its favour.

A traditional actively managed investment product with a benchmark index can be broken down into two components: an overlay comprising the difference between the actual positions of the product and the positions it would have if it were fully invested in its benchmark index; and an index fund invested in the benchmark index. As a traditional product cannot have short positions, any short position in the overlay has to be at least matched by a long position in the index fund. To illustrate this further, consider a two asset market comprised of 50% asset A and 50% asset B. Consider also a traditional active product where the manager is positive on asset A and negative on asset B.

Figure 2.2 shows how such a product might be invested as a combination of an index fund reflecting a capitalisation weighted benchmark and an active overlay that is long 10% of A and short 10% of B. Adding the two together gives the active portfolio.

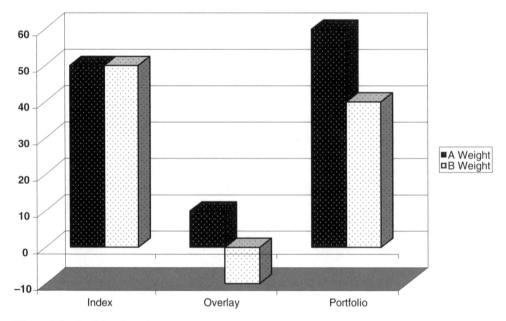

Figure 2.2   Traditional product

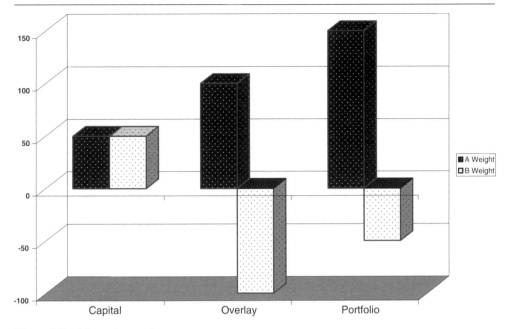

Figure 2.3   Alternative product

An alternative product that is allowed net short positions can have a much larger active overlay relative to its capital. To illustrate this further, consider an alternative product operating in the same two asset market as before and with the same benchmark, where the manager has the same positive view on asset A and negative view on asset B.

Figure 2.3 shows how such a product might be invested. The capital is invested in an index fund reflecting the benchmark as before, but this time the active overlay is 10 times the size so that the product has a net short position in B equal to half its capital.* As the gross size of the overlay is twice the capital, the product is leveraged.

The institutional investors described in the previous chapter can be thought of as overlays, which are long their asset holdings and short the promises they have made to their policyholders, in the case of insurance companies, or members, in the case of defined benefit pension schemes. Overlays and investment in overlays are not unique to the investment management industry. A bank is effectively an overlay, with a long position in loans, a short position in deposits and shareholders' funds acting as capital.

In addition to funding losses, the capital committed to an overlay maintains its net worth above the minimum level that triggers liquidation. The less liquid the assets and liabilities, the greater the investment professional running the overlay and his counterparties will want this minimum to be. This is because both stand to lose in the event that the fund achieves a negative net worth before its positions are finally liquidated. Further cash from investors under such circumstances is not a practical proposition.

The capital needed is consequently a function of the liquidity and risk of the overlay, rather than its gross volume. The riskier and more illiquid the assets and liabilities taken together, the more capital is needed. This point is key to understanding active overlays. A very large

---

* This investment strategy corresponds to a class of hedge funds known as long/short funds.

overlay in terms of gross volume, where the long position and the short position are closely related, will need less capital than a much smaller overlay in terms of gross volume, where the long position and short position are volatile and independent. For example, in the case of the illustrated alternative product, if A and B are perfectly correlated, the volatility of the overlay is zero so the product is not really leveraged at all.

2.4   CONCLUSION

The variety of financial securities that investors can choose from has resulted in the development of a range of pooled investment products designed to allow investors to delegate all or part of their investment decision making to investment specialists. The two main types of product are: closed-end vehicles, whose portfolios are unaffected by investor transactions but whose prices reflect marginal investor supply and demand; and open-ended vehicles, whose prices only reflect the values of their underlying assets but whose portfolios expand or contract as investors buy or sell at the margin.

A key difference in the investment strategies pursued by these products is between passively managed products, whose strategies mimic a package of securities or an index announced in advance, and actively managed products, whose strategies seek to achieve superior security selection. Any actively managed investment product can be thought of as a combination of an index product reflecting its benchmark and an overlay consisting of the positions owned by the product, that are not in the index, financed by sales of the components of the index, that are not in the product.

Open-ended products have proved more popular over time. A connection has emerged between type of product, regulation, investor access and investment strategy. Traditional products are heavily regulated, easier for investors to access but more constrained on investment strategy. Alternative products are lightly regulated, more difficult for investors to access but less constrained on investment strategy.

ENDNOTES

1. J.K. Galbraith, *The Great Crash 1929*, London: Penguin Books, 1992, pp. 85–90.
2. Department of Trade, July 1974, *Interim Report of Investigations under Section 165(b) of the Companies Act 1948*.
3. Financial Services Authority, May 2002, *Update Report on FSA's Enquiry into the Split Capital Investment Trust Market*.
4. C. Raw, B. Page and G. Hodgson, *Do You Sincerely Want to be Rich*, Newton Abbott: Readers Union, 1972, p. 41.
5. Raw *et al.*, p. 44.
6. Littlewood, p. 454.
7. E.J. Elton, M.J. Gruber and J. Rentzler, "The performance of publicly offered commodity funds", *Financial Analysts Journal*, July/August 1990.
8. *Managing Investment Portfolios*, Sponsored by the Institute of Chartered Financial Analysts. Boston: Warren, Gorham and Lamont, 1983, p. 400.
9. The FT index family has an explicit adjustment for what it calls free float or the freely traded component of the outstanding capitalisation of a stock. This is described in "Ground rules for the management of the UK series of the FT Actuaries Share Indices", available on www.ftse.com.
10. Raw data sourced from Pension Fund Indicators, UBS Global Asset Management, 2002, p. 47. [Primary sources credited in report]
11. Pension Fund Indicators, UBS Global Asset Management, 2002, p. 11. [Primary sources credited in report]

12. R. Lowenstein, *When Genius Failed*. US: Random House Trade Paperbacks, 2000, p. 33.
13. Lowenstein, pp. 30–38.
14. Lowenstein, p. 27.
15. Lowenstein, p. 187.
16. Author interview with Eric Rosenfeld, formerly a senior LTCM partner.
17. "If the fund suddenly failed...according to Long-Term, its seventeen biggest counterparties...would stand to lose a total of $2.8 billion." Lowenstein, p. 188.
18. Lowenstein, p. 234.
19. Lowenstein, pp. 163, 173.
20. Lowenstein, p. 210.
21. Raw *et al.*, p. 106.
22. Raw *et al.*, pp. 104–117.
23. Ironically, IOS itself prompted the net redemptions by switching sales emphasis from the Fund of Funds to IIT in 1969 on the basis of a "better" track record since the Fund of Funds launch in autumn 1962. A further irony was that IIT fell 30% from its launch in December 1960 to a bottom in October 1962 so the "better" track record was based on an incomplete performance series. Raw, p. 438.
24. Raw *et al.*, p. 445.

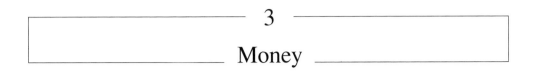

3
Money

Ah, take the cash and let the credit go, nor heed the rumble of a distant drum![1]

Investors needing to pay for something, who are reluctant to sell their portfolios, can always borrow against them. Other investors, who are nervous of stock market prospects, can use money as a safe haven for their wealth. As such, it is the asset class with no, or very limited, risk.

Many commentators view money as a sort of anti-investment, or something for the investor to hold as an alternative to getting invested. As discussed in Chapter 1, the simplest benchmark to compare the performance of any investment with is the performance that would have been achieved by not investing but retaining cash.

3.1 THREE DEFINING PROPERTIES

Money provides an investor with three things: purchasing power, return and a risk-free asset.

3.1.1 Purchasing power

For this role, money has to be a reliable store of value and acceptable for the widest possible range of goods and services. Legal tender or official currency often fails the acceptability test. In much of Latin America the US dollar is preferred to local currency. It is estimated that 30–40% of German banknotes in circulation before the introduction of the euro were held abroad.[2]

Official currency also frequently fails the store of value test, particularly during periods of inflation, usually in developing or undeveloped economies. But even Germany was not immune once. There are memorable newsreel images of people taking away their pay in wheelbarrows during the hyperinflation presided over by the Weimar government immediately after the First World War. The exchange rate of the Deutsche Mark against the US dollar declined from its gold standard rate of 4.2 Marks in 1914 to 2.5 billion Marks by the time the episode closed at the end of 1923. Figure 3.1 shows a Reichsbanknote for 500 million Marks. Printed on one side of poor quality paper, it does not give the impression that it is worth even the 20 US cents it could theoretically be exchanged for.

3.1.2 Return

The morality of receiving interest for the loan of money has been questioned or condemned from the earliest times.

He that hath not given his money upon usury: nor taken reward against the innocent. Whoso doeth these things: shall never fall.[3]

God has permitted trafficking and forbidden usury.[4]

Figure 3.1 Weimar currency

Western moralists and jurists* have justified interest by contrasting charging a fair rent for the use of money, or banking, with charging a predatory rent for the use of money, or loan sharking. In 1900, usury laws in US states restricted the rate of interest to a ceiling ranging from 5% in Louisiana to 8% in Wyoming.[5] Twentieth century inflation has progressively dismantled usury laws so that few, if any, remain now.

3.1.3 Risk-free asset

All money market instruments pay their returns in monetary terms. Analysts sometimes deflate these returns to express them in terms of constant purchasing power. Such numbers are more interesting to economists than investors, who are chiefly interested in stable nominal value and the difference between the return on money and the returns on other investments.

Investors expect a very high degree of stability. As illustrated in the example below, even very small fluctuations in nominal value can prompt severe reactions.

MAM's investors held their liquidity in an interest-bearing account known as an investment account. They also gave discretion to invest in money market instruments. One of the early situations that I had to resolve was caused when a money market trader, seeing that six-month money market rates were well above the investment account rate, had withdrawn a substantial proportion of cash from the accounts and invested it in liquid money market instruments of six-month maturity.

Shortly thereafter, there was a change in investment strategy, which resulted in the investment of most of the liquidity in the UK equity market. Most of the accounts holding the six-month instruments had to sell them, which they did with ease. The problem arose because interest rate fluctuations meant that there was a small capital loss of a few pounds per million. This was

---

* Some of their Islamic colleagues are less flexible and insist on special Islamic funds, which are low risk but derive their returns from trading rather than interest.

prominently displayed in the "realised capital loss" section of the accounts' quarterly reports, much to the embarrassment of the client relationship managers concerned who were unable to explain how cash investments could generate a capital loss.

It was agreed going forward to limit the maximum maturity of money market investments to one month. As the settlement period for UK equities was up to three weeks, this virtually guaranteed that no money market instrument would have to be liquidated at a loss to pay for UK equities.

3.2   EARLY FORMS OF MONEY

The most important early forms of money were gold and bank deposits. The return on holding gold is zero,* so the return on any asset was also equal to its return relative to gold. Bank deposits were introduced in the seventeenth century to give investors the opportunity to get a return on their cash.

3.2.1   Gold

Because of its rarity and desirability, a small weight of gold commands a lot of purchasing power. To the extent that currency is expressed as a weight of gold, it is a perfect store of value. Alternatively, it can be put to use as jewellery or tableware. Gold was in permanently short supply. Despite valiant attempts by the alchemists,† the problem was difficult to deal with in the laboratory. Fortunately, mineral prospecting in territories newly opened up from the discovery of America onward provided a solution.

69% of the 15.1 thousand tonnes of gold mined between 1493 and 1900 was dug out in the final 50 years, boosted by discoveries in North America, Southern Australia and South Africa.[6] Without this extra volume of metal, the international gold standard, whereby a group of primarily European economies from 1867 onwards made their currencies convertible to gold at fixed parities, would not have been possible. While some countries, such as the UK, had operated domestic gold standards, the international dimension, by removing exchange rate uncertainty, was a major boost to trade. However, it was a fragile arrangement that was quickly dissolved by the onset of the First World War in 1914.

There were two attempts to restore it in the twentieth century. The first, between the wars, dissolved in a series of competitive devaluations as countries tried to recover from the great depression. The second was a limited scheme for official currency transactions only, known as the Bretton Woods‡ system. This lasted from the end of the Second World War until 1971, when overwhelming demand from foreign governments for gold in exchange for their US dollars forced US President Nixon to suspend convertibility.

The enduring appeal of the international gold standard was that it automatically controlled inflation and prevented an economy overheating. This was because banks were required to hold

---

* A return can be achieved by lending it to an intermediary, but this introduces credit risk, or the possibility that the intermediary will disappear or default.

† Including the distinguished scientist Isaac Newton who devoted considerable efforts to finding the philosopher's tincture that would turn base metal into gold. Possibly influenced by his metallurgical interests, he gained the appointment of Master of the Royal Mint in 1697. His introduction in 1717 of the guinea coin with an overvalued gold content effectively put the UK on a domestic gold standard.

‡ The Mount Washington Hotel at Bretton Woods, New Hampshire was used in 1944 for the conference at which the post-Second World War system of fixed exchange rate parities, the International Monetary Fund and the World Bank were agreed. Keynes led the UK delegation.

reserves in gold and could only lend a multiple of these reserves. These loans then reappeared as deposits. Thus the money in any national system was a multiple of the gold held by its banks. Monetary theory argued that demand was a multiple of money and thus gold.[*] It also argued that, when demand exceeded the domestic supply of goods and services, imports would be sucked in. These imports had to be paid for with gold. The resultant gold outflow would cause a contraction of loans, a contraction of money and a correction of the excess demand.

A long-term problem with the gold standard was that its mechanism depended on the supply of gold growing at the same pace as real economic activity. Thus the great boost in real economic activity during the latter part of the nineteenth century was made possible by the coincident growth in gold production. Distortions in the supply of gold led to imbalances in the real economy unless countermeasures were taken.[†]

Despite losing its central role with the abandonment of the gold standard, gold has continued to feature as an investment medium. During the inflationary 1970s, its price was aggressively bid up, reaching over US$800 per ounce in 1980. At this stage the fluctuations in price were large and defied rational explanation.[‡]

Since then, the price has declined erratically, rather exploding gold's qualifications as an inflation hedge and disappointing investors such as the Swiss banker of my acquaintance whose savings consisted of an ounce of gold for every day that he expected to be retired.

3.2.2 Deposits

Deposit taking was established in London from the seventeenth century onwards when, during the English Civil War (1642–1649):

> Goldsmiths or new fashioned bankers began to receive the rents of gentlemen's estates remitted to town and to allow them and others who put cash into their hands some interest for it if it remained but a single month ... [7]

Receipts or notes for deposits began to be treated as money in their own right. As the deposit takers became bankers these notes became known as banknotes. The Swedish Riksbank, the first European central bank, issued the first European banknote in 1658. Both are credited to a Swede called Palmstruck.[8] At or before this time promises to pay fixed sums of money at a certain date in the future began to make their appearance, usually in connection with trade. An importer would make such a promise to pay an exporter's bill, timing the future date to coincide with the date he expected to have received and sold the goods. The exporter would expect the promise to be guaranteed by the importer's bank. He would then sell it at a discount to his own bank,[§] which reflected the delay, inconvenience and risk in obtaining payment.

The discount on the bills was closely related to the interest on deposits (A2.1). In both cases, you parted with a certain amount of cash today to get back more later. Bankers annualised the rate of return on the bills to make them directly comparable with the rate of return on deposits.

---

[*] The theory did not tell you how much gold was actually required. This had to be discovered by trial and error and varied from country to country. France, with a similar population and a smaller economy, needed twice as much gold as the UK.

[†] The story goes that in the USA during the gold standard era, the itinerary of the state bank examiner of a western state, where gold was in short supply, was published in advance. As he travelled from town to town he was preceded, unknown to him, by an employee of the banks he was visiting carrying a box of gold. When he arrived at each bank he was pleased to find that it had the required reserve of a box filled with gold available for inspection.

[‡] A colleague, who acted as our spokesman on gold to the press, had two ways to explain the inexplicable. The first was that the price had hit a chart point and the second was that the Russians were in the market. Neither could be checked and neither failed to satisfy.

[§] Banks serving merchants found it convenient to accept, or add their own guarantee to, a bill so they could sell it to investors unfamiliar with the foreign bank. In the UK, such banks became known as accepting houses or merchant banks.

Government short-term borrowing needs were often met by selling bills guaranteed by the treasury. Treasury bills have no credit risk and their returns are often used as a proxy for the risk-free rate by academics and other researchers. In practice, investors very seldom invest their liquidity in Treasury bills, preferring to use other instruments and products.

3.3   MODERN FORMS OF MONEY

In the twentieth century, the dissolution of the gold standard and the inflation that followed made gold a risky asset and paper currency a poor store of value. In order to fill the gap, a range of money products emerged, all providing yield, liquidity and minimum risk but each one tailored for a different class of investor.

3.3.1   Retail money funds

A relic of the old usury laws, Regulation Q of the US Federal Reserve Act, had the effect of creating a whole new class of product in the USA, the money funds. It did this by restricting the rate banks could pay individual investors on their deposit accounts to 5.25%. When rates soared above this in the late 1970s, there was a strong incentive to organise mutual funds investing in unregulated money market instruments with a higher return. Skilful packaging by brokerage houses linked them to brokerage accounts and provided chequebooks, credit cards, etc.

A constant one-dollar price (accrued interest was credited as additional units) even made them look like deposit accounts. The need to avoid breaking the buck, or letting the price drop below one dollar, set clear constraints on acceptable risk. As the price was the market value rounded to the nearest cent, sponsors could not afford to let the NAV of the unit fall below 99.5 cents. Where this happened they invariably made up the difference from their own funds.

In the UK, retail cash products developed rather differently. This was because income tax was charged at a lower rate than the standard rate on certain privileged savings accounts such as those offered by building societies, the UK equivalent of saving and loan institutions. Thus any individual paying marginal income tax at the standard rate or above (and virtually all savers come into this category) usually got a higher after-tax return from keeping his cash at the building society.*

3.3.2   Institutional money funds

In the USA, the 1974 ERISA triggered unbundling, or separation of investment management from safe custody, or holding and servicing a fund's assets. The financial institution responsible for custody, invariably a bank, swept, or collected, its clients' cash balances into a Short-Term Investment Fund (STIF), which was invested in the money market.

For UK pension funds, the dominant type of investment manager until recently was a merchant bank offering a bundled service of both investment management by its investment division and custody by its banking division. As deposits from the clients of investment management subsidiaries assumed an increasing importance in funding merchant banks' balance sheets, strenuous efforts were made to persuade investors that the credit standing of a merchant bank or accepting house was so good that bank exposure did not need to be diversified.

---

* In 1979, the merchant bank NM Rothschild, where I then worked, introduced a product known as a roll up fund. This invested in money market instruments. As the name implies, interest was rolled up into the principal value. For a while, until the tax code was changed, this had the effect of reducing the tax rate for investors from their marginal income tax rate to their marginal capital gains tax rate.

All this changed in 1994 with events at Baring Brothers, a merchant bank whose securities subsidiary had an apparently successful futures arbitrage trader in Singapore called Nick Leeson. Leeson, who was also in charge of his own back office,* took some huge futures positions. These went badly wrong, resulting in very large cash calls from the futures exchange. He was able to convince his management and the banking arm of Baring that these losses were offset by profits on forward positions which would not be payable until contract maturity, leaving him with a short-term liquidity problem. This was plausible as he was both supposed to have offsetting positions as an arbitrage trader and able to arrange for the supply of convincing documentary proof faxed directly from a creditworthy counterparty. Unfortunately the proof was forged. Baring's bank paid over £862 million, or more than its entire capital, before the real positions were unwound. At 0.1% of GNP, it was clearly not too big to fail and the Bank of England refused to bail it out. The illusion of merchant bank creditworthiness was lost forever.

In the short term, pension funds and their advisors panicked, insisting that much of their liquidity was placed overnight with banks that were deemed too big to fail. These institutions, awash with overnight funds they could not use, offered derisory rates. The long-term consequence was that custody and investment management in the UK became unbundled, with banks considered too big to fail acquiring the lion's share of the custody business.

3.3.3   Eurodollars

In the same way that investment products made their way offshore into regimes where they were lightly taxed and less regulated, so too did lending and depositing activities in all currencies, but particularly US dollars.

As with money market funds, the Eurodollar market had its origins in an action by the US authorities. In this case, it was a tax (the Interest Equalisation Tax) imposed on offshore investors in domestic US dollar interest-bearing instruments. By borrowing in US dollars offshore, banks could help investors avoid the tax and achieve better after tax-returns. At the same time, lighter regulatory arrangements offshore meant that banks could offer cheaper facilities to borrowers.

The resultant offshore banking business was called the Eurodollar market because the financial centres of Europe, particularly London, were quick to grasp the opportunity. The first round of Organisation of Petroleum Exporting Countries (OPEC) price rises in 1973 was a great boost for Eurodollar activity in London. The increased oil revenues resulted in a rapid build-up in the public and private US dollar cash holdings of the oil exporting nations. Temperamentally risk-averse and cautious about equity investment, they tended to keep very substantial proportions of their portfolios in the money market.

The Eurodollar money market was thus a natural place for the newly enriched OPEC nations to invest their liquidity. The growth of Eurodollar deposits, certificates of deposit (CDs), etc. presented the offshore banks with the problem of what to do with the money. They had to find borrowers. Fortunately a ready supply of these was at hand in the countries whose economies needed the money to pay for more expensive oil imports. This process was known as recycling the OPEC surplus.

The loans were called sovereign loans as the governments of the borrowing countries guaranteed repayment. Because the banks needed to match the interest payments on the loans with

---

* A back office is principally concerned with confirming, or verifying, transactions and settlement, or making sure that if something has been bought it is delivered against payment and if something is sold, it is paid for when delivered.

the payments they were making to their depositors, the interest floated, or was periodically reset to the London Inter-Bank Offer Rate (LIBOR) for the next period plus a mark-up. Such was the pace of loan-making activity that there was little time for extensive credit research. Some bankers believed that it was unnecessary.* Others developed facetious rules of thumb. One senior credit officer was reluctant to lend to any country whose flag contained the colour green.

Another less publicised recycling process developed whereby large chunks of many sovereign loans were deposited by members and officials of the borrowing governments in the private banks of Zurich, Geneva and Miami. These were often branches of the same banks that made the original loans. This created rapidly growing demand for private client investment management services.

The process was interrupted by the 1979 appointment of Paul Volcker as the Chairman of the Federal Reserve with a mandate to squeeze inflation out of the system with high short-term US interest rates. Loan interest floated up to unprecedented levels and the governments of many borrowers were unable or unwilling to service the loans, often arranged for and the proceeds spent by their predecessors.[†] The "Sovereign Debt Crisis" caused by this was eventually resolved by persuading the banks to accept a form of term debt in exchange for their short term loans.

3.4   ACTIVE CASH MANAGEMENT

Most money products are severely constrained on the risk they can take and the liquidity they can give up by their investors' expectation that they will act as a source of liquidity without risk. Nevertheless, some investors are able to take investment risk in pursuit of a higher return than the risk-free rate. There is thus a demand for active cash management.

This has the objective of doing better for short-term investors than they would have done through simply rolling over, or mechanically reinvesting, their maturing deposits or money market instruments. As with any other active investment product, active cash management can be viewed as a combination of a passive benchmark and an active overlay. In this case, the passive benchmark is very close to the risk-free rate. The active overlay is thus whatever risky asset the active cash portfolio actually owns less the risk-free rate. It is thus very similar to the risky asset itself as it has the same risk and the same return, less the risk-free rate. These active overlays tend to take two different types of risk.[‡]

3.4.1   Credit risk

The first is to take credit risk based on skilful credit analysis. This is effectively what a bank does when it makes short-term loans to risky borrowers. The opportunity to take credit risk in the Eurodollar money market is limited by its structure. Virtually all the early borrowers were banks that borrow from and lend money to each other at a market rate, LIBOR, that takes very little account of who the borrower is. Credit spreads in the Eurodollar money market were

---

* Walter Wriston, Chairman of Citibank in the 1970s, is supposed to have said that "Countries do not go bust".
 † In 1976, during a visit to La Paz in Bolivia, I had been shown the lamppost in Plaza Murillo from which an angry mob had hanged President Villarroel in 1946. It was easy to understand that these governments had more pressing priorities than repaying their foreign creditors.
 ‡ This list is not exhaustive. Other active overlays used for cash management that I have known about include currencies, equities and commodities such as gold.

therefore virtually non-existent. In any case the investors were very reluctant to take credit risk as this involved the risk of losing the entire investment if the borrower went bust. In contrast to the USA, active cash management in London involved very little credit analysis.

3.4.2 Maturity risk

The second way to take risk is by mismatching the maturity of the portfolio to the maturity of the benchmark. If the maturity of the portfolio is shorter than that of the benchmark and interest rates rise, the portfolio will outperform by reinvesting at a higher rate. Similarly, if the maturity of the portfolio is longer than that of the benchmark and interest rates fall, the portfolio will outperform by holding its higher yielding investments longer than the benchmark.*

This approach became the standard way of actively managing cash in offshore centres such as London. There are two preconditions for successfully bringing it off. First, you need to have superior short-term interest rate forecasting skill. Second, you need to have liquid instruments (which can be converted to cash without deposit-breaking penalties) so that you can quickly and cheaply rearrange the maturity of your portfolio when you change your view. The market responded to demand by introducing supplies of monetary economists to help with the first and new instruments such as the Eurodollar CDs to help with the second.

Another approach to taking maturity risk is to invest in floating rate securities, which are term securities whose coupons are reset every few months at the appropriate deposit rate plus a mark-up. As long as the mark-up exceeds the fee and the borrower has an acceptable credit standing, outperformance seems guaranteed. As the borrowers are usually the same banks that issue the CDs, credit is not an issue unless the security is subordinated to deposits. However, although the instrument can be sold in the market, the borrower only guarantees repayment at the end of a fixed term of several years. The market price is dominated by a judgement as to whether the mark-up justifies the extra risk created by the delay.

Initial offerings of such instruments performed well and gained in popularity as acceptable investments for cash portfolios. Some advisors took the view that successful cash management could be achieved through investment in these instruments without taking maturity risk. The issuing market responded predictably with permutations of cutting the mark-up, lengthening the maturity, reducing the credit status of the instrument and introducing lesser quality borrowers. This process culminated in the issue of "perpetual" floating rate instruments where the borrower never repaid. Again predictably, these instruments performed exceptionally poorly with downward trending prices and volatility often exceeding that of long-term bonds.

3.5   CONCLUSION

Money's place in an investor's portfolio is determined by its role as a risk-free store of value. The return on money is known as the risk-free return. The return on a risky asset is conventionally presented as its excess return after deducting the return that could have been earned by keeping the investment in cash.

Money has developed from metals such as gold to a wide range of financial instruments and investment products, each adapted to the needs of a different class of investor. Active cash

---

* This type of maturity risk is known as gapping. I believe that this is a reference to the gap between short-term and longer term interest rates created by a positively sloped yield curve. The gap provides the investor with a profit if rates do not move and a cushion of protection if rates move the wrong way.

management is a type of money product where an actively managed overlay is superimposed on a benchmark based on a mechanical or passive strategy of rolling over short-term money market instruments.

ENDNOTES

1. E. Fitzgerald, *The Rubaiyat of Omar Khayyam*, 4th Edition, 1879, stanza 13.
2. "Mattress money could harm euro", *Daily Telegraph*, 12 October 2001.
3. Psalm 15.
4. *Koran*, Sura 2.
5. *Encyclopedia Britannica*, 11th Edition. Cambridge: CUP, 1910–1911, vol. 18, p. 708.
6. 11th Edition, vol. 19, p. 269.
7. "The mystery of the new-fashioned goldsmiths or bankers discovered", pamphlet published in 1676, quoted in 11th Edition, vol. 3, p. 337.
8. 11th Edition, vol. 3, p. 335.

4

Fixed Interest

This asset class has two special properties. It can provide an investor with a fixed income without affecting his capital and it can match his future monetary obligations precisely. Money cannot perform either of these tasks because the risk-free rate varies from period to period. Fixed interest, or bond, market history is closely linked to the history of government finance, as the biggest borrower in any long-term debt market is usually the government.*

4.1 HISTORY

The rapid build-up of military budgets at the end of the seventeenth century led to state demands for finance that could not be met using the sovereign's personal credit supplemented by ad hoc imposts. Printing paper money provided a short-term solution, but one that rapidly prompted price increases and was in any case impossible for economies, like the UK, which were on the gold standard. To avoid inflation, governments had to borrow. When the war was over and the money was spent, they were still left with the burden of servicing the debt, or making the promised interest and principal payments. Before 1945, governments largely did this by running a peacetime fiscal surplus and using the surplus to repay enough of the debt to create a bull market for the rest. They then took advantage of the favourable market conditions to lower servicing costs by refinancing as much as possible of the remainder.

US and UK bond investors in 1945 thus expected that, as so many times before, peacetime fiscal surpluses would be applied to reducing government debt, causing bond prices to rise in an environment of stable consumer prices. They were to be bitterly disappointed by sustained bear markets in both countries.

Although the policies that caused these were reversed in the 1980s, the scars remain. The interesting question now is whether governments can be trusted in the future not to despoil their creditors in favour of more powerful constituencies. After the experience of 1945–1979, investors are likely to be extremely suspicious of any development that might herald a return to the policies of those years.

4.1.1 UK to 1945

Until the late seventeenth century, major state projects were financed creatively, often using one-off techniques. For example, the Ulster Plantation, James the First's attempt to solve the perennial problem of Ireland, had at least two original sources of funding.

First, there was a £60 000 "voluntary" contribution from the livery companies of the City of London. Second, there was revenue from the sale of newly introduced hereditary titles known as Baronetcies at £1095 each, a sum equal to the cost of paying 30 soldiers in Ireland for three years.[1] This is the equivalent of over £1 million in today's money at current rates of military pay.

---

* Government regulation of investors often has the effect of shifting assets from stocks to bonds. An example of this is presented in Chapter 7.

No fiscal advantages attached to Baronetcies, in contrast to hereditary titles sold in France,[2] where membership of the nobility carried the right to exemption from most forms of tax. Not surprisingly, sales progressed much better in France – at the cost of a permanent diminution in the French tax base.

All the sums of money involved were small. Even in 1684, the total annual English military expenditure was £283 775.[3] However, in 1689, William III led England into the "War of the Grand Alliance" (1689–1697), which cost £31 million, followed rapidly by the "War of the Spanish Succession" (1702–1713), which cost £51 million, all at a time when national product (GNP) was approximately £60 million a year.[4] A contemporary reminder of the costs of warfare comes from the discovery of the wreck of HMS Sussex, a 1200 ton, 80 gun ship[5] lost off Gibraltar in 1694. The Sussex was carrying the 800 000 piastre* subsidy required by the Duke of Savoy before he would start campaigning on William's side. Most of the money to pay for these wars was borrowed. In 1715, UK public debt stood at £49 million, or over 80% of GNP.[6]

This debt consisted of bonds and annuities. The technique of financing state deficits through the sale of annuities, or contracts where the buyer gets a fixed income for the rest of his life, was developed in Holland. The Dutch priced[7] annuities using the simple formula that if the money market rate was r, the rate of income allowed to an annuitant of any age was $2r$. It is easy to show (A2.15) that this is equivalent to assuming a low break-even life expectancy that falls as r increases, implying a unique connection between the money market and national mortality. Thus a 7% rate of return assumes a life expectancy of nine years, a 5% rate of return assumes a life expectancy of 13 years, etc. Despite the low life expectancies of the time, this was generous and the annuities sold well. Part of the problem of the high debt servicing costs that the government faced was because, as the annuitants inconveniently lived on, they were unexpectedly expensive to service. Another part of the problem was that most of the bonds had very long lives and coupons of 6.67% and upwards.[8]

The South Sea Chartered Company was an attempt to solve the problem by swapping equity in the company for the national debt. This manoeuvre works if the bondholders believe that the capital gains on the stock they are getting will more than compensate for the income lost by surrendering their bonds. The prospects of the company were based on a monopoly of the British trade with South America and the Pacific islands. As this was going to entail fighting the Spaniards, who were already in possession, the directors felt that prospects alone would not be sufficient to create the bull market they needed in South Sea stock. They therefore set out to get the price up by organising a speculative ramp. Such was their success that in August 1720, the company market capitalisation exceeded four times UK GNP.[9] As the business problems were unchanged, this proved unsustainable and the stock price collapsed in spectacular fashion, wrecking the scheme and creating a negative perception of joint stock companies that lasted more than a century.

The UK government then set about doing it the hard way. A cumulative peacetime budget surplus of £6.3 million between 1720 and 1739[10] allowed a modest debt reduction. It consolidated nine outstanding bonds together in 1751 as one perpetual bond, to improve liquidity and eliminate mandatory repayment.† But in 1740, it embarked on a series of global conflicts that culminated in the Revolutionary and Napoleonic Wars (1793–1815). All were expensive. In 1819, UK debt to GNP peaked at nearly 300%.

---

* Another name for a peso, the standard Spanish silver coin, which was equivalent to a thaler or dollar.
† These became known as the consolidated fund, shortened to consols.

By 1913, debt had fallen to 25% of GNP. The government had achieved this in two ways. First, there had been a century of peace, or at least inexpensive warfare, so enough fiscal surpluses had been generated to pay back some of the debt. Second, the economy had grown approximately nine times. The debt servicing burden as a proportion of GNP had fallen even further as the government had taken advantage of falling yields and the associated rising bond prices (A2.8) to reduce the coupon on consols, which represented the vast bulk of the outstanding debt, from 3% to 2.75% to 2.5%. It was able to do this because it had the option to repay the debt and refinance. This meant that the market price could not rise very far above par as the premium could be extinguished at any time. The lower coupon bonds could not be repaid until 1923, making them a more attractive investment for investors who expected yields to keep on falling.

In 1914, the UK embarked on another 30 years of global conflict. At the end of the First World War (1914–1918), debt to GNP stood at 130%. By the end of the Second World War (1939–1945), the ratio had risen to 270%, a level last seen at the end of the Napoleonic Wars.

4.1.2 USA to 1945

As the Continental Congress had no taxing authority until the new constitution of 1787,[11] printing money financed the first few years of the American War of Independence (1776–1782). Congress and the states printed $450 million of notes, which delivered $60 million worth of hard currency purchasing power, but were only worth some $2 million in hard currency by the time they were withdrawn from circulation in 1781. Ironically, most of the currency in circulation by then was hard currency imported by the British to pay their local expenses.[12]

The Federal government was able to issue bonds to pay for the American Civil War (1861–1865). At the end, debt to GNP had risen from virtually nothing to 50%. By 1913, this had almost all been paid back. By 1918, wartime expenses, both direct and through the role of the USA as banker to its allies, had taken this up to 30%, while by 1945 it was approaching 150%. In just over 30 years, the USA had transformed itself from a virtually debt-free state to the world's largest borrower, a doubtful distinction it retains to this day.

4.1.3 From 1945

In contrast to the post-war rallies experienced after every conflict up to then, both markets entered sustained bear phases. The nadir of the British government bond market came in 1974 when the consol yield crossed the consol price. This happened when the price fell below 15.8% of par and the yield rose above 15.8% (A2.10). In contrast, the lowest price during the 150 years to 1900 had been 47.4 in 1797 when mutiny at the Nore* introduced a serious element of credit risk. The bottom of the US government bond market came slightly later, in 1981. The same bear market almost took consols back to their all-time low, but they bottomed at a price of around 17.

With the benefit of hindsight, it is clear that bondholders had missed three important developments, which were to dominate bond markets over the period from 1945 to 1979. First, people now expected governments to deliver both full employment and a universal social welfare safety net. Second, the great depression had exposed one flaw in classical economics. This was that, if the economy was seriously depressed, increasing the supply of money did not necessarily increase demand if people were too frightened to spend. Keynes's solution to the

---

* Royal Navy anchorage at the mouth of the Thames. The UK was at war with France and only lack of control of the English Channel prevented the overwhelmingly superior French field army from mounting a successful invasion. Even adjusting for the coupon reduction noted earlier, the equivalent price would still have been 39.5.

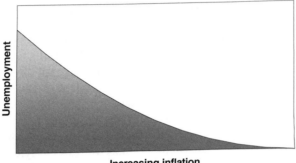

Figure 4.1 Original Phillips curve

problem was that the government should make up the difference by spending more than it took in taxes. Third, empirical analysis of rates of inflation and unemployment seemed to suggest that there was a trade-off* between the two, as shown schematically in Figure 4.1, with higher inflation being linked with lower unemployment and vice versa.

Thus, to caricature things somewhat, the welfare budget kept peacetime government spending at a high level, making it harder to generate a fiscal surplus. The resultant fiscal deficits were justified by Keynesian demand management arguments. The trade-off argument justified financing at least part of the deficits by printing money, in order to generate enough inflation to keep the economy at full employment.[†]

Initially, the impulse to inflate was moderate. Chapter 5 presents reasons why the Bretton Woods agreement probably contributed to this restraint. Between 1945 and the agreement's abandonment in 1971, annual inflation averaged 3.2% in the USA and 3.9% in the UK. Even so, the dollar lost over half its real value and the pound lost over three-fifths of its real value. Over the next decade, double digit inflation became common in the USA and the norm in the UK. By 1981, the dollar had lost four-fifths of its real value and the pound nine-tenths.

Because of falls in prices, bondholders had fared much worse. For example, a 1945 investor in consols would have seen the nominal price fall by three-quarters, leaving him with 2.5% of his original principal in real terms. By this time, the Bank of England was finding it increasingly hard to sell the huge volumes of gilts necessary to finance the UK fiscal deficit. From time to time, it resorted to what became known as the Duke of York tactic.[‡] This entailed first driving gilt prices down by increasing short-term rates, then pushing them up again by reducing short-term rates. The temporary bull market so created provided an opportunity to sell more bonds. Correctly anticipating this sort of thing proved very profitable for active maturity managers, who in any case were able consistently to beat the market by keeping their maturities shorter than those of the benchmarks against which they were measured.

Also by this time, it was increasingly apparent that the labour market anticipated inflation. The evidence suggested that, when inflation was as expected, the Phillips curve became a horizontal line (Figure 4.2).

The confusion may have been because the historical data upon which Phillips based his curve used periods when all inflation was unexpected. The policy implication now was that,

---

* This became known as the Phillips curve, after the New Zealand born economist Alban Phillips.
† Either directly, by creating more banknotes, or indirectly, by selling short term instruments to banks, which has the effect of providing them with the wherewithal to expand their lending.
‡ From the nursery rhyme: "The grand old Duke of York, he had ten thousand men. He marched them up to the top of the hill and he marched them down again. And when they were up, they were up. And when they were down, they were down. And when they were only half way up, they were neither up nor down."

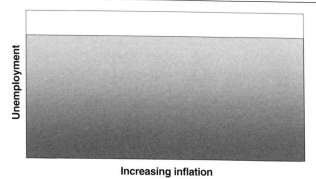

Figure 4.2   Revised Phillips curve

in order to keep unemployment artificially low, governments had not only to keep inflation rising, but also to keep it rising unexpectedly.

Another problem with inflation was that investors became reluctant to buy long term bonds, forcing governments to refinance more frequently at the higher rates. The real yield, or nominal yield less inflation rate, demanded by the market was now as high, or higher, than the peak nominal yields paid by the government during the eighteenth century.

For these and many other reasons, a consensus developed in both the UK and the USA that inflation had to be dealt with. Despite its drawbacks, inflation had managed one achievement: by 1980, despite consistent deficits since 1945 in both countries, debt as a percentage of GNP had fallen to some 50% in the UK and less than 30% in the USA.

Things changed in 1979, with the appointment of Volcker to the US Federal Reserve and the election of Margaret Thatcher as Prime Minister of the UK. The change in policy at the US Federal Reserve, which was echoed by new, less inflation tolerant policies in the UK, revolutionised the bond environment in both countries. This required some political courage, as another implication of the Phillips curve argument is that, if inflation is lower than expected, unemployment rises because higher real pay prices more people out of work. Unemployment rose in both countries, but particularly in the UK, where it peaked at rates last seen in the great depression.

Bond prices initially fell until 1981 under the influence of rising short-term interest rates. Subsequently, falling inflationary expectations powered falls in unemployment and a bond price rally, which recovered most of the losses of the previous 30 years and has lasted, with occasional setbacks, until the present day. Active maturity managers now had to keep maturities longer than benchmark for most of the time.

4.1.4   Performance experience

The Barcap database reflects the more recent of these developments. In the USA, since 1926, the average excess return of bonds over cash is 1.6%, while in the UK it is a barely positive 0.2% since 1900.

However, the experience varied from generation to generation. Figure 4.3(a) and (b) show the excess returns on stocks and bonds experienced by different generations of UK and US investors.

The UK chart shows that up to about 1950, the experience of returns on stocks of succeeding generations was consistently higher than their experience of returns on bonds, but the two kept

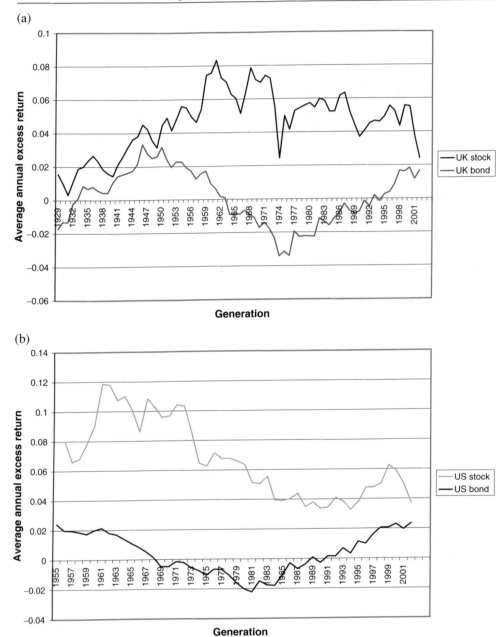

Figure 4.3 Excess returns for different generations
(Raw data sourced from Barclays Capital)

relatively close together so that improving stock experience was accompanied by improving bond experience and vice versa. For the next 25 years, improving experience of stocks was accompanied by deteriorating experience of bonds. This prompted a major shift from bonds to stocks.

During the final quarter of the century, relatively stable experience of stocks was accompanied by improving experience of bonds, albeit from a low base. The spread between the experience of stock and bond returns has reverted to that last seen in the first half of the century. The question for UK investors is therefore whether this is a temporary aberration or whether the last 50 years were an aberration themselves.

The US chart is missing the data from the first half of the twentieth century but shows the same pattern in the second half of divergence followed by convergence. The question for US investors is therefore also whether the huge discrepancies experienced by several generations of investors between stock and bond returns in the twentieth century were an aberration or whether they will set the pattern for the twenty-first century.

4.2   ACTIVE MATURITY MANAGEMENT

As foreshadowed by the discussion of market history, one key active strategy for bonds is active maturity management, or trying to extend maturities when yields are falling and to reduce maturities when yields are rising. The skill required for this is the ability to anticipate changes in yields. Active maturity management depends on knowing what effect a given change in yield will have on the active portfolio and on the benchmark. The tool evolved to deal with this problem is called duration.

4.2.1   Duration

Where one yield is used to value assets and liabilities, it can be shown (A2.18) that, for any change in yield, the change in asset value exactly matches the change in the present value of the liabilities if a simple condition is observed. This is that the value of the assets multiplied by their average life equals the value of the liabilities multiplied by their average life when the average life is calculated by weighting according to the present value of cash flow. Frederick Macaulay, who developed this proposition,[13] coined the term duration for an average life calculated in this way.

Thus a bank or insurance company or any other kind of financial overlay can immunise the overlay against positive or negative changes in overlay value resulting from changes in the interest rate. It does this by matching the durations of assets and liabilities when they are equal in value and the products of duration and value when they are not. The beauty of the concept is that the maturities of the individual assets do not need to relate to the due dates of the liabilities as long as the averages match so adjustment can take place by changing a fraction of the portfolio rather than the whole.

Duration is a useful tool for both active and passive bond portfolio management. For passive management, it determines which set of bonds matches a given set of liabilities. It is also the period for which the yield on a given collection of bonds has effectively been locked in. For active maturity management, the active overlay becomes the value of the portfolio multiplied by the difference between the durations of the active portfolio and the benchmark.

The idea was further developed to remove reliance on using the same yield to value assets and liabilities by introducing the concept of adjusted duration (A2.17). With equal adjusted duration, immunisation is achieved even if the internal rates of return on assets and liabilities are different. The difference between the two yields, or spread, is locked in whatever happens to rates.

Duration is the single number that tells you most about a bond portfolio or a single bond. In this way, it is similar to an equity price to earnings ratio. From equations (A2.17) and (A2.18), the average duration of a portfolio is the average of the durations of the individual bonds in the portfolio weighted by their market values. Thus the change in duration to a portfolio from substituting one bond for another is easy to work out.

4.2.2 Benchmarks

As credit strategies were little used for active bond portfolios managed in London, correctly identifying the benchmark duration was very important and not always straightforward as in the example that follows.

The index used by clients and investment advisors to measure the results of the sterling bond portfolios managed by MAM for UK pension funds was the All Stocks gilt index. This index was designed, as its name suggests, to reflect the entire gilt market. At first, we used the duration of this index as the fulcrum for our maturity bets. We were surprised to find that client feedback when we positioned the portfolios for a fall in interest rates was sometimes more positive when we got it wrong than when we got it right.

It turned out that clients and their advisors placed more importance on comparing our results with the return of the median UK pension fund sterling bond portfolio. As the median portfolio was not identified and changed from period to period, its duration was impossible to establish directly. Instead, we conducted an exercise to see which index had the best fit with the historical median results. This happened with the over-five-year gilt index, which had a duration some 20% more than the All Stocks. This explained the puzzling client reaction to positive bets and became the internal benchmark against which we managed portfolios of this type going forward.

4.2.3 Attribution

Duration is also useful in attributing, or explaining, the return from active bond management. Provided that the yield changes are small and the portfolio duration is constant over the period used it can be shown that the active return is made up of three separate components (A2.20).

The first is the difference between the yield on the portfolio and the yield on the benchmark multiplied by the period. This is the cash impact of the advantage or disadvantage in yield the portfolio has over the benchmark.

The second is the benchmark duration multiplied by the change in the benchmark yield less the change in the portfolio yield. This is the impact of the change in spread of the portfolio yield over the benchmark yield. If the spread narrows, the portfolio will gain capital value relative to the benchmark and vice versa. The first two components measure the effect of any spread bets.

The third component measures the effect of any maturity bets and is the change in the yield of the portfolio multiplied by the difference between the benchmark duration and the portfolio duration. Thus this difference defines an active maturity management overlay. If the portfolio yield rises and the portfolio duration is less than the benchmark duration, this number is positive. Similarly if the portfolio yield falls and the portfolio duration is greater than the benchmark duration, this number is also positive.

4.3 ACTIVE SPREAD MANAGEMENT

While the third component reflects the effect of active maturity management, the first two reflect the effect of active spread management, or trying to find bonds with the same maturity as the benchmark, but higher total returns. This is mainly achieved by skilful analysis and anticipation of spread changes, but as the mortgage example indicates, an active spread manager also has to understand any special features of the structures of the credit products in which he invests.

In 1980, the bulk of available spread products were investment grade* corporate bonds. The spreads were modest and closely related to the grade assigned.[†] The opportunities for distinction or disaster were rare. This rather dull world has been much changed by the increased importance of other types of spread product over the last 20 years.

4.3.1 Mortgages

A major development within the government securities market in the USA was the introduction from 1970 onwards of the mortgage pass-through. These consisted of shares in the cash flows generated by pools of fixed rate mortgages, all carrying the same interest rate and having the same final maturity. The administrator, usually the mortgage originator, collected the cash from the borrowers and passed it through to the bondholder. In the event of default by a borrower, the US government guaranteed the payments. With one important proviso, they were thus equivalent to government bonds with that coupon and that final maturity. The proviso was that there was no call protection as borrowers had the right to repay at any time so that they did not have to keep the debt going after they had sold the house.

The spread of mortgages over treasuries was one obvious incentive to hold them. Initially, it was thought that borrowers were relatively insensitive to market rates and that repayment patterns would be dominated by borrowers' propensity to move house. Historical analysis of repayments generated estimates of future repayments. Analysts used these to estimate the average lives and durations of mortgage securities.[‡] These estimates proved treacherous.

In practice, the pattern for active spread positions that were long mortgages and short treasuries using matched durations calculated in this way was that they outperformed if interest rates were steady and underperformed if interest rates either rose or fell. If interest rates went down, borrowers refinanced, or made use of their option to repay, not because they were moving house, but because they could take out a new loan on the same house at a lower interest rate. The shorter the life of the pass-through relative to its expected life, the worse it was for the bondholder who had to reinvest the unexpected repayments at lower rates.

If interest rates went up, refinancings slowed and the pass-through was repaid slower, leaving the holder receiving payments at less than the market rate for more time than expected. The longer the life of the pass-through relative to its expected life, the worse it was for the bondholder who had less than expected opportunity to reinvest at higher rates.

The historical data on repayments had been mostly gathered during the long bear market up to 1980 when refinancing was not an issue. But markets rallied strongly during the 1980s. Borrowers proved highly responsive[§] to movements in interest rates and high coupon pools were repaid very rapidly.

---

* Graded investment quality, or unlikely to suffer financial distress, by the rating agencies.
[†] Corporate bonds are priced using a matrix approach. That is, a spread is assessed based on the security duration, the effect of any call protection and the credit status of the borrower. This is added to the yield of the government bond of equivalent duration. The price is just the price that gives this yield. The Eurodollar bond market was an exception to this because of the Swiss Buy List effect. Swiss banks maintained lists of specific securities as suitable for purchase by their private clients. Thus different securities issued by the same borrower could trade at markedly different spreads over government bonds depending on which one was on such a list.
[‡] I remember being told by a salesman at the time that the life on issue of a mortgage-backed security was really 12 years and that any spread over a 12-year US Treasury was free money. Even then, the proposition seemed implausible.
[§] They were helped by aggressive advertising which included aeroplanes circling ballparks dragging banners screaming "REFI NOW".

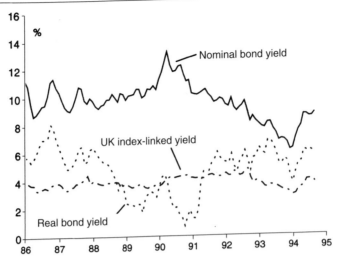

Figure 4.4 UK 10-year bond yields
Source: Goldman Sachs.

4.3.2 Index-linked bonds

With impeccable timing, from the perspective of minimising its debt servicing costs, the UK government began to issue index-linked gilts* in 1981. These securities were designed to match index-linked liabilities such as pensions upgraded to match inflation. As such, they were popular for portfolios where the priority was to match such liabilities. Unfortunately, as they were insulated from the effect of all inflationary expectations, including reducing ones, they completely missed the rally that took place after 1981 in conventional bonds. In 1997 the USA followed suit with the introduction of inflation-indexed treasury securities.

From the mid-1980s onwards, MAM took the view that it was better to mismatch in pursuit of higher return and we avoided this type of asset where we could. This was because, as Figure 4.4 shows, the real yield on conventional bonds was consistently higher than the yield on index-linked bonds with the exception of 1989 and 1990 when UK inflation temporarily spiked.†

4.3.3 Junk bonds and emerging debt

The origin of this market was the rather sad group of corporate bonds where poor performance of the underlying business had resulted in progressive credit downgrades. Because their very large spreads over treasuries made them attractive to yield-hungry investors, junk bonds could be used to finance highly leveraged hostile takeovers.

For example, at the end of 1988, the biscuit and cigarette manufacturer RJR Nabisco had total capital of US$30.1 billion of which US$24.6 billion was equity and US$5.5 billion was

---

* Coupons and principal tied to the UK Retail Price Index. Because of the lags involved in the computation formula, these instruments do not perfectly match movements in the index.
† The persistence of this anomaly was because the managers of UK government debt issuance did not see their job solely in terms of minimising borrowing cost. In the early 1990s, I served as a member of a panel advising the Bank of England and Treasury on sales of government securities. While open to many ideas, they were not receptive to the notion that they should increase the proportion of index linked sales even though, according to their own inflation forecasts, this would have substantially reduced costs.

high grade debt. As a result of such a takeover in March 1989, debt was increased to US$30 billion, equivalent to the entire pre-transaction capital. The proceeds were used to pay off the original shareholders and those bonds where the lenders had had the foresight to insist on their money back if leverage rose above a certain level.*

As the debt was serviced before tax, profits and hence the corporate tax burden were reduced. The market grew rapidly. From year-end 1976 to 1986, the junk market grew from US$15 billion to US$125 billion, or from 7% to 17% of outstanding corporate bonds.

This kind of transaction was particularly popular with ambitious individual predators, or financiers specialising in making hostile takeover offers, with limited resources. This was because the target effectively paid for itself through bond issuance without the predator having to produce cash. It required two things: a steady cash flow from the target to pay the bonds' coupons and proof that the predator could find buyers for the bonds. The first requirement was often met by finding a company involved in consumer staples. The second requirement was met for a fee by an investment bank.

The leading practitioner in this field was Drexel Burnham whose junk bond expert, Mike Milken, issued highly confident (that Drexel could raise the money through a junk bond issue) letters to predators, which were treated with the same respect as irrevocable bank credit lines.[14]

Junk bonds never really took off in Europe and MAM took the decision not to develop the capability to deal with them. This was just as well as yield-hungry junk bond investors had a mixed experience. Stripped of most of their equity protection, many of the highly leveraged takeovers completed in the 1980s, including RJR Nabisco, subsequently experienced financial distress including default and bankruptcy. Milken himself also came to grief by falling foul of securities law and serving time in jail.

Another spread product that MAM ducked was the emerging debt market. This was revived when the Sovereign Debt Crisis was resolved by reorganising US dollar syndicated credits, whose borrowers were unable to pay, as securities with low fixed payments and principal repayment guaranteed by attaching a US Treasury strip.† When these rallied, the market for emerging market government borrowings was reopened. Spreads were as volatile as spreads on junk bonds and the incidence of financial distress was comparable.

4.3.4 Swaps

From the early 1980s onwards investors, who had the flexibility to do so, could take leveraged positions in bank debt through the swap market. A typical investor of this type would be a proprietary trader for a bank or investment bank. An investor with a standard fixed – floating swap would receive a fixed rate known as the swap rate and pay LIBOR at regular intervals over the term of the agreement. The effect is identical to having an overlay that is long a bank bond and short money market borrowings. The difference between the yield on the fixed side of a swap and the yield on a government bond of the same maturity is known as the swap spread and is usually positive to reflect the better credit of the government paper.

Sometimes it is not. In the 1980s and early 1990s, the lira swap market was priced at a yield under the government bond yield. This was because the Italian government deducted withholding tax from their bonds and the market priced the swap over the net yield. An investor who could

---

* Such restrictive covenants tended to be absent from Eurobond prospectuses. Thus many holders of AAA corporate Eurobonds, including the Belgian dentists who were supposed to be the archetypical Eurobond investors, had the unpleasant experience of seeing their securities reduced to junk by some unwelcome US corporate convulsion.
† Called Brady bonds after the eponymous US Treasury Secretary of the time.

recover the tax captured the spread by taking a position that was long Italian government bonds and short lira swaps.

4.4   MARKET EFFICIENCY

Efficient market theory suggests that prices reflect all the available information about a security. The theory is more fully discussed in Chapter 6, where it is shown to provide the intellectual justification for passive management. Active maturity management is impossible when markets are efficient because future yields are already discounted in current yields. Similarly, active spread management is impossible because positive spreads will be cancelled by future losses.

An efficient market also implies that arbitrage, or simultaneously buying or selling an identical security or package of securities for a profit, is impossible. Common sense suggests that an arbitrage is particularly unlikely in markets, such as government bond markets, where the range of securities is limited and transaction costs are low. Fortunately, there are always sufficient inefficiencies, even in government bond markets, to keep active bond managers and market makers in business. Sometimes government creates the inefficiency.

4.4.1   UK tax arbitrage

When I started my career, profit opportunities in the gilt market for investors and traders alike were dominated by two tax arbitrages, both stemming from the peculiar way in which the UK tax authorities treated accrued interest, or the interest earned on a security since its last coupon payment. In the USA (and any other bond market including, now, the UK), accrued interest earned that is subsequently sold is treated as income and taxed as such. However, until the mid-1980s, gilts were quoted with dirty prices, where the accrued interest was not formally separated out, allowing market participants to argue successfully to the UK Inland Revenue that accrued interest should be treated as a capital item. Capital gains tax was much lower than income tax in the UK, with plenty of opportunities for deferral.

Pension schemes, which were exempt from tax, could thus buy gilts from insurance companies, which paid corporation tax, just before they paid a coupon and sell them back after receiving the coupon. The net result was that the insurance company paid a lower rate of tax on its income and was able to share the benefit with the pension scheme and the broker who arranged the transaction. Insurance companies were not allowed to wash, or eliminate the taxable income on, individual bonds in this way so that if one company sold the bond another company had to buy it back (and vice versa), but the process averaged out to the same result. The effect of this activity could be seen very clearly from another quirk of the system. This was that at a certain stage, the market simultaneously quoted both dirty and clean, or net of coupon, prices. The difference between the two was always less than the coupon by a margin that reflected the arbitrage opportunity.

The underwriting syndicates of Lloyds of London, mainly comprised of UK tax-paying individuals, benefited from a version of this arbitrage. Because they calculated profits each year, they tended to keep syndicate reserves in securities with one year or less to maturity. Most of these were not quoted with dirty prices. They therefore persuaded the Inland Revenue to grant them an important concession. This was that they could take up to 80% of their income by selling accrued interest and count it as capital gain (this was known as the 80/20 rule). As going over 80% made all income taxable, the only thing that mattered in running a syndicate portfolio was to realise 79.9% precisely. Some specialised investment managers were established to accomplish just that.

Several things happened in the 1980s to eliminate these activities. First, a wholesale modernisation* of the UK securities markets in 1986 eliminated dirty prices along with much else. Second, the marginal rates of income tax and capital gains tax converged as a result of government policy. Third, severe underwriting losses resulted in most of the Lloyd's syndicate reserves being paid away as underwriting claims.

4.4.2   The US Treasury market

Government bond market inefficiencies are not always dependent on government policy. The US government has worked hard over the years to streamline the US Treasury market. Final maturity at original issue has been restricted to a small number of set terms and call features[†] have been progressively eliminated by the simple expedient of not attaching them to new issues.

Coupon and maturity payments have been synchronised to a set day of each month to simplify comparisons of different bonds and stripping, or breaking up bonds into their component cash flows. In the early days of these instruments, when US treasuries still suffered withholding tax, or tax deducted at source from coupons paid to foreign owners, foreigners had to be careful to buy principal strips, or cash flows arising from principal repayments, as opposed to income strips, which suffered this tax. Most trading in US treasuries is now done with buyers and sellers matched electronically to minimise transaction costs.

Despite this simplicity and efficiency, there have been consistent anomalies between the prices quoted for on-the-run bonds, or those that have been recently issued, and off-the-run bonds, or those issued some time in the past. This is because the on-the-run bonds are more liquid than the off-the-run bonds. Many of the latter have either been stripped or been locked away, often in dedicated portfolios. Because of this higher level of liquidity, active maturity managers prefer to own on-the-run bonds and they trade at lower yields than off-the-run bonds of identical maturity.[‡]

As off-the-run bonds have been issued some time ago, their coupons tend to be significantly higher or lower than those of on-the-run bonds of the same maturity, whose coupons are at or near current market rates so the bonds trade at or close to par. This is because interest rates will have changed over the years since they were issued. Off-the-run bonds thus typically trade at either a premium over par or a discount to par.

Arithmetically, a premium bond is equivalent to a bond trading at par plus a short position in the final maturity cash flow while a discount bond is equal to a par bond plus a long position in the final maturity cash flow (A2.13). It can be shown, by comparing on-the-run bonds with appropriate combinations of off-the-run bonds and strips, that identical packages of US government cash flows are priced differently. This suggests the paradox of a perfect arbitrage being common in a market thought to be close to perfect.

For example, on 24 February 1991, there were three five-year US Treasury securities outstanding, all maturing at par in February 1996. The only difference between them was the

---

* Another effect of this change, which the market rather self-importantly called Big Bang after the prevailing theory about the origin of the universe, was to eliminate the restrictive practice whereby only a specialised member of the stock exchange known as a jobber could make market prices. Before Big Bang, two jobbers dominated market making in gilts. As over 20 institutions took the opportunity to set up as gilt market makers, there was a shortage of skilled gilt traders. This became obvious in early trading as some market makers offered bonds at below the prices other market makers were prepared to pay. In the aftermath of Big Bang, a Darwinian process caused the numbers to fall rapidly as losses mounted.

† Including issues known as flower bonds because the nominal value could be used to pay estate taxes. This feature effectively gave the owner's heirs the right to force the government to prepay the security on the owner's death. The securities were consequently unique in that the life expectancy of the marginal buyer drove the price.

‡ By definition, these are bonds that were originally issued at a longer maturity and have now shortened up to match the maturity of the on-the-run bonds.

coupon rate. The oldest had a coupon of 8.875% and was offered at 105.25 with a yield to maturity of 7.59%. The next oldest had a coupon of 7.875% and was offered at 101.12 with a yield to maturity of 7.57%. The third note had been auctioned three days before. It had a coupon of 7.5% and was offered at 99.72 to yield 7.57%. The differences in yields were thus barely noticeable.

But an investor could also buy a coupon strip maturing in February 1996 at 68.44 to yield 7.78%. He could then use (A2.14) to combine the strip with the high-coupon five-year to duplicate exactly the cash flows of either of the two lower coupon five-years.

Thus $100 nominal of the 7.875% coupon could be matched by a combination of $88.73 nominal of the 8.875% coupon and $11.27 nominal of the strip at a price of $101.10 or $0.02 less than the actual offer price. $100 nominal of the new on-the-run 7.5% coupon could be matched by a combination of $84.51 nominal of the high coupon and $15.41 of the strip at a price of 99.49 or $0.23 less than the actual offer price.

The 7.5% note was thus $0.21 more expensive relative to the arbitrage price of its cash flows than the 7.785% note. The same calculations performed on prices from the day of the auction three days earlier give an arbitrage value of the 7.875% coupon $0.07 below the offer and an arbitrage value of the 7.5% coupon $0.18 below the offer, making the latter $0.11 more expensive than the former.

Such anomalies were consistently available with the arbitrage opportunities for longer dated securities tending to be greater. Also on 24 February 1991, there were two securities maturing in February 2001. One had a coupon of 7.75% and was priced at 98.97 to yield 7.90%. The other had a coupon of 11.75% and was priced at 125.84 to yield 7.95%. The coupon strip was priced at 44.66 to yield 8.25%. The arbitrage combination of $65.96 nominal of the high-coupon bond and $34.04 of the strip was priced at $98.21 or $0.76 less than the actual offer price.

The obstacles to being able actually to make money out of a matched cash flow overlay which is long the combination of off-the-run and zero and short the on-the-run are formidable. First, you have to be able to deal at these prices. Second, you have to be able to borrow the low-coupon bond cheaply. Third, you cannot be subject to withholding tax. In effect this limited the field to primary dealers* and specialist investors with the right dealing skills, credit status and tax status.

For those in a position to capture the arbitrage, the returns are modest as the capitalised arbitrage value is realised over the life of the bond so the 10-year arbitrage works out at about eight basis points a year. The repo, or sale and repurchase, market in US treasuries compensates for this by allowing leverage of 50 times or more, raising the potential excess return to a respectable 4% or so. Positions that were long off-the-run treasuries and short on-the-run treasuries were standard for both the Salomon Arbitrage Group and LTCM.[15]

When the US government auctioned bonds, the old on-the-run bonds were supplanted by the new bonds and became off-the-run. Primary dealers offer bonds before the auction as when issued (WI), so that active managers could switch into the new on-the-run without waiting for the auction itself. Primary dealers who had sold bonds WI had to make sure of getting sufficient bonds in the auction to cover their commitments as otherwise they would be squeezed by those who had been successful.

---

* A group of some 40 investment banks granted the right to bid in US Treasury auctions in return for a commitment to make markets in these securities. Any other bidders had to use a primary dealer as agent.

4.4.3   Salomon episode

On one occasion that I am personally aware of, these inefficiencies had some help. The story starts when, to my surprise and alarm, I received a letter in April 1991 from the US Treasury telling me that my desk had bid through Salomon Brothers for US$3.15 billion or 35% of the 21 February five-year note auction and that the bid had been accepted into the auction. My surprise was because MAM's auction participation was very limited as we preferred to buy either WI or in the after-market. Salomon was then the leading US investment bank specialising in bonds. It had received an important seal of approval when the well-known US investor, Warren Buffett, had acted as white knight and taken a controlling stake[16] as a defence against a junk bond financed hostile takeover bid in 1987. I knew so little at the time about auction mechanics (US Treasury trading and our day-to-day relationship with Salomon Brothers being the responsibility of a colleague, then unavailable) that my first concern was that the bid had been kept in a bottom drawer and was now a colossal late booked bargain.*

The reason for the letter was that our parent owned a small primary dealer and this entity had bid for US$100 million at the same rate. The Treasury felt that, as we were affiliated, the two bids should be treated as one and were therefore in technical breach of a rule introduced to stop any one bidder cornering the market by limiting bids to 35% of the auction.

I then took a call from Paul Mozer, a senior managing director, who had been in the Arbitrage Group but was now Head of US Treasury trading at Salomon. Mozer told me that there had been an embarrassing error and that Salomon had put our name down mistakenly for a bid made by another client. He asked if we could acknowledge the letter and leave it to Salomon to make the appropriate explanations to the Treasury. I was relieved that there was no late booked bargain problem but noncommittal about his request, telling him I would discuss it with colleagues.

My cautious reaction was because my then chairman was very sensitive about our relationships with US investment banks. Our parent organisation was making strenuous efforts to break into the US investment banking business and my chairman was on the parent board. He had recently made his displeasure known in no uncertain terms when my team had suspended an unsatisfactory dealing relationship with another major US investment bank, with which our parent had a close relationship.

I therefore checked the matter with him and other interested internal parties and found that no one wanted to risk crossing Salomon by denying the auction bid directly and all were in favour of letting them straighten it out themselves. After all, even the best run financial institutions made embarrassing administrative errors and the US Treasury, while peripheral to our activities, was central to theirs.

As anyone who is familiar with this story knows, Mozer had in fact used our name to evade the US Treasury 35% limit. He had done the same thing with our name[†] and others' several times in the past without being caught, so the bid from our primary dealer affiliate must have come as an unpleasant surprise.

Taking the shift in relative value over the three days after auction day as a measure of the impact on prices of the squeeze, the value to Salomon of the extra bonds he obtained by

---

* Unscrupulous traders have been known to delay, or put in the bottom drawer, allocating a bargain until they know whether it has gone up or down. In order to police such activity, discretionary investment managers are given a brief window in time in which to record or "book" transactions. Transactions recorded after this deadline are called late booked bargains and can be repudiated by the investor, who effectively gets an option on the transaction.

† Mozer probably chose MAM from among Salomon's large clients both because it was a very infrequent auction participant and because it ran one of the largest single portfolios of actively managed US treasuries outside the USA at the time.

violating the auction rules was an unremarkable 0.1%, which probably explains why nobody outside Salomon noticed at the time. US$1.7 billion face value of bonds was allocated to the rule-breaking bid, implying a potential profit of US$1.7 million. Ironically, Salomon are reported to have lost US$14 million on the auction, suggesting that any advantage from the squeeze was swamped by poor positioning.[17]

As a further irony, Mozer seems to have been sufficiently worried by my noncommittal response to brief his boss, John Meriwether, about the bid. However, he presented it as a one-off aberration. They had then told John Gutfreund, Salomon's chairman (known at the time as the King of Wall Street), Thomas Strauss, Salomon's president and Donald Feuerstein, Salomon's chief legal counsel. Mozer was given a severe reprimand, promised not to do it again and all let the matter drop.

In the May 22 auction of two-year notes he acquired 94% of the total offered. "According to Buffett, that particular bid by Mozer was 'almost like a self-destruct mechanism. It was not the act of a rational man'."[18] The abuse was so blatant that it triggered SEC and Justice Department investigations. In the course of these, the April letter came to light and a group of us had to cross the Atlantic to explain ourselves* to the SEC. Mozer went to jail and Meriwether, Gutfreund, Strauss and Feuerstein were all forced to leave Salomon. Buffett temporarily took over as chairman but Salomon never recovered, eventually losing its independence to Travelers Insurance in 1997.

4.5   CONCLUSION

Fixed interest assets, or bonds, are attractive for investors who want reliable future income as they deliver a fixed and therefore predictable set of future payments. Until the twentieth century, they were the asset class of choice for investors. Unprecedented inflation during the twentieth century meant that bonds significantly underperformed stocks. As a result of this, there has been a tendency for investors to deploy their risky asset investment into stocks and confine bonds to acting as matching assets, or assets designed to meet defined monetary obligations.

Much of the early impetus to develop bond markets came from government borrowing and government bonds still form an important part of the bond market of each country. Financial economists consider government bond markets to be close to the theoretical ideal of perfect markets. Even so, tax and liquidity effects have been sufficient to create many long-standing inefficiencies.

Active bond management seeks to exploit these and other inefficiencies by using either maturity strategies or spread strategies based on the wide range of instruments trading at a yield premium or spread over government bonds. The spread is usually attributable to credit or the probability of borrower default, but not always. It sometimes reflects the right of the borrower to repay or call the bonds back when rates move against him.

ENDNOTES

1. 11th Edition, vol. 3, p. 423.
2. C. Northcote Parkinson, *The Law and the Profits*. London: John Murray, 1960, p. 33.
3. *The Oxford History of the British Army*, ed. D. Chandler. Oxford: Oxford University Press, 1996, p. 63.

---

* To his credit, Meriwether rang me to apologise personally for Salomon's behaviour and the embarrassment this was causing my colleagues and me.

 4. J. Macdonald, *A Free Nation Deeply in Debt*. New York: Farrar Strauss, 2003, p. 339.
 5. *Sunday Times*, 9 September 2001.
 6. This and all subsequent debt to GNP figures up to 1945 are taken from Macdonald.
 7. The information on Dutch annuities comes from two papers (vol. ii, p. 222 and vol. iii, p. 93) contributed by Frederick Hendriks to the *Assurance Magazine*, a precursor to the *Journal of the Institute of Actuaries*.
 8. Macdonald, p. 187.
 9. Macdonald, p. 219.
10. Macdonald, p. 236.
11. Johnson, p. 176.
12. Macdonald, pp. 293, 294.
13. "Some theoretical problems suggested by the movement of interest rates, bond yields and stock prices in the United States since 1856", National Bureau of Economic Research, 1938.
14. C. Bruck, *The Predators Ball*. New York: Simon and Schuster, 1988, p. 166.
15. Lowenstein, pp. 43–45.
16. Lowenstein, p. 18.
17. *Independent*, 5 January 1992.
18. *Financial Post*, 9 September 1991.

5

Foreign Assets

These are the fourth main asset class and comprise stocks, bonds, cash and other assets from outside the investor's home market. Foreign, or overseas, assets have a long history. In the Middle Ages, Kings Henry II and Richard I of England thought more about their possessions in the Loire Valley than anywhere else, even choosing to be buried at Fontevrault rather than Westminster Abbey. The village in which I live was given after the Norman Conquest to the Abbey of Bec in Normandy. King Henry V expropriated it in 1414[1], an early example of one problem with overseas assets. Another problem with overseas assets is that of exchange rates, leading to many early international obligations to be specified as weights of gold and silver, a system that eventually led to the international gold standard.

With all these difficulties, there have to be good reasons to get involved. There are two main ones. The first is that some overseas assets give a better return than domestic assets of the same type while others give a worse return. Being able to predict which is which creates the potential for a successful active overlay. The second is that, by having returns linked to a different economy, overseas assets provide an investor with diversification.

5.1   HISTORY

Foreign securities developed from the seventeenth century onwards. As a domestic security for a resident of one country is a foreign security for a resident of another country, the history of foreign securities is really the history of global securities. Although the literature on foreign securities concentrates on stocks, the bulk of foreign securities measured by value was and still is bonds. However, while global growth in the volume of bonds has been impressive, their return has been eclipsed by the return on global equities with the result that equity market capitalisation has caught up.

5.1.1   To 1900

Some securities in the seventeenth and eighteenth centuries were issued by businesses with actual or intended overseas operations. We have already seen examples of these in the East India Company and the South Seas Company. Contemporary examples in other countries were La Compagnie des Indes in France and the Darien Company in Scotland.* The Darien Company also attempted to sell its securities outside Scotland. By the nineteenth century, it was commonplace for securities to be issued in one country and sold as overseas securities to investors in other countries.

---

* La Compagnie des Indes was the vehicle for a scheme promoted by the expatriate Scots financier John Law to develop the Mississippi basin and pay off the French national debt. The Darien Company was the vehicle for a scheme devised by another Scot, William Paterson, who also played a leading role in founding the Bank of England, to develop a trading settlement on the Isthmus of Panama. Both attracted a substantial proportion of the financial wealth of their respective countries but both ended badly. In 1720, only months after being created Duc D'Arkansas by a grateful French government, Law had to flee for his life from the Paris mob. The Darien Company was said to have bankrupted the Scottish business community and paved the way for the Act of Union with England in 1707.

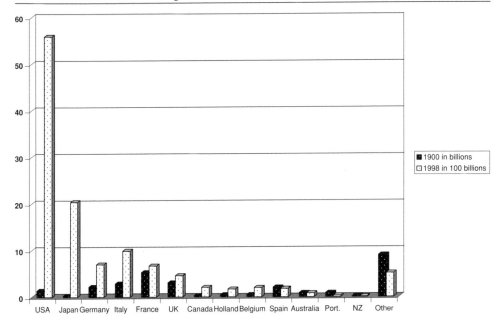

Figure 5.1 World government debt

The Suez Canal Company, a pioneering global security issue to finance one of the major infrastructure projects of the time, was established in 1858 in Egypt with a paid-up share capital of 200 million French francs. This was raised as follows: 104 million from French nationals, 7 million from other foreigners and 89 million from the Egyptian government[2]. To protect investors from any depreciation of the franc, its fixed obligations were specified in gold francs.*

As a natural extension to their business of accepting overseas paper, the London merchant banks became heavily involved during the nineteenth century in raising finance for overseas borrowers. In anticipation of the Baring episode of 1995, there was a Baring crisis in 1890. Baring got overextended in Argentine debt and was unable to meet obligations totalling £21 million. As this was approximately 2% of GNP, the Bank of England obviously considered that Baring was too big to fail and organised a rescue.[†]

5.1.2   Foreign bonds from 1900

By 1900, the global total of outstanding government debt was US$31.3 billion[3] as compared with a global total a century later[4] of US$11.9 trillion, an average growth of 380 times. Figure 5.1 shows outstanding debt by country.

The pattern of borrowing has changed since 1900. The largest borrowers now, the USA and Japan, were relatively insignificant then. The Iberian peninsular, Australia and New Zealand

---

* In 1973, the French government sold bonds effectively denominated in gold francs as they were convertible to gold at fixed parity. They were known as "Giscards" after the then French Finance Minister (later President) and proved a very good investment when the gold price rocketed.

† Before this happened, at least one retired partner was approached for help. The following conversation ensued. Emissary: "My lord, the house may fall." Retired Partner: "Then call in a builder. Good day to you Sir."

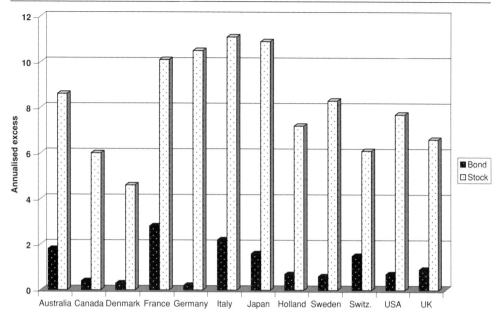

Figure 5.2   Twentieth century returns
Source: ABN AMRO

have managed to restrain the growth in their borrowings to less than a factor of 100. The very slow growth of "Other" has been because a number of important borrowers in 1900 either have ceased to be important now or have been reclassified as "emerging debt". This casualty list includes Russia, India, China, Brazil, Argentina and Hungary.

5.1.3   Foreign returns from 1900

Studies of the returns on stocks and bonds over the last century have to omit returns from the markets of countries where there are large gaps in the financial data. These lacunae bias the results upwards because they are often associated with a financial or economic disaster such as expropriation or market abolition. We will return to the topic of survivorship bias in Chapter 6.

Figure 5.2 shows the average annualised percentage excess return over money market rates of the stock and bond markets of countries for which complete or almost complete time series are available for the twentieth century.[5] This is the survivors' roll of capitalism. Its composition would not have been obvious in 1900.

For these successful capitalist countries, the pattern of financial return is absolute. All excess returns over money market rates are positive and no stock market has an average excess return that is less than that of any bond market.

This experience has had a profound effect on investment policy. While global overseas and domestic holdings of equities were small relative to bonds in 1900, equities had caught up by 1995. The global total of private and institutional holdings of equities, at US$16.3 trillion, just exceeded the global total holdings of bonds, at US$15.7 trillion. Within these figures, overseas holdings of equities, at US$2.8 trillion, still lagged overseas holdings of bonds, at US$3.9 trillion.[6]

5.2 GLOBAL INVESTORS

The collapse of the gold standard and the emergence of equities as the asset class of choice complicated overseas investment in two ways: investing in equities required a specialised knowledge of overseas business conditions; exposure to foreign currencies required a specialised knowledge of exchange rate conditions. US individuals and institutions are now the most important overseas equity investors, with two-thirds of global overseas equity holdings. Of this, individual holdings total US$1.5 trillion while institutional holdings of overseas equities total US$0.4 trillion.[7]

5.2.1 Modern portfolio theory

During the nineteenth century, the USA had imported capital. In its early career as a capital exporter, foreign investment had largely taken two forms: direct foreign investment by US companies and government loans such as the US$4.3 billion to the UK immediately after the Second World War. As explained in 5.3.2, the terms of this loan made it of little use to the hard-pressed UK economy. "Keynes thought the loan to be grudging and inadequate and the strain of negotiating it left him exhausted and contributed to his early death the following year."[8]

The development of modern financial techniques of analysis based on the proposition, expanded in the next chapter, that an investor is trying to maximise the ratio of return to standard deviation of return of his portfolio gave a big boost to the credibility of overseas security investment in the USA. This was because such analysis placed a premium on securities or groups of securities that had low correlations with the US stock market. Overseas was the obvious place to look and a number of academic papers were published from 1970[9] onwards with this message.

5.2.2 US overseas equity investors

When the benchmark is domestic equities, the active overlay that corresponds to an overseas equity strategy is long foreign equities and short the domestic equity index. The performance of such an overlay is dominated by broad market and currency effects and tells the investor little about the active manager's skill in picking overseas stocks and sectors. A demand therefore arose for an overseas stock index both to measure actively managed overseas stock portfolios and to form the basis of passively managed overseas stock portfolios. US investors use an EAFE (Europe, Australia, Far East) index.[10]

Because their marketing departments need access, US mutual fund sponsors generally prefer to use in-house investment professionals to manage their products investing in overseas securities. However, the 1974 ERISA specifically encourages US pension fund sponsors to use the services of qualified professional investment managers. This had the effect of creating a level playing field on which foreign-based investment management firms could compete with US-based firms on equal terms for the overseas components of US pension funds.

Although UK overseas investments were small in scale, they required an infrastructure of analysts, strategists and portfolio managers to support them. The opportunity to compete for US business gave UK investment management firms the chance to leverage these sunk costs.

However, there was a problem. In order to manage portfolios for US pension funds, you had to register a firm of investment advisors with the SEC. The regulations required that it should be an independent entity. Cautious legal counsel interpreted this to mean that it should have separate personnel, infrastructure and investment policies. In short, that it should be enclosed in a soundproof glass box. The only firms that could leverage their existing infrastructures and avoid creating new ones were those whose investment professionals worked together on a common investment strategy. Such firms could argue that US investors needed access to the existing team. They could also put forward the track record achieved for non-US-sourced portfolios as a valid indication of the track record US investors would have experienced.

5.2.3   US overseas bond investors

In order to justify strategic investment in foreign bonds, it is not enough to apply the mathematics of diversification to domestic bonds. This is because foreign bonds, including those hedged using short-term forward foreign exchange contracts, are no longer matching assets. Foreign bonds have to be treated, like foreign equities, as an additional risky asset class. Their lower returns make them less attractive as such. US institutions, including insurance companies, own US$0.2 trillion of overseas bonds. Overseas bonds held by US individuals are negligible.[11]

The US investors that did acquire overseas bond portfolios tended to divide into three groups. One elected for international portfolios comprising only overseas bonds and currencies. The argument for this was that they already had plenty of US assets and did not want their overseas manager to buy any more. One elected for global portfolios, which allowed the overseas manager to allocate actively between US and overseas currencies and assets. The last group elected for hedged portfolios on the basis that these represented a lower risk diversification from US bonds.

As with stock portfolios, overseas bond portfolios need indices to form passive portfolios and to measure active portfolios. During the 1970s and early 1980s, the indices that were available were of indifferent quality. Good quality overseas bond indices only became available in the mid-1980s.[12]

5.3   GOVERNMENT POLICY

Government policies towards overseas investment tend to have two simplistic objectives. First, minimising any tax leakage. The US Interest Equalisation Tax is an example of this. Second, discouraging overseas investments that create jobs for foreigners where the money could be used to create domestic jobs. The UK provides good examples of distortions arising from both kinds of policy. In recent times, there has been a return towards the open capital markets of the nineteenth century. This in turn has encouraged governments to relax policies directed against overseas investment.

5.3.1   Tax

Apart from Americans, MAM's main overseas clients with fixed interest portfolios were governments (including those newly enriched by the oil price boom), offshore insurance subsidiaries of US companies* and offshore corporations. With the exception of governments, which had sovereign immunity, investors had two tax problems.

---

* Known as "captive" insurance companies. They were essentially a mechanism to allow corporations to self-insure and not to pay tax on the income from their reserves. In order to maintain their tax status they had to underwrite other risks as well, which sometimes resulted in disaster. Poorly advised single parent captive insurers became known in the underwriting business as "innocent capacity". A second generation known as "offshore mutual" insurance companies grouped participants together so that they insured each other's risks, thus keeping it all in the family.

The first problem was that of withholding tax, at one stage deducted from almost all government bonds.* This was addressed by bond washing, or selling bonds about to pay coupons and reinvesting the money in bonds of similar maturity that had just paid their coupons, at considerable trouble and expense. The second problem was the attitude of the UK Inland Revenue. This was that, if a foreign company had its portfolio managed by a UK investment firm, it was carrying on business in the UK and the income from the portfolio was subject to UK tax. The industry solved this with the "echo system".

This device required the UK investment management firm to have an investment subsidiary in the Channel Islands or some other offshore location. This became the entity foreign corporate clients legally contracted with. No pretence was made at creating any investment management expertise offshore. The subsidiary was supposed to follow London's investment advice. To substantiate this and create a paper trail, the London "advisor" had to telex a "recommendation" to Jersey or Guernsey. The Channel Islands subsidiary then had to telex back an acceptance (hence the echo) before a transaction could take place. The system was cumbersome to operate, particularly in fast moving markets, and required extra clerical activity both in London and offshore. In addition, the tax status of the whole portfolio was compromised if one step in the chain was missed or taken out of sequence. Furthermore, it was not tax efficient. Taxes on investment income that could be recovered through double taxation treaties could not be recovered for portfolios set up in this way.

Despite the disadvantages for both investors and investment professionals, the echo system survived into the 1990s when the Inland Revenue finally adopted a more rational position. This was probably due to the benefits the system generated for UK investment management firms, which may have reduced the energy they put into lobbying for change. By booking the fees from such portfolios offshore, substantial tax savings were generated which more than outweighed the cost of the extra clerks.

5.3.2   UK exchange control

From the East India Company onwards, investors living in the UK had looked overseas for higher returns and the UK had accumulated a very substantial net position in overseas assets by 1914. However, the exigencies of the two world wars had eliminated this by 1945. Between 1914 and 1919, the UK had reduced net foreign assets by about £1 billion and incurred extra net foreign debt of about £1.2 billion.[13] Between 1939 and 1945, the UK reduced its net foreign assets by a further £1.1 billion and added £2.9 billion to its net foreign debt. Raising the foreign exchange needed for wartime supplies thus eliminated the £4 billion positive net position in foreign assets that remained in 1939.[14]

The balance of payments problems caused by the loss of foreign assets resulted in a system of exchange controls that were introduced at the beginning of the Second World War and were still in place 40 years later. The most onerous condition of the post-war US loan was that sterling had to become fully convertible. Convertibility was reintroduced on 15 July 1947 and suspended indefinitely on 21 August 1947, by which time less than 10% remained of the dollars originally advanced.[15]

In order to invest a dollar overseas, you had to buy it from an investor who already had overseas investments and was planning to reduce them. Such people were hard to find and in

---

* There were certain exceptions. Canada was for a while the only major borrower not to deduct tax from coupons paid to overseas holders of its government securities. Other countries had special classes of bonds designed to allow overseas investors to avoid their own taxes. For example, the UK had FOTRA (free of tax to residents abroad) bonds.

order to give them an incentive, a dollar premium was introduced, which was effectively the market clearing price for the UK overseas investment pool. If you wanted to invest a dollar in US stocks and the premium was 25 cents, you had to pay US$1.25 for your investment. Thus if the dividend yield on your investment was 5%, your effective yield was only 4%. In addition, as the premium fluctuated wildly, you were not only experiencing market and currency risk but also premium risk.

Not surprisingly, there were a number of attempts to circumvent the premium. One of the more ingenious was that devised for IOS.[16] Investments gathered by the IOS sales force in the UK were redefined as premium payments on life insurance policies written by an IOS subsidiary and reinsured abroad with another IOS subsidiary. The reinsurance payments were then invested in the IOS Fund of Funds without having to buy investment dollars.

Despite the premium, overseas investment showed some growth. In 1964, the average allocation to overseas stocks of UK pension funds was zero. By 1979, after a cumulative real return on UK stocks over 15 years of -32%, desperate investors had raised pension funds' average allocation to overseas stocks to 5%. They had also invested in precious metals, works of art, farmland, indeed anything that might arrest the continuous loss of real value their portfolios were experiencing. The abolition of exchange controls in October 1979 thus released a pent up wave of demand. The dollar premium, quoted at 23–26 cents, became worthless overnight and the proportion of UK pension funds invested in overseas stocks climbed to 8% over the next year.

5.4   ACTIVE CURRENCY MANAGEMENT

Currency strategy is an important part of managing foreign assets. It is sometimes separated from securities management and packaged as a freestanding currency overlay service, where the investment firm has discretion to implement its views through currency forwards, or a currency advisory service, where the advisor does not have discretion. Currency strategy can be passive, as with decisions to hedge everything all the time or never to hedge anything ever, but it is often active. Active currency strategies that have proved useful in the recent past include those based on yield and those based on convergence. Sometimes the currency strategy forms an integral part of the investment logic, as in the hedged overseas bond example described in this section.

5.4.1   Theory and practice

Economists offer two theories about currencies, both based on arbitrage arguments. The first theory, Purchasing Power Parity (PPP), assumes that the real or inflation-adjusted prices of tradable goods, or those capable of being moved from country to country, are the same as otherwise entrepreneurs would ship goods from where they are cheap to where they are expensive (A2.23). Thus if inflation is higher in country A than country B, currency A must depreciate relative to currency B to keep real prices the same. In addition, if currency A undergoes a step depreciation, or devaluation, relative to currency B, goods in country A immediately become cheaper, or more competitive, than goods in country B. PPP explains why inflation was possible in the USA despite Bretton Woods, why foreign demand for the gold in the US depository at Fort Knox grew from a trickle to a flood between 1945 and 1971, and why UK inflation could be higher than US inflation.

Despite wartime inflation, the US dollar was competitively priced against gold in 1945. This was because President Roosevelt devalued the US dollar against gold, and thus the currencies tied to gold, by 41%, or from US$20.67 per ounce to US$35 per ounce, between April 1933 and

January 1934.[17] In addition, the fortunes of war had directed the vast bulk of the world's gold in official hands into Fort Knox. These two factors gave the US authorities plenty of scope to inflate without triggering an exchange rate crisis. However, as they inflated, the declining real value of the dollar made gold look progressively cheaper at US$35, prompting more and more demand from foreign governments. In contemporary parlance, the 1945 'dollar shortage', became, by the 1960s, a 'dollar glut'. Although sterling was overvalued in 1945, the UK was able to sustain annual domestic inflation about 1% higher than the US between 1945 and 1971. This was because sterling was devalued over the period by a cumulative 40% against the US dollar.

The second theory is a combination of covered interest arbitrage (A2.24) and efficient market theory. Covered interest arbitrage sets the rate at which you can buy or sell a currency forward, or in the future, against another currency at the spot, or current, rate adjusted for the interest rate differential between deposits in the two currencies. Efficient market theory suggests that this forward rate should be the best possible forecast of the spot rate at that time.

While they provide explanations for long-term effects, neither theory works very well over the short or medium term. The currencies of high inflation countries frequently appreciate relative to the currencies of low inflation countries. The real value of the Mark was famously volatile during the Weimar inflation.[18] Keynes lost heavily by speculating against it, having to be saved from bankruptcy by loans from his publishers and a friendly financier.[19]

As all successful active currency managers know, currencies appreciate more often than not when they are at a forward discount, even though the theory predicts depreciation. There is a lot of discussion in the financial economics literature about this latter anomaly and why it occurs. In simple terms, the reason why both theories fail is that the total return, or yield plus currency movement, on higher yielding money market investments tends to be greater than the total return on lower yielding money market investments because investors tend to chase yield and bid up the higher yielding currencies. High inflation countries tend to have high money market rates, which is why purchasing power parity is so inaccurate as a practical tool for active currency management.

Thus a good naïve active currency strategy is systematically to hedge out of lower yielding currencies into higher yielding currencies. This introduces exchange risk as the active overlay is now long the high-yielding currency and short the low-yielding currency. The active overlay manager needs something to give him confidence that the currency depreciation will be less than the spread. This usually turns out to be a government policy designed to manage the exchange rate. Two very common strategies that depended for their success on government intervention of this kind were emerging high-yield strategies and European convergence strategies.

5.4.2   Emerging high-yield strategies

Emerging high-yield strategies took advantage of certain currencies such as the Mexican peso where the exchange rate had a peg, or official support, at a set dollar rate, which sometimes crawled.* The long position of the active overlay was therefore the emerging currency while the short position was the US dollar. The problem with this strategy was that such currencies were prone to large and unpredictably timed devaluations.† This pattern of steady gains over

---

* A crawling peg describes a rolling series of small adjustments to the support level, usually of a currency with a high domestic inflation rate.
† When flying into Mexico City in 1976, I was struck by the assiduity with which the cabin crew were distributing a brochure showing that the Mexican peso had been stable against the dollar for over 20 years and that peso investors could get 4% more yield than dollar investors. Within days, the peso devalued by 50%.

long periods punctuated by large losses has been studied in the literature of financial economics where it is known as the "peso problem".

In common with most of its European competitors, MAM had minimal exposure to such strategies. This was not the case in the USA, where such products were packaged as "Global Money Funds". We therefore escaped the problems that our US opposite numbers had in 1994 after a round of emerging economy currency devaluations caused substantial capital losses.

5.4.3 European convergence strategies

MAM did make extensive use of European convergence strategies. These took advantage of the long-held ambition of a widening group of the constituent countries of the European Union to merge their currencies together. This started, after the events of 1971, with commitments to limit currency fluctuations against other European currencies, which were known as the snake and the snake in a tunnel.*

The early versions of this system had a turbulent history, with member currencies leaving and rejoining frequently as their finance ministers and central bankers juggled membership with domestic policy priorities. Over time, commitment grew and arrangements for mutual support became stronger so it became more difficult to drive a currency out of the system with a speculative raid.

The opportunity was that member currencies all had parities against the Deutsche Mark that were officially fixed but all had money market rates that were above German money market rates. It was thus possible to create a synthetic money market instrument in any currency by owning a high-yielding European money market instrument and "cross-hedging" it back through forward sales of the Mark into the currency of choice. The synthetic instrument would deliver the European yield spread over the domestic money market instrument. The active overlay corresponding to this strategy was long the high-yielding European currency and short the Mark. In order for it to work, the high-yielding European currency had to stay within its tolerance against the Mark.

The ultimate success of EMU (European Monetary Union) has meant that this strategy has been extremely successful in the long run. Starting with the Dutch guilder, successive currencies converged with the Mark by achieving a constant exchange rate and identical money market rates. The path has not been smooth. From time to time there have been crises[†] when currencies have left the system or devalued against the Mark.

The existence of the convergence opportunity has acted as a substitute for credit strategies for London-based fixed income managers over the last 20 years. Its elimination through EMU after a final five years when there were no crises has prompted a new emphasis on credit analysis and research.

---

* So called because the pattern formed by plotting the exchange rates of member currencies against the dollar over time was reminiscent of a writhing and thrashing snake. The fatness of the snake reflected the degree by which member currencies could fluctuate against each other. The tunnel represented a rather short-lived attempt to manage the fluctuations of the whole system against the dollar.

[†] The last major one was in 1992 when sterling was forced out of the system and speculators made a killing. While it has never admitted a figure, rumour has it that the Bank of England lost £4 billion mounting a futile defence of the currency. Hedge funds managed by George Soros made £1 billion and he became known as "the man who broke the Bank of England". Sterling money market rates, which had been kept high to defend the currency, were subsequently cut substantially, which diminished the hedged bond opportunity for UK investors.

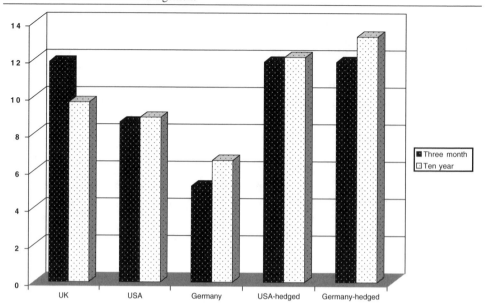

Figure 5.3 1988 Yield curves
Data sourced from Wall Street Journal

5.4.4   Hedged overseas bonds

Until 1988, the exposure of UK pension funds to overseas bonds was close to zero. In that year, an unusual opportunity presented itself. As discussed in Chapter 4, the UK government of the time was running a tight monetary policy. In addition, helped by the tactic of privatisation,* it had achieved a fiscal surplus. It was using the surplus to buy back government bonds with the result that the UK yield curve was negatively sloped with the 10-year bond yield lower than the three-month deposit rate. The 10-year gilt rate was still high relative to the 10-year rate in other bond markets, but these had differently shaped yield curves. The USA, for example, had a flat yield curve with the 10-year rate very similar to the three-month rate. Germany, for example, had a positively sloped yield curve with the 10-year rate higher than the three-month rate. Stylised versions of these yield curves are shown in Figure 5.3.

The figure[20] also shows stylised versions of the yield curves achieved by hedging US and German government bonds into sterling using three-month forwards. Because a hedged three-month deposit rate equals the three-month deposit rate in the hedging currency, all these curves coincide for short maturities. But because a hedged yield curve preserves its shape, the curves diverge at longer maturities. The strategy of hedging non-UK bonds back to sterling can be thought of as creating synthetic bonds with a yield curve arrived at by superimposing the short-term yield differential on the non-UK yield curve.†

An important property of hedged bonds should now be apparent. This is that, if the bond market being hedged has a more positively sloped yield curve than the bond market of the hedging currency, the synthetic yield of the hedged bond will be higher than the yield of the

---

* The process of selling off state-owned businesses to the public. Unlike the South Sea scheme, this equity for debt swap was successful as the market had a positive view of the business prospects of the privatised companies.

† Captured through the forward discount at which the hedge contract bought sterling. The greater the differential, the greater the discount.

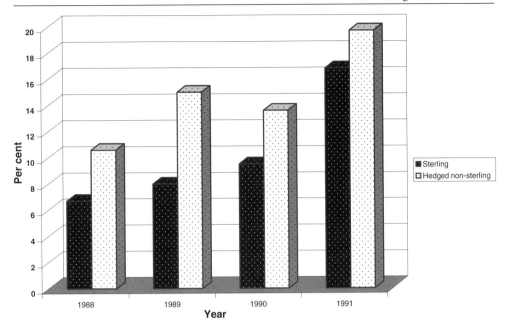

Figure 5.4   Hedged bond performance
Data sourced from JP Morgan

bond of equivalent maturity denominated in the hedging currency. As the UK yield curve was more negatively sloped than the yield curves of all the other major global bond markets, sterling hedged bonds had very attractive yield characteristics relative to gilts.

In October 1988, MAM launched a product to take advantage of the opportunity to capture the spread between such synthetic sterling government bonds and gilts. Although the currency strategy was to be permanently hedged, it formed part of a currency neutral active overlay, which was long hedged foreign bonds and short gilts. The product was described to our investors in the following way:[21]

> The fund will be able to exploit long-term structural anomalies in global capital markets. For example: the UK yield curve is, on average, very much flatter than the German yield curve. If these circumstances persist, this implies that German government bonds hedged into sterling will, in the long term, outperform gilts because the forward premiums captured will, on average, be significantly greater than the long term yield differential given up.

The risk was that the capital performance of sterling bonds relative to non-sterling bonds would exceed the spread. We judged this to be acceptable relative to the potential upside. Figure 5.4 shows the performance of sterling bonds and hedged non-sterling bonds[22] over the four years when these conditions obtained.

The average annual outperformance of 4.1% was achieved over a period when UK government bond yields fell by 0.46% while yields rose in Germany by 0.96% and fell in the USA by 2.53%. The dramatically different fortunes of the US and German bond markets demonstrate the benefit of adopting a diversified approach to overseas bond investment.[23]

As we will see in Chapter 8, the product and its imitators grew rapidly and by 1991 the UK pension fund allocation to overseas bonds had caught up with the allocation to index-linked bonds. Because MAM's product was organised as a pooled vehicle rather than segregated

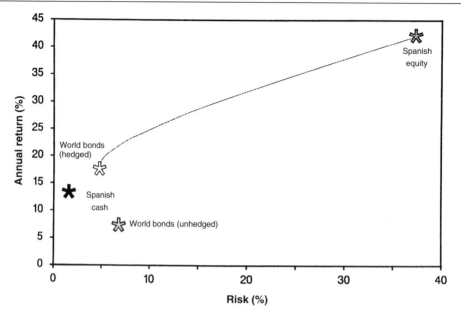

Figure 5.5   1988 Spanish perspective
Raw data sourced from Salomon Brothers

portfolios it then represented, at US$4 billion, one of the largest actively managed global bond portfolios in the world outside the USA, with the consequences described in 4.4.3.

Coincidently, we secured a mandate from a Spanish bank to manage a global bond portfolio for Spanish retail investors. These investors measured the performance of fixed income products like this against what they could get in the Spanish money market. This was a tough benchmark. Peseta rates were high and the peseta was strong. We proposed hedged bonds first because their synthetic yield was higher than peseta cash and second because of the reduction in volatility from combining hedging with the effect of diversifying across a number of different bond markets. Figure 5.5 comes from the original presentation of this concept.

Once again it worked well and we were invited to run several of the limited number of Spanish global bond mutual funds. The strategy was finally stopped by the Spanish regulatory authorities who decided, despite our representations, that it was speculative to hedge overseas assets back into pesetas.

5.5   CONCLUSION

The case for holding overseas assets rather than their domestic equivalents relies on two arguments. First, selected overseas assets give better returns than their domestic equivalents. Second, by having returns linked to a different economy, overseas assets provide an investor with diversification that reduces his investment risk.

The case against holding foreign assets is also twofold. First, government policy generally discourages overseas investment. Domestic owners of foreign assets have historically been penalised while foreign owners of domestic assets are more vulnerable to expropriation than domestic owners. Second, the denomination of foreign assets in foreign currencies changes their nature. Foreign cash is no longer a risk-free asset, foreign bonds no longer match domestic liabilities and foreign stocks have an extra overlay of currency volatility.

Despite these problems, the increased emphasis accorded to diversification by modern thinking about risk has powered a general increase in the representation of overseas assets in investment policies around the world. This has been helped by a trend for governments to dismantle measures directed against overseas investment such as taxes and capital controls. Investors in overseas assets have to address the currency issue. This can be dealt with by using the passive currency strategy of hedging a fixed proportion (usually zero) of currency exposures. Alternatively, investors can follow active currency strategies or active strategies for which currency strategy is an integral component.

ENDNOTES

1. J.C. Blomfield, 'Deanery of Bicester', 1887, part 3, pp. 10, 11.
2. "You have it, Madam" (words supposed to have been said by the Rothschild of the day to Queen Victoria when he had acquired the Khedive's shares on behalf of the UK), Lord Rothschild, privately published, 1980, Annex 4, pp. 54, 55.
3. 11th Edition, vol. 18, p. 269.
4. "Size of major bond markets at year-end 1997", Salomon Smith Barney, 1998.
5. Data sourced from: E. Dimson, P. Marsh and M. Staunton, The Millennium Book: a century of investment returns, ABN AMRO, 2000, pp. 50, 57.
6. Data compiled as at 1995 by Intersec.
7. Intersec.
8. *Sunday Times*, 2 June 2002.
9. The earliest I can find is: H. Levy and M. Sarnat "International diversification of investment portfolios", *American Economic Review*, September 1970.
10. Available through Capital International, subsequently Morgan Stanley Capital International, since 1970.
11. Intersec.
12. The Salomon global hedged bond indices provided data from March 1985 onwards while the JP Morgan global hedged and unhedged indices provided data from December 1985 onwards.
13. J.M. Keynes, *The Economic Consequences of the Peace*, chap. 7, p. 9, available on www.j-bradford-delong.net.
14. Littlewood, p. 19.
15. Littlewood, p. 29.
16. Raw *et al.*, p. 212.
17. J. Brooks, *Once in Golconda*. London: Victor Gollancz, 1970, pp. 168–178.
18. During the whole period, the mark depreciated against the US dollar by a factor of 70 million. Nevertheless, between February 1920 and September 1921, and again between November 1922 and February 1923, the mark was stable. Within those periods, it actually appreciated by 150% between February and May 1920 and January and February 1923. Figures from: Supplement to 11th Edition, vol. 2, p. 225.
19. R.F. Harrod, *The Life of John Maynard Keynes*. London: MacMillan, 1963, p. 296.
20. Yields taken from the *Wall Street Journal* as at 30 September 1988.
21. Quoted from letter written by the author explaining the fund sent out during the fourth quarter of 1988 to UK investment consultants.
22. Performance sourced from JP Morgan Government Bond Indices.
23. Yield changes between 30 September 1988 and 30 September 1992, from *Wall Street Journals* of those dates.

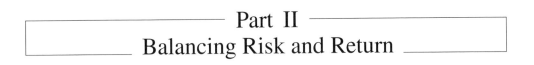

Part II
Balancing Risk and Return

6

Measuring Risk

I returned and saw under the sun, that the race is not to the swift, nor the battle to the strong; neither yet bread to the wise, nor yet riches to men of understanding, nor yet favour to men of skill; but time and chance happeneth to them all.[1]

Investments do not usually* involve physical danger. The risk to an investor, whether a man of understanding or not, is the chance that, at some critical time in the future, he will either lose more wealth than he can afford to lose or become unable to meet financial obligations when they fall due.

6.1   THE CHANCE OF MISFORTUNE

The problem of measuring the chance of a particular adverse combination of events in the future can be solved precisely when the odds of future events are known precisely. In the more realistic case where the odds of future events are not known precisely, risk measurements are always estimates.

6.1.1   Fixed odds

Probability theory[†] shows that, if the odds of individual events are known with certainty, the probabilities of all possible outcomes, including the bad ones, of any strategy based on these events is also known with certainty. The expected value or average pay-off of the strategy is therefore also known with certainty. A gambler can use these probabilities to check not only that the expected value of a strategy is positive, but also what chance he has of losing the maximum he can afford to lose.

This was fine for games involving cards, dice or coin tossing where the odds are simple to calculate and obvious in advance but what of more complex games where the odds are unknown? Jakob Bernoulli[‡] was able to demonstrate for independent trials that, if the results of past trials (outcomes of past bets) were available, it was possible to estimate what the odds were to within a tolerance that depended on the number of trials.

6.1.2   Uncertain odds

Bernoulli's result was helpful as far as it went, for example in analysing whether a given coin or die was weighted, but what of situations where there were no previous trials or where it was

---

 * Huntingdon Life Sciences, a company specialising in testing pharmaceuticals on animals, became the target in 2000 of aggressive direct action by animal rights groups. This included a serious assault on its managing director. It was forced to implement a rarely used shareholding structure to protect its investors from physical intimidation by preserving their anonymity.

 † Pascal and Fermat devised the binomial theorem in 1654 to solve, for the Chevalier de Méré, the problem of how the stakes should be divided in an unfinished game of dice.

 ‡ Lived from 1654 to 1705. This is a consequence of his Law of Large Numbers.

not clear that the unknown probability distribution remained unchanged over time? As Keynes put it in 1937:

> By uncertain knowledge ... I do not mean merely to distinguish what is known for certain from what is only probable. The game of roulette is not subject, in this sense, to uncertainty ... The sense in which I am using the term is that in which the prospect of a European war is uncertain, or the price of copper and the rate of interest twenty years hence, or the obsolescence of a new invention ... About these matters, there is no scientific basis on which to form any calculable probability whatever. We simply do not know.[2]

Although we simply do not know, we often have to make a guess. Without any special knowledge about the future, our guesses normally involve looking at the experience of the past:[3] "The thing that hath been, it is that which shall be; and that which is done is that which shall be done: and there is no new thing under the sun." The alternative is worse as it involves assigning arbitrary probabilities or using some arbitrary rule of thumb. We have already seen an example of this with the seventeenth century Dutch method of valuing annuities, which linked mortality to money market rates.

The method of valuing annuities that has been generally accepted since the eighteenth century is to look at historical mortality rates and treat them as trials of future mortality rates. This technique forms the basis of actuarial science. It is not certain as it depends on using data from past deaths to estimate probability distributions of deaths in the future. Actuaries do not know when a given individual will die, they can merely predict his chance of dying within a given time interval.* There is the further problem that mortality rates change with advances in medical science. Actuaries have had to develop techniques to factor in projections of such advances. Thus projected mortality rates are only guesses but, unless there is specific local knowledge to the contrary, they are the best guesses available.

6.1.3   Historical prices

Using historical security price movements to develop estimates of the probability distributions of their future price movements usually provides the best guess available. There are two exceptions to this. First, there may be special local knowledge. If you know that a takeover bid will be announced tomorrow, or the company will be declared bankrupt, the historical pattern of daily returns will not be of much use. Second, as we will see later, information about the distribution of future price movements can be inferred from the options market.

Using historical distributions of security returns in this way relies on assuming some stability in the return generating process. For example, the assumption suggests that you can assign a probability of two-fifths to the chance that next year's UK stock market return will be less than the return on cash because a year drawn at random from the past UK stock market return sequence has a probability of two-fifths of showing a negative excess return. For an actively managed investment product, a change in either the people involved or what they do is likely to compromise this assumption.

The assumption that the price generating process remains unchanged for securities and markets is also open to question, particularly over long periods. Why should the processes that drove price changes in the UK in 1900 and the USA in 1926 be the same as those that drive

---

* Except, as the joke goes, for Sicilian actuaries who can give you his name and address.

them now? The people and institutions involved have cycled through several generations and the securities they buy and sell have changed substantially.

Two further factors argue against the assumption. First, historical data can be distorted by unusual periods. We saw in Chapter 1 that the price generating process for US small stocks seems to have been rather different between 1975 and 1983 than it was for the rest of the period since 1926. Second, the constant growth model presented in Chapter 1 suggests that the market may have memory. That is, past price movements may influence future price movements. This is because the model says that, if the price goes up and the dividend stays the same so the dividend yield falls, the expected return should fall (A2.22). The reverse should happen if the price falls. Thus periods of strong performance should be followed by periods of weak performance and vice versa.

6.1.4   Measuring risk from historical prices

Industry convention sets these caveats aside and assumes that the past distribution of returns is a valid guide to the future distribution of returns.* Quantifying the risk, or chance of a specified loss at a specified time horizon, of a portfolio of financial assets is then straightforward in principle. First, the analyst reconstructs the historical return distribution of the portfolio using the portfolio's weights and the historical returns over intervals equal to the specified time horizon. This distribution becomes his estimate of the distribution of returns of the portfolio at the next time horizon. Then he adds up the probabilities of all the returns that are worse than the cut-off. This is then the quantitative estimate of risk.

The problem with this approach is that the analysis has to be repeated from scratch every time the portfolio changes, the time horizon changes or the unacceptable loss changes. Investors have made various attempts to simplify the task of estimating quantitative measures of risk.

One simplification is to focus on the worst case observable from historical data. This measure, known as drawdown, was originally developed for futures portfolios, where it reflected the maximum cumulative cash calls experienced. The concept has been extended to hedge funds, where it represents the maximum cumulative loss experienced from a peak. The advantage is that it is simple to calculate.

However, there are several disadvantages. One is that the longer the product has been going, the greater the chance of a bad performance run and the larger the maximum recorded drawdown is likely to be. Another is that the historical composition of the portfolio may be different from the current composition of the portfolio. Another is that the definition of what constitutes a peak and a trough is necessarily arbitrary. For futures positions, the futures exchanges and futures clearing house procedures for making cash calls on losing positions and returning cash on winning positions provide one definition. For hedge funds, monthly performance cut-offs provide another.

6.2   A SIMPLIFYING PROPOSITION

A much more coherent and elegant simplification of the task of measuring risk is made possible by a combination of two empirically observed characteristics of security price distributions.

---

* If this were not the case, there would be no point in analysing historical performance time series.

Table 6.1

Secular distribution	Skewness	Excess kurtosis
UK equity	−0.34 (−1.4)	6.07 (12.6)
UK bond	0.49 (2.0)	1.13 (2.3)
US equity	−0.76 (−2.7)	0.83 (1.5)
US bond	0.28 (1.0)	−0.27 (−0.5)

Raw data sourced from Barclays Capital

6.2.1   The chance curve

The distribution of returns from securities has much in common with the distribution of returns from flipping coins or rolling dice. Before inventing duration, Macaulay made the following remarks on the topic of forecasting security prices:

> Macaulay observed that there was a striking similarity between the fluctuations of the stock market and those of a chance curve which may be obtained by throwing dice. Everyone will admit that the course of such a purely chance curve cannot be predicted. If the stock market can be forecast from a graph of its movements, it must be because of its difference from the chance curve.[4]

Another name for Macaulay's chance curve is the normal distribution. The normal distribution (A1.10) was already familiar to statisticians and researchers. It has the properties that it can be described fully by two numbers, the mean (A1.11) and the variance (A1.12) and its relationship with another normal distribution can be described fully by another number, the covariance (A5.1) between the two distributions. For example, the chance of losing more than any given amount of money on a portfolio of securities with normally distributed returns can be precisely calculated from the portfolio variance. This in turn can be precisely calculated from the variances of the securities and the covariances between them.

Thus, when asset returns are normally distributed and expected variance equals historical variance, historical variance of returns over a specified interval becomes a unique measure of risk for the time horizon that matches the specified interval. The ability to simplify the measurement of risk in this way is so useful that investors and their advisors make extensive use of it even though the evidence that security returns are normally distributed, with expected variance equal to historical variance, is mixed.

Tests of normality are conducted by measuring a distribution's skewness (A1.14), which quantifies its degree of asymmetry, and its kurtosis (A1.15), which quantifies the relationship between the probability mass at the extremes and the probability mass at the centre of a distribution.* Table 6.1 shows the skewness and excess kurtosis of the returns relative to cash of equities and bonds in the USA and the UK. For a normal distribution, both these should be zero. The numbers in brackets are the t values.†

Only the return distribution of US bonds has neither skewness nor excess kurtosis significantly different from zero. All the others tend to have fat tails or asymmetry or both. Both US asset classes have distributions that are closer to being normal than their UK equivalents.

---

* The extremes are sometimes called the tails of the distribution. A distribution that has more probability mass at the extremes than a normal distribution is called "fat tailed".

† (A1.16) gives the formulae for t values. The higher they are, the more chance the underlying distribution is abnormal. The probability that a t value of a certain level is consistent with a normal distribution can be read off from the normal probability distribution table. As a rule of thumb, a t value of more than 2 is unlikely to have arisen by chance.

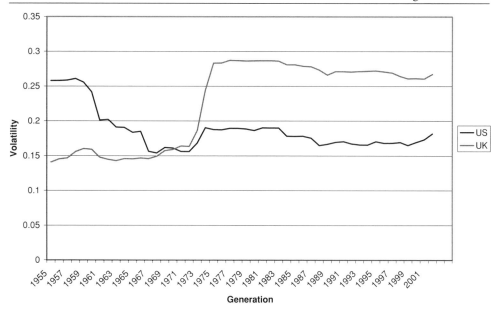

Figure 6.1 Volatility over time
Raw data sourced from Barclays Capital

If expected standard deviation or volatility is accepted as the measure of risk, the usual approach is to infer it from historical volatility. The actual volatility experienced by any given generation of market participants will tend to vary.

Figure 6.1 shows that up to the late 1960s, market participants had experienced more stock market volatility in the USA than in the UK. The turmoil in the UK in the early 1970s reversed this, so that market participants in the UK have experienced more volatility than those in the USA over the past 30 years.

An alternative to inferring volatility from historical returns is to infer it from option prices. This can produce dramatically different results. Figure 6.2 shows implied volatility or the volatility necessary for the market price of three-month options on the UK FTSE 100 (large capitalisation) stock index to equal their value calculated from the Black–Scholes option price formula. The two lines track the implied volatilities of options that are 5% out-of-the-money between January 1997 and October 1998. The dark line plots the implied volatility of an option to put the index 5% below its current level, a typical position for investors seeking to put a floor under their equity returns. The dotted line plots the implied volatility of an option to call the index 5% above its current level, a typical position for an investor holding cash and anxious not to miss the market.

Over the two-year period covered, implied volatilities varied between 10% and 50% compared with the long-term average of 18.6% and the volatility experienced by the 1997 generation of 26%. The market clearly did not expect the FTSE 100 to have a return distribution that reflected history. In addition, the steady difference between the implied volatilities of the put and the call meant that the market consistently attributed a higher volatility to downward moves than it did to upward moves. This could have reflected supply and demand, or an expectation that the FTSE 100 had a negatively skewed distribution, or both.

As mentioned in Chapter 2, one of LTCM's largest losing positions was in options. Much of it was because they had sold options to European financial institutions, who needed to cover

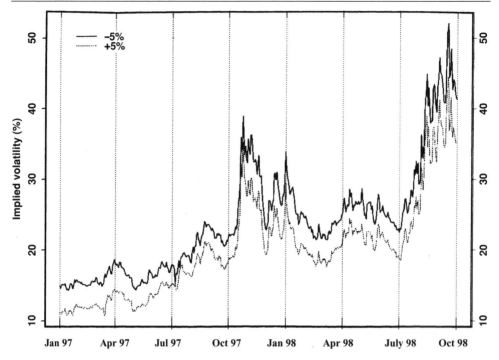

Figure 6.2 Option implied volatility
Source: Salomon Smith Barney

the exposures generated by selling CDs with equity kickers.[5] For LTCM, this was equivalent
to going short of equity volatility. As volatility followed the same pattern in the third quarter of
1998 irrespective of market or time horizon, the figure illustrates how LTCM's option position
deteriorated.

6.2.2   Interval and variance

Changing the time horizon over which risk is calculated means that the intervals used to estimate
the expected return distribution from historical return data have to be changed. A standard
theory of statistics is that the accuracy of an estimate is inversely proportional to the square
root of the variance and proportional to the square root of the number of observations (A3.6).
If you chop the time series up into a larger number of observations by measuring performance
over shorter intervals, you get a larger number of observations and greater accuracy if the
variance is unchanged. But this is not the case. On average, quarterly price changes are greater
than monthly price changes, which in turn are greater than weekly price changes.

The hypothesis that, for a give time series, the variance of performance is proportional
to the interval is very convenient. For then, the accuracy of estimates based on historical
numbers is independent of the interval used (A3.7) and variance at any time horizon can be
converted into variance at any other time horizon. Thus, where returns are normally distributed
and where the variance is proportional to the time horizon, annualised variance becomes the
single number measure of risk from which the probability of any loss at any time horizon can
be calculated. Putting this another way, the further the actual distribution of returns is from
being normally distributed, with variance proportional to the time horizon, the less accurately

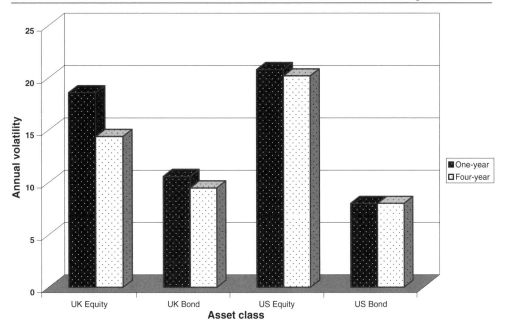

Figure 6.3   Market memory
Raw data sourced from Barclays Capital

will annualised variance predict the chance of losing a particular amount at a particular time horizon.

If the interval hypothesis is correct, it should not matter what time period is used to calculate annualised volatility. This provides a practical test. Figure 6.3 shows the annualised volatility of all possible one and four-year excess returns over cash for stocks and bonds in the UK and USA.

The annualised volatilities calculated using both four and one-year data are broadly similar, although for both UK asset classes and US stocks, the four-year number is lower than the one-year number. In particular, the annualised volatility of UK stocks calculated using four-year data is substantially less than the annualised volatility using one-year data. This suggests that both stock markets have some memory, as a sequence of bad years has a slightly higher than average chance of being followed by a good year and vice versa. If this is so, the chance at the time of writing that UK or US stocks will beat cash in 2003, thus ending the last three years' sequence of negative excess returns, is somewhat higher than three-fifths and two-thirds, respectively.

The existence of market memory leads naturally to active strategies using market timing. For example, investors believing that the UK stock market has the kind of memory it has exhibited in the past will buy stocks after a bad run and sell stocks after a good run. By the same token, if the market has no memory, market timing strategies are unlikely to succeed.

6.2.3   Random walk hypothesis

The theory that rationalises these two hypotheses about security price movements is the random walk* hypothesis, which proposes that security prices follow Brownian[†] motion. The three

---

* The same mathematics governs the distance a drunk will manage to get from a lamppost by taking random steps.
† The random movement of microscopic particles. First observed by the botanist Robert Brown in 1827. The French mathematician Louis Bachelier first proposed that security prices follow Brownian motion in 1900.

elements of the random walk hypothesis are:

1. The probability distribution of price changes is normal with variance proportional to the length of time over which the price changes occur.
2. Future price changes are independent of past price changes (the direction of a price's next movement over a given time interval is not affected by the direction of any of its previous movements).
3. The probability distribution of future price changes is identical to the probability distribution of past price changes.

For a return generating process of this type, a reliable estimate of annualised standard deviation of return can be used to generate reliable estimates of the probability of any loss at any time horizon in the future. Thus expected risk is identical to historical annualised standard deviation. Investors who accept that risk is measured by standard deviation or variance are known as mean variance investors. There is a huge literature on mean variance investing, starting with an article by Harry Markowitz* about constructing portfolios for investors "Who consider expected return a desirable thing and variance of return an undesirable thing".[6]

The theory developed to predict the behaviour of mean variance investors is sometimes called Modern Portfolio Theory (MPT). Much of the history of modern applied financial economics is that of the development of models based on this theory. Hundreds of billions of dollars change hands every day using practical applications of these models such as option valuation tools, financial risk analysers and optimisers.

Perhaps the most commonly used of these practical models is the Black–Scholes option valuation formula, which relies on the price of the optioned security following Brownian motion and which has already been mentioned in this chapter and Chapter 2. The formula is simple, elegant and depends only on the time horizon and exercise price of the option, the variance of the security price and the risk-free rate.

The assumption of normality is so closely linked to the assumption of independence that they are effectively the same. To see why, remember that we can chop our time series up into sections of any length. It follows that any given observation of a price change over a time period of length L is the net or average effect of a whole series of price changes over much shorter time periods of length l. If the price changes over these shorter periods are not normally distributed but are independent of each other, we can invoke the Central Limit Theorem (A1.13), which tells us that the distribution of price changes over period L will be much closer to normal than the distribution over period l. Thus lengthening the observation time period will force any distribution towards normal provided the subperiods are independent of each other.

Despite the elegance of the theory, the match with empirically observed data is mixed. Studies, including the simple analysis of US and UK secular return data presented earlier in this chapter, have shown that many security price distributions are not normal. However this is not an insuperable problem as, thanks once again to the Central Limit Theorem, the abnormality diminishes if the distribution is combined with other distributions provided there is a degree of independence.

---

* Although he received the Nobel Prize for Economics, Markowitz's background was in linear programming, which concerns itself with maximising one quantity (usually output) while holding another quantity (usually input) constant. This approach translated naturally to maximising return while holding variance constant. Quantitative investment analysts make extensive use of a concept they call the efficient frontier. This is just the plot of the maximum feasible return for each level of variance over the range of all possible variances.

In addition, the Brownian motion assumption that the variance is proportional to the length of the time period is also sometimes violated. Some studies, including that presented earlier in this chapter, show that very low frequency observations of equity prices have a tendency to revert to the mean, as suggested by the constant growth model.

6.3   THE CASE AGAINST ACTIVE MANAGEMENT

If future returns have to be independent of past returns in order to be normally distributed, there are uncomfortable consequences, not just for market timing strategies, but for all active investment management. As pointed out by Paul Samuelson,[7] a winner of the Nobel Prize for Economics and a leading sceptic about active management, the only way future returns can be completely independent of past returns is if all the information from past prices is fully discounted in the current price. If there is information embedded in past prices that has not been discounted, it can be used as a signal to predict future prices. If future prices can be predicted by past prices, they are no longer independent of them. Adding value from active management in such a world is not just elusive, it is an illusion.

Markets with prices that follow such a pattern are known as efficient markets. The hypothesis that financial markets are efficient is known as the Efficient Market Hypothesis (EMH). The EMH leads directly (A5.20) to the Capital Asset Pricing Model (CAPM). Both the EMH and the CAPM are central to modern financial economics. The EMH does not have to hold absolutely before it governs people's practical behaviour. Markets merely have to be sufficiently efficient to make unpredictable both inefficiencies leading to abnormal returns and the ability to exploit them by active management:

> Despite all the evidence to the contrary, suppose an investor still believed that superior investment management really does exist. Two issues remain: first, it is clear that such skill is very rare and second, there appears to be no effective way to find such skill before it has been demonstrated over time. Paul Samuelson sums up the difficulty in the following parable. Suppose it was demonstrated that one out of twenty alcoholics could learn to become a moderate social drinker. The experienced clinician would answer, "Even if true, act as if it were false, for you will never identify that one in twenty and in the attempt five in twenty will be ruined". Samuelson concludes that investors should forsake the search for such tiny needles in huge haystacks.[8]

This then is the real case for the prosecution against active management. It is not that inefficiencies do not exist. Human fallibility makes this highly implausible. It is that they may be too elusive to justify the risk and expense to investors of trying to seek them out. If this is so, the EMH holds for all practical purposes and all investors will want the same risky asset weights for their portfolios. The only way for all investors to have the same risky asset weights is if they all own risky assets in proportion to their outstanding capitalisations. This is why capitalisation-weighted indices form the basis of passive products.

The EMH is clearly of immense practical significance. During 1999, 26.8% of the 937 articles submitted to and 32.2% of the 59 articles published in the *Journal of Finance* were in the single subcategory "Information and Market Efficiency".[9] Researchers test the EMH by investigating whether the information hypothetically discounted by one of three versions under review is capable of producing predictable abnormal returns. The version of the EMH where only historical price information is discounted in the price came to be called the weak form. This was to distinguish it from the semi-strong form, where everything but private information is discounted in the price, and the strong form, where everything is discounted in the price.

6.3.1 Testing the weak form

In tests of the weak form, the focus was on technical analysis or chartism and products, such as commodity funds, that relied on technical analysis. The essence of technical analysis is that historical price movements can be used to predict future price movements, a direct violation of the hypothesis.

Initial statistical tests of well-known technical rules suggested that they produced results that were no better than random. Harry Roberts, a Chicago University professor, used a random number generator in the 1950s to construct "charts", which he showed to technical analysts who were unable to distinguish them from the real thing.[10] The performance achieved by commodity funds was also analysed and found worse than random.[11]

But subsequent research on momentum or historical price trends shows that, under certain circumstances, they had predictive power.[12] If momentum, the simplest technical rule of all, worked it was clearly impossible to write off technical analysis completely.

6.3.2 Testing the semi-strong form

Initial tests of the semi-strong form focused on the published recommendations of security analysts. Studies[13] from the 1970s onwards showed that published recommendations could be found that did indeed generate excess returns before costs with a high degree of confidence. However, the average excess returns were of the same order of magnitude as the costs involved in executing them. In addition, the bulk of the excess returns seemed to occur at the time of the recommendation, suggesting that early information was valuable.

Research on size, as defined by market capitalisation, and value, as defined by the ratio of book value per share to share price, showed that both had predictive power.[14] This allowed at least the possibility that publicly available information could form the basis of an investment approach that performed better than random at predicting market movements, in violation of the hypothesis.

6.3.3 Testing the strong form

Tests of the strong form of the EMH focus on whether private information can produce abnormal returns. Because of the nature of private information, the fewer people who know it, the more valuable it is to the holder. It is therefore difficult for researchers to gather data on it that allows them to research its effects directly. Research studies involving private information tend to be opportunistic responses to databases that become available for a variety of unpredictable reasons. Because of this handicap, most tests of its predictive power tend to be indirect.

One such indirect approach is to assume that all actively managed investment products are attempting to outperform by use of private information and then test to see whether they do outperform and if so with what degree of confidence. Tests of this kind focus on the average performance of mutual funds as compared with market indices. Because poorly performing products tend to get terminated, the performance of surviving products is higher than the average performance of all products. The annual effect is estimated to be 0.5–1.5% for mutual funds, 3.6% for commodity funds and 3.0% for hedge funds.[15]

Once the problem of survivorship bias had been recognised and accounted for, studies consistently find that, on average, the funds underperform by approximately the margin of their expense ratios. One study of UK unit trusts analysed a sample of 752 products between

January 1978 and December 1997, including 279 that had closed during the period. They found that the average annual active return was -1.08%, net of an average expense ratio of 1.35%.[16] Similar results are to be found for US mutual funds.[17] This evidence is conclusive. However, it is not necessarily a proof that the EMH is valid for all practical purposes. Two other interpretations are possible.

First, there is the possibility that some funds consistently outperform but are balanced in the averages by other funds that consistently underperform. Some tests have focused on persistence, or whether funds that have performed well (badly) in the past perform well (badly) in the future. One such study found evidence of persistence for badly performing mutual funds with high expense ratios.[18] This raises the question as to why investors allow such funds to continue to exist. Evidence of persistence for mutual funds that perform well has been harder to find, suggesting that a strategy of selecting mutual funds that have performed well in the past is unlikely to confound the EMH by producing abnormal returns in the future.

The alternative interpretation is that there is something in the way traditional products such as mutual funds and unit trusts are structured that makes it very hard to predict their future success. Thus, the poor average performance of traditional products is not evidence that markets are efficient, but evidence that traditional products need to change if they are successfully to provide investors with access to active management strategies. This possibility is explored in some detail in the second half of this book.

6.4   GUARANTEES

Once an investor has recognised investment risk he has to decide how to deal with it. The only way to be sure of eliminating the risk of unacceptable loss is to buy a guarantee. But this always comes with a cost.

A common form of guarantee is that a risky asset portfolio P will be worth a minimum of X at a fixed time in the future. This is usually presented as a guarantee that an investor will get his money back and is simple to execute. The guarantor merely has to monitor the value of P and the risk-free investment R required, in say a Treasury strip, to deliver X at the correct time. P has to start above R. If P falls to equal R, it is liquidated and the proceeds reinvested at the risk-free rate. In deciding when to liquidate, the investor or his agent has to adjust for frictional effects such as time lags and the cost of the transactions involved. The choice of the riskiness of the initial portfolio P will determine the trade-off between potential upside and probability that the guarantee will be triggered. The cost of such a strategy comes when the guarantee is triggered and P then recovers to finish above X. P minus X is then called the investor's opportunity cost.

Another common form of guarantee, which is more expensive but avoids the chance of such an opportunity cost, is where the guarantor promises the investor the better of the risk-free return and the risky return, less the cost of the guarantee. There are two ways of meeting such a guarantee and thus two ways of establishing the cost.* The first is to establish a reserve using the principles of insurance. The second is to buy options in the capital market.

Because of the cost of guarantees, normal practice is to run risks that are acceptable and only seek guarantees for risks that are unacceptable. One of the topics of the next chapter is to identify what constitutes an acceptable investment risk.

---

* These costs can be dramatically different. In late 1998, MAM conducted an exercise to compare the insurance reserve required to support a particular guarantee with the cost of hedging the guarantee by buying options. The cost of the options was some 20 times the insurance reserve. This was mainly because of the difference between historical volatility and expected volatility, as shown in Figure 6.2.

6.5   CONCLUSION

Financial risk is the chance that adverse market movements mean that an investor does not have the money he needs available when he needs it. Different investors are interested in different levels of loss and different time horizons. They will therefore have different measures of risk for the same financial asset. From this it is clear that a measure of risk is only unique if it allows the calculation of the probability of any level of loss at any time horizon.

Empirical observation of financial asset returns shows that these are approximately normally distributed with variance proportional to time horizon. When this approximation is exact, the annualised standard deviation of return can be shown to be a unique measure of risk. Modern Portfolio Theory relies on the risk of a financial asset being equal to its standard deviation. Thus normally distributed asset returns lead to both risk being equal to standard deviation of return and MPT.

Fault lines arise because the Efficient Market Hypothesis postulates that investors can only expect asset returns to be normally distributed when markets are efficient so that asset prices reflect all available information. As active managers rely on inefficiencies to add value, successful active management is impossible in such circumstances. Thus, the more an investor believes that successful active management is possible, the less he can believe either that standard deviation of return is an accurate measure of risk or that MPT is an accurate tool for wealth management.

ENDNOTES

1. *Ecclesiastes*, Chapter 9, Verse 11. Traditionally attributed to King Solomon.
2. "The general theory", *Quarterly Journal of Economics*, vol. LI, February 1937 [quoted in P.L. Bernstein *Against the Gods*. Chichester: John Wiley, 1998, p. 229].
3. *Ecclesiastes*, Chapter 1, Verse 8.
4. *Journal of the American Statistical Association*, vol. 20, June 1925 [quoted in Seigel, p. 242].
5. Author interview with Eric Rosenfeld.
6. "Portfolio selection", *Journal of Finance*, June 1952.
7. "Proof that properly anticipated prices fluctuate randomly". *Industrial Management Review*, 1965.
8. B.G. Malkiel, *A. Random Walk Down Wall Street*. Norton, 1999, p. 377.
9. Report of Editor, *Journal of Finance*, vol. 55, August 2000.
10. Bernstein, p. 145.
11. Elton *et al.*, 1990.
12. Siegel, pp. 245–252.
13. F. Black, "Yes Virginia there is hope: tests of the value line ranking system", *Financial Analysts Journal*, 1973 and E.J. Elton, M.J. Gruber, and S. Grossman, "Discrete expectational data and portfolio performance", *Journal of Finance*, July 1986.
14. E.F. Fama and K.R. French, "Multifactor explanations of asset price anomalies", *Journal of Finance*, March 1996.
15. W. Fung and D.A. Hsieh, "Performance characteristics of hedge funds and commodity funds", *Journal of Financial and Quantitative Analysis*, September 2000.
16. G. Quigley and R.A. Sinquefield "Performance of UK equity unit trusts", *Journal of Asset Management*, July 2000.
17. Malkiel, pp. 374, 375. Seigel, pp. 272–277.
18. M.M. Carhart, "On persistence in mutual fund performance", *Journal of Finance*, March 1997.

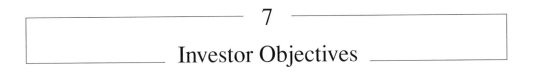

7
Investor Objectives

The only way of expressing emotion in the form of art is by finding an "object correlative"; in other words, a set of objects, a situation, a chain of events which shall be the formula of that *particular* emotion.[1]

Because they have such profound consequences for future personal and family financial well-being or even survival, investments have great capacity to generate emotion. Considering what investment policy or degree of active manager discretion to pursue can evoke fear and greed, while the effect of market movements on portfolio values can trigger elation or despair.

7.1 SELECTED INVESTOR INSTRUCTIONS

If an investor employs one or more advisors or investment firms, he has to give instructions, usually in written form. These are not easy to frame, as they have to capture needs that are emotional as well as financial. Winston Churchill managed to compress his into three words:

> I sent my £10,000 to my father's old friend, Sir Ernest Cassel, with the instruction "Feed my sheep". He fed the sheep with great prudence. They did not multiply fast, but they fattened steadily, and none of them ever died. Indeed from year to year they had a few lambs; but these were not numerous enough for me to live on. I had every year to eat a sheep or two as well, so gradually my flock grew smaller, until in a few years it was almost entirely devoured. Nevertheless, while it lasted, I had no care.[2]

Cassel either interpreted Churchill's instructions more conservatively or did not try as hard for him as he did for another client, King Edward VII. He is credited with making over £1 million for the King. He is also credited[3] with having said: "When I was young, people called me a gambler. As the scale of my operations increased, I became known as a speculator. Now I am called a banker. But I have been doing the same thing all the time."

7.1.1 UK pension funds

Modern client instructions leave less to interpretation and therefore lack Churchill's brevity. Institutional guidelines often run to several pages. Here is an extract from officially recommended practice for UK pension funds, which sets out what the author believes are the key elements of a practical investment mandate.[4]

> Trustees should set out an overall investment objective for the fund that:
>
> Represents their best judgement of what is necessary to meet the fund's liabilities, given their understanding of the contributions likely to be received from employer(s) and employees; and
>
> Takes account of their attitude to risk, specifically their willingness to accept underperformance due to market conditions.

Trustees should agree with both internal and external investment managers an explicit written mandate covering agreement between trustees and managers on:

An objective, benchmark(s) and risk parameters that together with all the other mandates are coherent with the fund's aggregate objective and risk tolerances;

The manager's approach in attempting to achieve the objective; and

Clear timescales of measurement and evaluation such that the mandate will not be terminated before the expiry of the evaluation timescale other than for clear breach of the conditions of the mandate because of significant change in the ownership or personnel of the investment manager.

Objectives for the overall fund should not be expressed in terms which have no relationship to the fund's liabilities, such as performance relative to other pension funds or to a market index.

In this case, benchmark(s) are both the policy* that is consistent with the fund's objectives and the benchmarks set for mandates that form a part of the whole. These benchmarks have to be components of the policy benchmark. The risk parameters are the degree to which each active manager can deviate from his benchmark. They thus determine the maximum risk his active overlay can have. This ability to take risk relative to benchmark is what determines an active manager's scope to add or subtract value.† The manager's approach is the style he adopts. The timescale sets the period over which the active manager's skill will be evaluated.

7.1.2   Individual investors

Individual investors tend to take less elaborate approaches to setting up their investment mandates. Best practice for advisors appears to be to ask them a series of questions designed to tease out both their attitude towards taking risk in pursuit of higher return and their liabilities or financial commitments. Because of the large numbers involved, they are sorted by objective.
Here are five objectives designed to span most private client investor profiles:[5]

Achieve above average capital growth over a three to five year time period with no concern for income.

Accumulate wealth rather than income over a three to five year time period.

Achieve a balance between bonds for current income and stocks for growth of principal and dividends over a three to five year time period.

Obtain a continuing, secure income stream with some emphasis on protection of principal over a three to five year time period.

Protect principal with some emphasis on income over a three to five year time period.

We will see in Chapter 9 that the three to five-year time horizon corresponds both to average investment professional tenure as product manager and to the assessment period normally used to evaluate historical performance. This is no coincidence.

---

* Policy is tailored to investor objectives and forms the asset allocation benchmark of the fund. Policy setting is described more fully in the next chapter.
† One of the mandates in place when I joined MAM in 1985 was one from a Middle Eastern airline, which gave no scope to take either maturity or credit risk. The client was disappointed that the return was equal to the benchmark less fees and took the money away before I could negotiate some investment flexibility.

7.2   THREE ESSENTIALS

In principle, an investor's objectives are very simple. He wants to eat well and to sleep well. Another way of putting this is that he wants to make as much money as possible after meeting his commitments, all without taking too much risk. The information needed to define his objectives in these terms can be boiled down to one currency and two numbers.

7.2.1   Risk-free asset

The investor's "home" currency is the currency in which his risk-free asset is denominated. This is usually obvious, as for example in the case of a UK pension fund, but sometimes less so.*

7.2.2   Liabilities

Any fixed liabilities, or promises to pay fixed amounts at fixed times in the future, have to be identified. There is an important difference between promises to pay projected liabilities, or estimated amounts at estimated times in the future, and promises to pay fixed liabilities. This is that an investor can construct a portfolio that precisely discharges a promise to pay fixed amounts by buying the appropriate bonds. Any portfolio designed to discharge a promise to pay uncertain amounts will always end up with too much or too little, depending on how market uncertainty and liability uncertainty are resolved. A useful test of whether a promise is a liability in this sense is therefore to consider whether a portfolio of bonds can be constructed that discharges it precisely.

As presented in Chapter 4, there are two ways of constructing such a matching portfolio. The first is to dedicate, or buy bonds with cash flows that exactly match the liabilities. The second is to immunise, or match the product of the value of the liabilities and their duration with the product of the value and duration of the asset portfolio. This technique allows the investor to match his fixed liabilities with a standard bond index. The weight he needs in the index provides a standard number, or normalised, definition of his liabilities. For then, if the value of the liabilities is v and their duration d, the normalised matching value required of an index with duration D is dv/D.[†]

For defined benefit pension funds, pensions in payment are liabilities as they are fixed either in money terms or real terms. Bonds can match the former kind, while index-linked bonds can match the latter kind. Pensions promised to scheme members who are still active can only be projected, as final salary and years of service have yet to be determined. Consistent with this, as noted in Chapter 1, pensions in payment have legal priority over promised pensions.

7.2.3   Attitude to risk

He has to identify his attitude to risk from both policy and active management. The only way he can avoid risk altogether is by keeping his investments in cash and receiving the risk-free rate. Any investment policy or active strategy designed to beat cash can fail to do so and will on occasion. Thus his attitude to risk is really his appetite for risk. This will be dominated by his

---

* I had a colleague in the 1970s, who was appointed to manage a conservative actively managed offshore cash portfolio. He went into the first review meeting quite pleased to have consistently outperformed dollar deposits by a modest margin. The client was furious and showed him a chart demonstrating that his performance relative to Swiss franc deposits was both poor and erratic.

† To match the present value of the liabilities with the value of the matching assets, the investor would also have to hold cash in the matching portfolio of $v(1 - d/D)$.

memory of how he has responded to economic events in the past. If small market changes to his wealth have resulted in strong emotions, he will want to manage his assets in a risk-averse way.

As we have seen in the cited examples, investors articulate their appetites for risk in terms of metaphor or behaviour, such as a preference for income over capital growth. Their advisors and portfolio managers have to create practical mandates by interpreting such statements. As different people often use the same words to mean very different things, this interpretation is not easy.

7.3 TRADE-OFF BETWEEN RISK AND RETURN

Chapter 6 defined risk as the probability of unacceptable loss and showed that this was equivalent to annualised variance for normally distributed returns. By this reckoning, the risk of policy is the standard deviation of policy return while the risk of active management is the standard deviation of active return. Knowing what risk is does not tell you how much to take.

The Efficient Market Hypothesis suggests that investors will all own the market portfolio of risky assets. It does not say whether a given investor will keep money in the bank or borrow money to invest in more risky assets. Whether he owns cash or levers himself is determined by his risk aversion. The first step in solving this problem is to recognise that there is normally a trade-off between return, which is good, and risk, which is bad. A risk-averse investor will be prepared to take more risk to get more return. However, the more risk averse he is, the more return he needs to find a given level of risk acceptable.

One approach to understanding the trade-off is to talk it through with the investor and plot the levels of risk he finds acceptable for a range of different levels of return. There are two problems with this. First, it is very cumbersome. Second, it is a very unusual investor who can give precise answers to questions such as: "What level of variance would you accept in order to get an expected return of X?"

The practical way forward is to have a simple but robust model, which allows the advisor to calculate the trade-off between any level of risk and return for any investor. Ideally, the investor's attitude to risk should be defined by one number.

7.3.1 Utility theory

The first step in developing such a model came in the work of Daniel Bernoulli. In 1738, he published a paper arguing that the price an individual would pay for a risky strategy was not its expected value but its utility or risk-adjusted expected value. Further, he argued that "the utility resulting from any small increase in wealth will be inversely proportional to the quantity of goods previously possessed"[6] and that "The utility is dependent on the particular circumstances of the person making the estimate. There is no reason to assume that the risks anticipated by each individual must be deemed equal in value". Thus different people will assign different utilities to the same risky strategies depending on both their attitudes to risk and their existing levels of wealth.

Bernoulli used this proposition to analyse the Petersburgh Paradox. This was a complex gamble, which had an infinite value according to standard probability theory. The paradox was because professional gamblers gave it a finite value. Bernoulli effectively proved that the amount they were willing to pay was consistent with a utility function that was equal to the natural logarithm of wealth (A1.9). He was unable to state his conclusion in quite this way as his result anticipated Euler's discovery of e, or the base of the natural logarithm, by 10 years.

The Expected Utility Hypothesis (EUH) that developed from such thinking assumes that each investor maps wealth into utility, or satisfaction arising from that wealth, through a utility function with two characteristics. The first is that he always prefers more to less. Thus a graph of utility against wealth is always sloping upwards. The second is that the more wealth he has, the smaller the incremental utility for a given increment in wealth. The implication that the emotional significance of a particular level of wealth for a given investor is always the same is not obvious and may not always be true. However, like mean variance analysis, it provides a very useful tool for modelling investor behaviour.

For example, consider an investor whose wealth is entirely in houses. The EUH implies that he will always be happier with one more house. However, the extra happiness from one more house will be more if he only already has one house than if he already has 10 houses.

The EUH also implies that investors with utility functions of this form are risk averse. That is, the maximum they will pay for a risky gamble is always less than its expected value. This allows the two forms of utility, satisfaction and risk-adjusted expected return, to be married up.

If our real estate investor has 10 houses, he will not hazard the tenth on a 50:50 gamble between 11 houses and nine. However, there will be odds in his favour that will incline him to take the bet. There will also be odds at which he is indifferent between taking the bet and not. Thus 60:40 has an expected value of 1.2 houses. If he is indifferent between taking a 60:40 gamble and not, the gamble has a certainty equivalent (A4.1) of one house. This certainty equivalent can be interpreted in two ways. First, it is the expected utility or satisfaction of the gamble. Second, it is the expected value of the gamble less the investor's risk adjustment, so the risk adjustment in the example is 0.2 houses. The degree to which the odds have to be stacked in his favour before he takes the gamble measures the compensation he requires for bearing risk and thus serves as a measure of how risk averse he is.

It turns out that the degree of risk aversion can be derived from the slope and the slope's slope of the utility curve. The more it bends, the more risk averse the investor is. A consequence of the EUH is that for very small gambles relative to an investor's wealth the relevant segment of the curve is almost a straight line, so the investor acts as though he is risk neutral. This is why even risk-averse people are happy to gamble as long as the stake is small relative to their total wealth.

7.3.2   Varying appetite for risk

Unless an investor's attitude to risk is constant over time, measuring past risk aversion does not help in assessing current risk aversion. The evidence that investors have risk appetites that change over time is that they vary their risky asset holdings over time, with a tendency to reduce their holdings of equities and increase their holdings of bonds and cash. Some US advisors use the rule of thumb that the percentage of bonds in an investor's portfolio should equal his age.[7] This is sometimes taken as evidence that investors become more risk averse as they grow older. But it could equally well be taken as evidence that investors' financial liabilities also increase with age, for example after retirement when they need to replace work income.

The tax and regulation of investment can also motivate investors to eliminate or run down their risky asset holdings even though their attitude to risk is unchanged. For example, in the UK, the government insists that a money purchase pension fund is invested in an annuity when the investor retires. This is effectively a compulsory liquidation of risky assets on retirement.

The regulation also introduces the risk that the annuity will be purchased on adverse terms. As annuity rates are closely correlated with the internal rate of return of a portfolio of long-dated bonds, this happens when bonds are expensive relative to equities. Investors can average into the rate at which they make their compulsory annuity purchase by reducing their equity holdings and building up their long-dated bond holdings over the years leading up to retirement.*

7.3.3   Constant risk aversion

When investors' attitudes to risk are constant over time, economists[8] have been able to develop a mathematical treatment of utility that derives simple formulae for utility functions from different hypotheses about investor attitudes to risk. The two main hypotheses are that the investor either has constant absolute risk aversion or has constant relative risk aversion.

Constant absolute risk aversion assumes that an investor has a fixed appetite for investment risk, whatever his level of wealth. In other words, if his wealth grows, he will wish to reduce the proportion of risky assets in his portfolio while if his wealth falls, he will wish to increase the proportion of risky assets.

Constant relative risk aversion assumes that an investor's appetite for risky assets as a proportion of his portfolio is part of his personal make-up and not dependent on the level of wealth he happens to hold. Equation (A4.16) defines such an investor's utility of wealth. The behaviour of investment advisors suggests that constant relative risk aversion is the dominant model as they uniformly present their recommendations as percentage weights. Any who believed that their clients had constant absolute risk aversion would present their recommendations as money weights.

The form that constant relative risk aversion utility takes (A4.16) is known as a power function because it consists of a constant plus an expression given by wealth raised to the power of one minus a special constant divided by one minus the special constant. The special constant is known as the investor's risk aversion and usually given the Greek letter gamma.[†]

Bernoulli's result that the utility function is the natural logarithm of wealth is equivalent to setting gamma equal to one (A4.16). This represents a very high level of risk tolerance, as one might expect from a professional gambler. Gammas between two and six appear to represent the risk aversions of most investors prepared to have more than token weights in risky assets.

7.3.4   Modelling the risk-return trade-off

Knowing an investor's gamma allows the analyst to calculate the trade-off he will make between risk and return. When the investor is either the mean variance investor assumed by MPT or owns a portfolio with a normal expected return distribution, the calculation is particularly simple. In order to make the expected utility of a risky strategy comparable with the expected utility from investing in risk-free assets, a risk adjustment has to be deducted from the expected return to give the certainty equivalent of the risky strategy. The risk adjustment is equal to half the product of the expected variance and gamma (A4.7).

---

* In December 2002, the UK government published a green (consultative) paper on pension reform [Simplicity, Security and Choice: Working and Saving for Retirement, Department for Work and Pensions]. This included the proposal that the excess of the value at retirement of an individual's money purchase pension portfolio over £1.4 million be taxed at 33%. If enacted as legislation, this will inevitably lead to demand from investors for bond portfolios designed to deliver £1.4 million on retirement.

† The reciprocal of gamma is known as risk tolerance.

Faced with a choice between risky assets providing an excess return over the risk-free asset and the risk-free asset itself, an investor will switch out of risk-free assets into risky assets until the marginal incremental return equals the marginal incremental variance multiplied by half gamma. The larger gamma is, the more rapidly this point is reached and the more risk-free assets the investor needs to be comfortable. Thus gamma uniquely determines the trade-off between return and risk.

Reducing the complexities of altruism, envy and other human emotions to one number is clearly a massive simplification. Financial economists and psychologists have developed a school of behavioural finance* to analyse and chronicle the occasions when humans make economic decisions at odds with the smooth utility curve embedded in the model's logic. Another obvious shortcoming is that equation (A4.7) requires either normally distributed returns or mean variance investors. Utility theory itself does not, although the expression for certainty equivalent (A4.11) becomes more complicated. Positive skewness improves the desirability of the asset while negative skewness lessens it. The greater the excess kurtosis, or the fatter the tails of the distribution, the less desirable the asset is.

Expression (A4.12) gives the risk adjustment for skewness relative to the risk adjustment for variance. It is equal to the product of the return distribution standard deviation, the distribution return skewness and the investor's risk aversion plus one, all divided by three. Thus the relative importance of skewness depends not only on skewness itself, but also on risk aversion and return volatility.

7.4   ACTIVE MANDATE DESIGN

Despite the concept's elegance, practitioners do not usually calculate an investor's policy and degree of active overlay risk by reference to his numerical risk aversion. Neither do they include risk adjustments in performance presentations. There are a number of good reasons for this.

The first is a philosophical one. Performance represents a concrete change to net worth (you can eat it) while certainty equivalent is a more metaphysical concept and, as such, more difficult to explain.

The second is a technical one. To adjust for risk correctly, you have to know not only what an investor's utility function is, but also what else he owns. Such information is hard to come by.

The third is a practical one. Even if the investor's utility function is known, the risk adjustment is hard to estimate with precision from actual performance data as only a few observations are usually available.

The fourth is that there is often ambiguity as to who the investor is. An example of this is the uncertainty as to whether the investor(s) in a defined benefit pension scheme are the members of the scheme or the sponsoring firm.

However, the limits set on active management risk in traditional mandates appear, either through serendipity or through design, to keep reported returns from active management close to risk-adjusted returns. To illustrate this, consider a traditional product designed to deliver a complete solution to a pension fund's investment needs, including active management. It will consist of the desired policy plus an active overlay.

Suppose that the investor wants the incremental risk from active management to be negligible so that the incremental risk-adjusted return equals the incremental return. He would design a

---

* Daniel Kahneman, awarded the 2002 Nobel Prize for Economics for work in this field, trained as a psychologist.

mandate that constrained the variance attributable to active management to be small relative to the variance attributable to policy.

Analysis of historical data suggests that the active overlays of pension fund mandates are indeed small enough to make the variance of return attributable to active management a small fraction of the variance of return attributable to policy. One study[9] concluded that: "Investment policy dominates investment strategy [market timing and security selection], explaining on average 93.6% of the variation in total [pension] plan return." Another reason why pension fund investors keep the risk from active management low may be lack of confidence in active management skill. This possibility is discussed further in Chapter 9.

7.5   CONCLUSION

An investor wants to make as much money as possible after meeting his liabilities, all without taking too much risk. His instructions to the advisors and investment firms he employs therefore have to explain: what he considers is money; what, if any, his liabilities are; and what his attitude to risk is. These can be reduced to a currency and two numbers. The first number is the weight in his domestic bond index he needs to match his liabilities.

The second number is his risk aversion, which defines his attitude to risk. Risk aversion can be used to calculate the risk adjustment needed to model the way an investor trades off expected risk with expected return. For normally distributed expected returns, the risk adjustment equals half the investor's risk aversion multiplied by the expected variance of his risky asset portfolio.

Despite the simplicity of the formula, risk adjustments are not calculated in practice as, for each investor, they require accurate estimates both of his risk aversion and of the variance of his portfolio. However, investors and their advisors appear to arrange traditional active mandates in such a way that the variance of the active overlay returns is low relative to the variance of policy returns. This eliminates the need to make risk adjustments to the active returns of traditional products.

ENDNOTES

1. T.S. Elliot, "Hamlet & His Problems", *The Sacred Wood*, 1920.
2. W.S. Churchill, *My Early Life*. London: The Reprint Society, 1944, pp. 377–378.
3. E. Chancellor, *Devil Take the Hindmost*. London: Macmillan, 1999.
4. "Institutional Investment in the UK, a Review", HM Treasury, 2001 (Myners report), p. 149.
5. "Global Research Highlights", Merrill Lynch, 2000.
6. Bernstein, pp. 103, 105.
7. Malkiel, p. 371.
8. J. von Neumann and O. Morgenstern, *Theory of Games and Economic Behaviour*. Princeton: Princeton University Press, 1944.
9. G. Brinson, L.R. Hood, and G.P. Beebower, "Determinants of Portfolio Performance", *Financial Analysts Journal*, July 1986.

8

Setting Policy

To defend a bad policy as an "error of judgement" does not excuse it – the right functioning of a man's judgement is his most fundamental responsibility.[1]

Investment policy is the asset allocation between cash, bonds and stocks that best meets an investor's objectives in the absence of any special market knowledge. The concepts presented in the previous two chapters allow an alternative definition as the asset allocation that maximises the risk-adjusted return of an investor who rejects active management.

Assume he knows both his risk tolerance and his liabilities. Suppose also that he believes, following the random walk hypothesis, that the future distribution of risky asset returns is identical to the historical distribution of risky asset returns. Such an investor can judge which asset allocation policy to follow and execute it by taking the following three steps. First, he collects the historical data on asset class performance. Second, he determines his asset class weights by calculating the solution to (A5.5). Third, he invests his wealth in asset class index funds using these weights.

Because policy depends on historical returns, it is market neutral, i.e. contains no market view. Provided there is plenty of historical data, the historical estimates of return and volatility will be stable, i.e. new data will have very little effect on the historical averages. This means in turn that new data has very little effect on policy weights. This combination of stability and market neutrality makes policy an attractive benchmark for actively managed portfolios and it is commonly used as such, as described in the previous chapter, which also describes why most of the risk and return from actively managed pension fund portfolios now comes from policy.

Of course, practical policy setting is not usually just a matter of collecting data and performing some simple calculations. The complications, which affect policy and therefore active benchmarks, include: policy uniqueness; liability matching; pension fund cash; active asset allocation. The balance of this chapter will deal with these in turn.

8.1 POLICY UNIQUENESS

The process of policy review for a pension fund suggests that policy advice is a unique solution to the pension fund's specific circumstances. But there is evidence that the policy advice for a fund with a specific set of objectives varies depending on the advisor and the time the advice is given.

8.1.1 Policy review

The opportunity for trustees to review pension fund policy comes from a procedure, known as asset liability modelling, which the advisor conducts every few years. The procedure is similar to the first two steps outlined above as its main inputs are long-term historical asset class performance together with contribution and payment projections for the fund. The main difference is that the advisor does not establish the fund's risk tolerance in advance. Instead, he calculates the probability distributions of the return, net of projected contributions and payments to pensioners, from different mixes of stocks, bonds and other asset classes. Trustees are invited to indicate their risk tolerance by choosing one of these mixes, which then forms the investment policy of the fund going forward. The more stock in the mix they choose, the more risk tolerant they are electing to be.

By limiting trustee choice to level of risk tolerance rather than different policies for a given level of risk tolerance, the procedure implicitly assumes that policy for a given level of risk tolerance is a unique solution to the pension fund's profile and cannot be compared with anything except itself. A unique policy suggests little or no competition in policy setting and therefore secure advisor tenure: "Many [UK pension] funds retain the same advisors for twenty years or more."[2]

In effect, advisors have exchanged security for the ability to demonstrate, and thus justify payment for, the investment value added from policy. This helps explain why annual investment management fees in the UK are estimated to total £4.9 billion while annual consulting, or advisory, fees are estimated to total £80 million[3] despite the fact that risk-adjusted return from policy is a large multiple of risk-adjusted excess return from active management.

8.1.2 Policy variation

And yet different policies are set for the same set of objectives. Anecdotally, different advisors will come up with different solutions to the policy problem for the same pension fund. But perhaps the best evidence of policy variation comes from the way average policy has changed over time. Figure 8.1[4] shows average asset allocation over time for UK pension funds. As the difference between average asset allocation and average policy is made up by net active asset

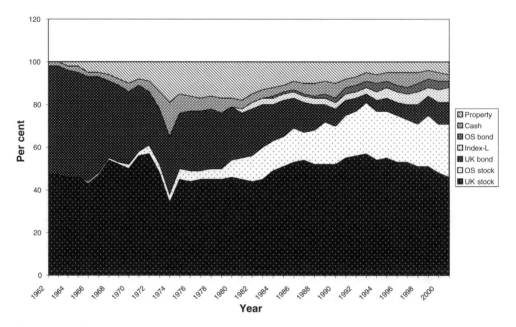

Figure 8.1 UK investment policy
Source: UBS Global Asset Management

allocation positions, which average to zero over time, the figure also shows how average UK pension fund policy has varied since 1962.

In 1962, average policy was 47% UK stock, 51% UK bonds and 2% cash. Over the 23 years after that, four new asset classes were introduced: property in 1964; overseas stock in 1966; index-linked bonds in 1981; overseas bonds in 1984.* This suggests that the number of asset classes considered suitable for pension fund policy by UK advisors more than doubled over this period. In addition, only UK stocks and cash had relatively stable allocations over the period. All the other allocations changed substantially. Index-linked bonds together with overseas assets increased, while UK bonds fell and property first increased and then fell away.

If a suitable methodology could be found for measuring the performance of policy setting, there is thus no reason why policy setting during asset liability modelling exercises could not be opened up to competition. Advisors able to demonstrate policy-setting skill could charge higher fees, but advisor tenure would become less secure.

8.2   LIABILITY MATCHING

Many advisors argue that the starting point for setting policy for institutional portfolios should be to match both fixed and projected liabilities. This means that a matching asset has to be assumed for projected liabilities. For example, when regulators[†] calculate the capital adequacy of UK pension funds, they assume that UK equities should be used to pay the pensions of, or match the projected liabilities attributable to, those not yet retired and gilts should be used to pay the pensions of, or match the liabilities attributable to, those already retired.

At first sight, an objective to match liabilities is rather different from the objective proposed in the previous chapter of maximising risk-adjusted return after paying fixed liabilities. However, it turns out that the resultant polices are identical if two conditions are met. First, the matching portfolio that the investor chooses for his projected liabilities coincides with the way he would invest his wealth if he had no fixed liabilities. Second, risk and return for bonds, risk and return for stocks and the correlation between bonds and stocks have to interrelate in a particular way. The different degrees to which this condition has historically been met in the USA and the UK may explain the different bond policies in the two countries.

8.2.1   The liability matching condition

Equation (A5.14) shows that the condition for bonds to equal normalised liabilities exactly in a risk-adjusted return maximising policy is for the ratio between the expected bond Sharpe ratio[‡] and the expected stock Sharpe ratio exactly to equal the expected correlation coefficient (A5.2) between bonds and stocks. This is therefore the condition for a liability matching objective to be the same as a risk-adjusted net worth objective. It is independent of the investor's risk aversion.

---

* The figure also shows how the weighting in overseas equities advanced rapidly from 1979 and that in overseas bonds advanced rapidly from 1989, as discussed in Chapter 5.

† The rules for calculating the Minimum Funding Ratio (MFR), or prescribed minimum ratio of assets to liabilities are set out in the UK Pensions Act 1995 as: "The scheme's assets are valued at current market levels; the scheme's liabilities are divided between pensioners and those who have not yet retired and discounted to a capital value at different discount rates. For pensions in payment, the rate is the prevailing market yield on gilts. For pension rights of scheme members not yet retired, the rate is broadly the assumed long-term rate of return for UK equities..."

‡ The ratio calculated by dividing excess return over cash by standard deviation of excess return over cash. Named after William Sharpe, who received the Nobel Prize for Economics for his contribution to developing the Capital Asset Pricing Model, which flows from the Efficient Market Hypothesis (A5.20).

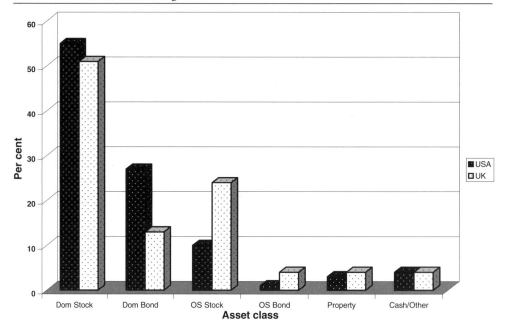

Figure 8.2   Policy in 2000
Source: UBS Global Asset Management

8.2.2   Historical evidence

Over the full period spanned by the Barcap database, the correlation coefficient between domestic bonds and domestic equities is 0.5 in the UK and 0.2 in the USA. The ratio of Sharpe ratios is 0.1 in the UK and 0.7 in the USA. Thus the historical experience of bonds suggests that they should be overweighted relative to liabilities in the USA and underweighted relative to liabilities in the UK.

It may be that the relevant period is a shorter one to reflect the actual experience of policy setters active in the market. For the period 1970–2000, the correlation coefficient between domestic bonds and domestic equities is 0.7 in the UK and 0.3 in the USA. The ratio of Sharpe ratios is 0.6 in the UK and 0.7 in the USA. Once again, this suggests that bonds should be overweighted relative to liabilities in the USA and underweighted relative to liabilities in the UK. However, the match is closer.

Average pension fund weights[5] as of January 2000 in both countries are shown in Figure 8.2. The most striking differences between the two are in domestic bonds, where the USA has more than double the weight of the UK, and in overseas equities, where the UK has more than double the weight of the USA. If the actual weight of liabilities is similar in both countries, the low weight in bonds in the UK relative to the USA probably reflects the poor bond experience in the UK relative to the USA. In other words, UK policy setters may have taken a collective decision, based on their experience, to undermatch liabilities while US policy setters may have taken a collective decision, based on their experience, to overmatch liabilities.

8.3   PENSION FUND CASH

With the exception of the freak years of 1973, 1974 and 1975, the chart of UK pension fund policy shows that UK pension funds held between 2% and 7% cash at all times. As any pension fund

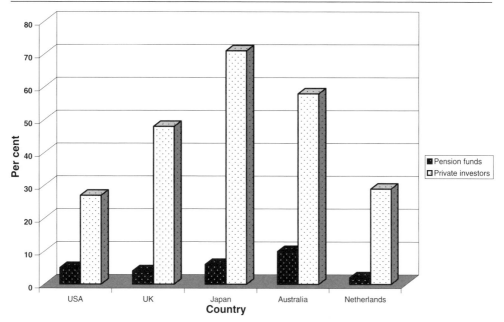

Figure 8.3 Cash in policy
Source: UBS Global Asset Management, Intersec

has to hold a certain amount of frictional cash to support its operations, this meant that UK pension funds were effectively fully invested in other asset classes. Indeed, as noted in Chapter 3, many advisors do not consider cash to be an investment at all. In contrast, private investors seem consistently to maintain a large portion of their net worth in cash. Figure 8.3 shows the 1995 allocation to cash of both pension funds and private investors in five countries.[6] For both types of investor, these figures overstate the cash held for investment purposes only as they include cash held against short-term spending needs and, in the case of pension funds, private equity investment. The UK experience therefore seems to be supported by international evidence.

Equation (A5.7) tells us that the more risk averse an investor, the more cash he will want to hold. Equation (A5.8) tells us that an investor will only not want to hold cash when his risk aversion happens to coincide with the expected ratio of return on risky assets to variance of risky assets. The evidence that pension funds are fully invested at all times, after taking frictional cash into consideration, while individual investors all hold large cash positions, leads to two questions. First, as pension funds are collective investment schemes for individual investors, why is their risk aversion so different from that of private investors? Second, why does their risk aversion always exactly equal expected return divided by variance?

The first question is a particular problem for trustees, who are expected to endorse policies that are considerably more risk tolerant than those the average private investor is comfortable with, while also being expected to treat the money with the same care as they would their own. UK law states that: "It is the duty of a trustee to conduct the business of the trust with the same care as an ordinary man of business would extend towards his own affairs."[7]

There are two possibilities here: either trustees are specially selected to have exceptional risk tolerance, or there is something special about pension funds. There is no evidence for the former. Indeed trustees are selected to be representative of a scheme's beneficiaries and are therefore likely to have average tolerances for risk. However, there is a good argument for the latter.

This runs as follows. As discussed in Chapter 1, a defined benefit pension scheme is essentially a tax-advantaged savings vehicle designed to help the sponsoring company deliver on promises it has made to its employees about retirement benefits. The important point is that the employees ultimately rely on the company, not the scheme, to make good on its promises to them.

The assets and liabilities of the scheme are thus extensions of the assets and liabilities of the company and the portion of the portfolio that is intended to pay for promised pensions, effectively the net worth of the scheme, forms part of the company's net worth. But the shareholders of the company expect its net worth to be invested, not held in cash.* The company will therefore try to use the net worth either to invest in its own business or in equities issued by other businesses. Thus pension funds' insignificant exposure to cash does not represent a risk tolerance that mysteriously varies as expectations of risk and return vary. Rather, it meets the needs of the shareholders of the sponsoring companies.

Pension fund regulation takes a hand to allow people to justify having more risk tolerance when they act as trustees than they do when they act as private investors. For example, UK law allows trustees to take advice on complex matters outside their normal area of expertise. The elaborate machinery of liability matching objectives and asset liability modelling to reach these objectives is clearly one such complexity. It can therefore be interpreted as a mechanism for making the fund more risk tolerant[†] than the trustees without making them uncomfortable.

As we have also seen in Chapter 1, the trend is away from defined benefit schemes and towards defined contribution schemes. If this continues, it is likely that pension fund policy will converge with private client wealth management policy for individuals with similar characteristics.

8.4   ACTIVE ASSET ALLOCATION

Pension fund policy acts as the benchmark for active asset allocation. The active asset allocation overlay consists of overweight and underweight positions in asset classes based on views about their short or medium-term performance prospects.[‡] The UK is unusual in that two third-party vendors, Russell/Mellon CAPS and the WM Company, carry out performance measurement for pension funds. Each vendor assembles a universe of results, the distribution of which is representative of the whole range of UK pension fund results.

UK advisors have in the past set pension fund policy benchmarks by taking the median or average asset class weights of one of the two universes. There are two problems with this, the practical consequences of which are making this behaviour less common.[§] First, even though

---

* Stockholders usually demand the return of any cash that is surplus to the operating requirements of the company either as dividends or as stock buy-backs.

[†] Some UK actuaries now argue that bonds are the correct matching asset for all pension liabilities ["Actuarial tempers running high", *Financial Times*, 24 August 2002]. Such a shift, by eliminating exposure to equities, would make a pension fund less risk tolerant than its trustees. In addition, by using a lower discount rate to value the accrued liabilities of active members, it would cause a major deterioration in funding ratios. The last time investing the assets of active members in bonds was popular was in the USA in the early 1980s, when market yields on bonds rose above the actuarial discount rate for equities. Schemes were able to save money by immunising the liabilities due to both retired and active scheme members. Sadly, even though bonds subsequently did well, equities did better, so reduced pension expense in the short term led to increased expense later.

[‡] Active asset allocation overlays are marketed as separate, or freestanding, Tactical Asset Allocation (TAA) products, which take long and short positions in bonds and equities through the futures markets.

[§] Regrettably, it still seems to be common for UK investment firms to advise the trustees of charitable endowments to use average endowment asset allocation as policy. This has the consequence that those charities, which support their activities through fund raising and therefore need to use their endowments as working capital, get the same policy as those charities, which support their activities through endowment income and can consequently take a much longer term view.

pension fund conventions and regulations make risk tolerance uniform, liabilities themselves are not uniform so that such a policy is only optimal for funds with average liabilities. Second, the averages include active asset allocation positions.

This can be illustrated by a recent example, the effect of which can be seen in Figure 8.1. In 1996, one of the four leading UK investment firms took a cautious view of markets and switched out of UK equities into cash. Because of the concentration of UK investment firms, this was enough to shift the average allocation to UK equities down and the average allocation to cash up by noticeable amounts in the two universes. Those investment firms trying either to match the average or to maintain a given active asset allocation overlay then had to reduce their weights in UK equities, which resulted in a further reduction in the average allocation to UK equities, and so on over two years.

8.5   CONCLUSION

Investment policy is the allocation between asset classes that best meets the needs of an investor without special market knowledge. As such, it forms the investment portfolio of an index fund investor. Because it does not contain a market view, investors also use policy as a benchmark for measuring active performance. As an active overlay is an active portfolio less its benchmark, policy defines it.

While policy is not sensitive to market views, it varies over time as new historical data comes in and advisors consider new asset classes. Despite this, policy is not set competitively. This reduces the revenues of advisors skilled in policy setting but strengthens the tenure of all advisors. Policy is sometimes set with a view to matching committed liabilities. Policy set with this objective coincides with policy set with a return-maximising objective when the expected returns on risky assets and liability matching assets have a particular relationship with each other. Despite being collective investment schemes for individual investors, pension funds have more risk-tolerant policies than individual investors.

Active asset allocation reflects active views on asset class returns. Tactical asset allocation products represent freestanding active asset allocation overlays. Using average investor asset allocation as policy can cause problems for pension funds different from the average, as it incorporates average liabilities, average risk tolerances and average policy active overlays.

ENDNOTES

1. *Life of Robert, Third Marquess of Salisbury*, Lady Gwendolen Cecil, 1921–1932, vol. 3.
2. Myners, p. 65.
3. Myners, p. 64.
4. Data sourced from Pension Fund Indicators, 2002, UBS Global Asset Management, p. 18. [Primary sources credited in report]
5. Data sourced from Pension Fund Indicators, 2000, UBS Global Asset Management, pp. 7, 11. [Primary sources credited in report]
6. Sourced from Pension Fund Indicators, 2000, UBS Global Asset Management, pp. 7–11 and Intersec. [Primary sources credited in report]
7. Judgement in Bartlett vs. Barclays Bank 1980 [quoted in Myners, p. 42].

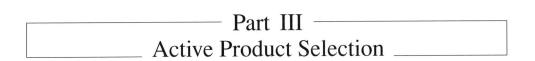

Part III
Active Product Selection

9

Finding Skill

Chapter 6 pointed out that the Efficient Market Hypothesis is incompatible with successful active management. As well as financial economists, many practitioners argue that investors should avoid active products:

> There is a lot of show biz in active fund management. Investors pay a lot for a promise that can only be delivered by chance. It signifies the greed of people – they are willing time and time again to suspend their rational judgement in the hope that someone has the magic touch.[1]

The empirical evidence from unit trust and mutual fund performance that supports the proposition that active management fails to add value was also presented in Chapter 6. In addition, there is the practical consideration that an investor who decides not to use active products saves himself a great deal of trouble and expense.

An investment management industry where active management was discredited would consist of a small number of suppliers of index products competing on price. Although the index fund sector takes this form, the rest of the investment management industry does not. As we saw in Chapter 2, indexation, although growing, is not the dominant form of investment product, even by asset volume. By revenue, index products are insignificant relative to actively managed products. It is therefore clear that many investors and their advisors still believe that it is possible to find superior actively managed products and wish to invest in them.

The global investment management industry that has developed to meet this need is very diverse, with hundreds of product types, thousands of investment management firms and tens of thousands of products. Most of these products are of the traditional type. In the USA, investment firms serving pension funds offer 7953 products collectively controlling US$3.1 trillion.[2] In addition, there are 5357 mutual funds controlling US$2.1 trillion.[3] In the UK unit trust and OEIC sector there are 1874 products, 150 firms and 35 product types[4] controlling a dollar equivalent of some US$0.4 trillion.[5] Either natural selection does not occur or it is very slow. Dozens, sometimes hundreds, of products survive together within the same product type for decades.

If the industry procedures for identifying skill with confidence worked well, one would expect a Darwinian process to operate within each product category. A consensus that certain products were good and others were bad would emerge and investors would transfer their investments from one to the other. The fact that this does not happen suggests that investors and their advisors have great difficulty in identifying, with confidence, which products to withdraw from and which products to transfer their investments to.

To understand why this might be the case, it is useful to consider what an investor needs to do if he decides to invest his money in actively managed products. First, he has to find good, or skilfully managed, products. Second, he has to decide how to divide his wealth between the products he has identified. The first problem is the subject of the rest of this chapter.

9.1   EVIDENCE OF SKILL

Active overlays allow a very precise definition of investment skill as only skilfully managed overlays have reliably positive returns, or profits. The more reliable the profits are, the more skilful the management is. A skilful investment professional, or team of investment professionals, can confidently be expected to manage an active overlay profitably. Even when a skilful investment professional, or team, manages a product, it will not be skilfully managed from its investors' perspective if fees and other expenses exceed the profit. Thus the skill that is important to an investor is product skill, or the skill delivered to him. He is only interested in estimating the skill of an individual, or team, as a means of estimating product skill.

In looking for skill, it is important to know whether it resides in a team or an individual. Opinion is divided about this point. Some industry practitioners seem to believe that the investment firm, or a team of investment professionals working within it, takes the investment decisions. Some industry practitioners seem to believe that an individual* independently takes the investment decisions for each product. Chapter 11 will identify when skill is likely to reside in a team and when it is likely to reside in an individual. In either case, investors and their advisors consider two types of evidence when looking for investment skill.

9.1.1   People

The first type of evidence is the human factor. Analysis of this has to conclude with a judgement based on evidence of the experience, talent and motivation of the investment professional or team responsible for handling an active overlay. When making this judgement, it is important to know whether to look at individuals independently or as a team. Here is a leading advisor's view of what needs to be considered:[6]

> The experience of a manager's professional staff, both individually and more importantly in working together, is an important element in the evaluation process. The sponsor also needs to assess whether the prior experience of key professionals is applicable to their present responsibilities and whether it was acquired in an organisation with the same investment approach . . . As another consideration, examine how professionals within the firm are motivated and compensated.

9.1.2   Past performance

The second type of evidence is past performance. Once again, it is important to know whether the individual is key, in which case the analyst has to focus on the product track record since the individual was appointed to manage it, or whether the team is what matters, in which case the analyst has to focus on the team's track record in running the product. In either case, finding skill from past performance is far from easy.

> I have been increasingly convinced that the past records of mutual fund managers are essentially worthless in predicting future success. The few examples of consistently superior performance occur no more frequently than can be expected by chance.[7]

> Past returns are no indication of future performance, for a number of reasons. One is simply luck. A manager selects securities in the belief that the market has mispriced them. Whether the market corrects itself within the time period under management, particularly if it is a short or ill-defined

---

* US regulations require that a designated individual be identified as portfolio manager for each US mutual fund or pension fund portfolio.

period, is often a matter of chance. A second factor is that the manager's approach or style may be particularly favoured by the market during the period under measurement – or may be particularly hard-hit. A third factor is that there may be an optimal size at which a manager can continue to generate outperformance using its existing personnel, strategy and so on.[8]

The second statement articulates the main limitations of using past performance to predict skill. The first is that the shorter the evaluation period, the more chance that a skilful manager will underperform. The second is that the effect of market movements that are unrelated to skill can swamp the influence of skill on historical performance. The third is that, owing to changes in the manager's ability to add value, skill shown in the past may not be the same as future skill.

Despite misgivings about it, investment consultants and advisors do in fact make extensive use of past performance, usually using it as a preliminary screen in the process of developing a recommended list of products for the investor to choose from.

> A pre-occupation with recent performance (i.e. the last 3–5 years) which, despite worthy statements from consultants and clients alike, continues to dominate the manager selection process.

> It appears that most consultants are chiefly driven by recent performance in making recommendations for a shortlist. Although they claim that other factors such as the quality of the investment process or personnel are just as important, in practice the 3–5 year performance track record is the critical consideration in being included on a shortlist.[9]

When investors and advisors focus on a three to five-year time horizon, they are implicitly taking the view that the individual drives performance and the historical track record to look at coincides with the tenure of the individual manager.

Historically, the probability of a US mutual fund changing the individual designated as manager in a given year is approximately one in five,[10] corresponding to an expected tenure of five years. In 2002, 636, or 31.2%, of the managers of 2039 UK funds had completed less than one year's service.[11] This corresponds to an expected tenure of just over three years.

9.2   MEASURES OF SKILL

The studies of unit trust and mutual fund performance data referred to in Chapter 6 suggest that average skill for such products is negative. Thus a traditional product picked at random is more likely to destroy value than to create it. This in turn means that investors and their advisors have to find products that are significantly above average to have a good chance of profiting from the experience. To help them do this, the industry uses a statistical approach to estimating confidence in whether skill exists. From this, it has evolved the quantitative measures of information ratio and active risk.

9.2.1   Confidence

This approach starts with the probability P that the active overlay return observed in the past is a statistical fluke and that the true performance-generating process of the product gives an expected active overlay return of zero. In order to simplify matters, analysts adopt the convention that the overlay return is normally distributed.* To find P, analysts also adopt the convention that skill is constant. P is then determined from a historical track record by calculating a quantity given by the annualised average excess return multiplied by the square

---

* According to MPT, an equivalent assumption with the same effect is that all investors are mean variance investors.

root of the length of the track record in years and divided by the annualised standard deviation of the excess return (A3.7). This quantity is known as the confidence interval, C^*. The probability P that the overlay return is really zero or less is equal to the probability that a normal distribution will be C standard deviations or more from the mean. Thus, the higher C is, the lower P is and the more confident the analyst can be that the process really is generating a positive overlay return.

9.2.2   The information ratio

An analyst can distinguish between products with different track records by calculating each product's C. The product with the highest C is the product for which the analyst will have the highest confidence that its skill will be positive.

When all time series have the same length, the quantity that drives the confidence interval, from equation (A3.7), is the mean overlay return divided by the standard deviation of overlay return. This is known as the information ratio (A5.21). The product with the highest C will also have the highest information ratio.

To get from information ratio to expected skill as defined at the beginning of the chapter, you have to make two assumptions. First, you have to assume that skill is constant so that skill calculated from historical data is a good estimate of expected skill. Section 9.3.3 considers the potential limitations of this assumption. Second, you have to assume that overlay profit equals risk-adjusted overlay profit. Although we have implicitly made this assumption so far, it is obviously only true when the risk adjustment is zero. From (A5.18), the risk adjustment attributable to the overlay is only negligible if the weighting in the overlay is small and the overlay is independent, i.e. does not correlate with anything else in the portfolio of passive products and active overlays that the investor already owns.

Because calculations of the relationships between the overlay return and the return on the rest of the investor's portfolio are usually very imprecise, it is hard to disprove that the overlay is uncorrelated with his existing investments. Assuming that the overlay return is independent is very convenient. In addition to equating historical information ratios to demonstrated skill, independence means that it is no longer necessary to know what investors already own to judge what value a product will add to their portfolios.

If a product is not independent so that some part of its return correlates with the investor's existing portfolio, it is possible to show that the only part of the product return that affects weights and value added is the independent component. Equation (A6.29) shows that an investor who owns a portfolio P will buy a weight in a new asset A that depends on that part of A's return that is independent of P. Similarly, equation (A6.30) shows that the maximum value added from A depends on the independent component of A, or A's alpha relative to P. This can be demonstrated intuitively by remembering that if P comprises optimal weights of the various index funds and active overlays, extra weights in these, by the definition of optimal weights, will not increase risk-adjusted return. Thus the only source of incremental risk-adjusted return has to be from the independent component.

An important class of product where the active overlay cannot be assumed independent is the large group of products where the benchmark portfolio is cash, so that the information ratio

---

* Confidence intervals are closely related to the t values introduced in Chapter 6. The confidence intervals that stocks really do beat cash can be calculated from the Barcap data by multiplying the Sharpe ratios (0.28 for US stocks and 0.21 for UK stocks) by the square roots of the lengths of the time series (8.8 for US stocks and 10.1 for UK stocks) to give 2.5 for US stocks and 2.1 for UK stocks.

becomes the Sharpe ratio. For most such products, there is evidence of correlations between their excess returns and the excess returns on components of their investors' policies. For example, the CSFB Tremont hedge fund index has correlations of 0.5 with the S&P 500 and 0.4 with the MSCI EAFE.[12] A calculation to isolate the independent component of this index is presented later in this chapter.

Despite the assumptions necessary for its validity, the information ratio is so commonly used that it has acquired a number of alternative names: alpha–omega ratio; signal–noise ratio; return–variability ratio; appraisal ratio; selection ratio.[13] If the overlay is separately available, it can be added to any benchmark to create excess return against that benchmark.*

9.2.3   Active risk

Active risk, or the standard deviation of overlay return expressed either as a dollar amount or as a percentage of capital, has two main uses. First, it is a better measure of the size of the active overlay than assets under management. This is because from (A5.21), for a given information ratio, the standard deviation of overlay return multiplied by the information ratio gives the expected profitability of the overlay. In addition, (A6.4) shows that the active risk investors want exposure to from a given overlay is proportional to the skill with which the overlay is being managed.

Second, it is used as a measure of the risk introduced for the investor by active management.† Its popularity in this role has given it its name. Chapter 12 will analyse its effectiveness in this role.

9.3   ELUSIVENESS OF SKILL

Knowing what to look for does not mean that you will find it. As already noted, the behaviour of investors and their advisors suggests that they have great difficulty‡ in establishing which traditional products are skilfully managed and, equally importantly, which are unskilfully managed. A sceptic or an efficient market theorist would have an easy answer. He would argue that the reason why skill is hard to find is that it does not exist, at least in a form accessible to investors.

But there is another answer. This is that there are reasons embedded in the career structure of the industry, the form into which traditional products have evolved and the nature of skill itself that make skill hard to find. This section looks at the way manager tenure, benchmark ambiguity and the stability of individual skill all have the potential to intensify the difficulty of the task.

9.3.1   Manager tenure

We have already seen that average manager tenure for traditional products is in the range of three to five years. As already discussed, (A3.7) indicates that the confidence interval that an

---

* This is why hedge funds, which together with TAA and currency overlay products are the nearest things currently available to freestanding overlays, are sometimes known as "portable alpha".

† As discussed in Chapter 6, if the overlay return is normally distributed, the mean and standard deviation of overlay return define the distribution and therefore the chance of exceeding any level of loss.

‡ The generally low confidence in traditional product skill explains both why regulators dismiss historical performance as a way to predict skill and why investment firms do not publish confidence intervals. Regulators currently address the issue in the form of a performance health warning that is often buried in the small print. There is a case for them to insist that, when investment firms use historical performance to sell their products, they also publish the confidence interval, or the probability derived from it, that product skill has actually been demonstrated.

active overlay is being managed with positive skill is equal to skill multiplied by the square root of the length of the time series of data available.

To illustrate how the numbers work, consider an investment professional capable of running an active overlay that generates an annual average of one dollar of profit for every three dollars of active risk, giving him a skill rating of 0.33. If he runs a product for four years, the confidence interval that skill has been shown is 0.33 multiplied by the square root of four, or 0.66. This translates to a probability that skill exists of 0.75, or a 75% confidence level. In order to achieve 95% confidence over this period, an investment professional would need a skill rating of 0.82 and in order to achieve 99% confidence he would need a skill rating of 1.16. Such talent is truly exceptional.

A manager with skill of 0.33 would need 50 years to raise the confidence level that he had skill to 99%. Tenure of that length is a practical impossibility. In any case, as we will see later, the average skill shown over decades may not be the best estimate of skill to be shown over the next year.

Unless the manager is exceptional, it is therefore very unlikely that an analyst seeking to prove or disprove skill from active management track records will assemble enough historical performance data to achieve the 95% or 99% confidence level that statisticians normally require. Instead, the industry seems to treat top quartile performance as a skill cut-off for traditional actively managed products.

9.3.2 Benchmark ambiguity

By definition, changing the benchmark of an active product changes its active overlay by an equal and opposite amount. It follows that the risk and return of the active overlay measured from historical data depends on the definition of the benchmark portfolio. There is little benchmark ambiguity for hedge funds, which are almost invariably measured against cash.

However, there is a great deal of benchmark ambiguity for traditional products. It frequently happens that different investors measure the same product using different benchmarks. Inevitably they conclude from the same data that the product has demonstrated different information ratios. They also make different estimates of skill and have different levels of confidence that skill exists. In addition to causing confusion among investors about skill, this ambiguity has a further adverse consequence. The active manager becomes uncertain as to which of his positions is creating active risk and which is not.

A related problem for traditional products is that, even when all investors agree on what benchmark to use, the benchmark may not exactly reflect what the manager is doing. (A5.25) is an expression for the skill calculated when the difference between the benchmark actually used and the true passive portfolio is treated as a noise factor N with zero excess return.*

The greater the variance of the noise factor, the lower the calculated skill relative to the true skill and the longer the time taken to achieve a given level of confidence. If the variance of the noise factor equals the variance of the active overlay, the length of the time series needed to achieve a given level of confidence doubles. Thus an active overlay with a 0.33 skill rating will have to generate an eight-year track record to give analysts even a modest 75% confidence level that skill exists.

---

* When the noise factor is independent and has a positive excess return, it can increase the information ratio. For example, consider a product with a cash benchmark that has a proportion permanently invested in equities. (A6.36) shows that the optimal proportion in equities will improve the product's Sharpe ratio by a factor that depends on the ratio between the equity Sharpe ratio and the skill ratio of the active overlay.

As we saw in Chapter 7, investors and advisors constrain traditional product active risk relative to benchmark active risk. But the consequence of this is that a small difference between the benchmark portfolio and the true passive portfolio can still result in a noise factor that has a high variance relative to the variance of the active overlay.

For example, consider a pension fund whose advisor wants the proportion of total variance not attributable to policy to be no more than the US industry average of 6.4%.[14] Suppose that the product's true passive portfolio and the pension fund's policy benchmark are almost indistinguishable but there is a small noise factor such that the correlation between the two is 0.983. If the noise factor is independent of both the active overlay and policy, this correlation implies that its variance is equal to the variance of the active overlay. This in turn means that the time taken to establish a given level of confidence in active management skill will be twice the time taken if the noise factor did not exist.*

9.3.3 Experience and age

The assumption that skill remains constant over time, while necessary when using information ratios calculated from historical performance to measure skill, is not intuitively obvious, particularly when measured over long periods. For a team, the quality and cohesiveness of the group may vary as individuals come and go. For an individual, skill is likely to vary with experience and age.

He is likely to experience a gain component, which increases skill over time. Factors important for the gain component might include the investment professional's investment aptitude, risk-taking experience and learning opportunities, particularly to develop sources of proprietary market insight. He is also likely to experience a loss component, which decreases skill over time. Factors important for the loss component might include mental flexibility, physical fitness, enthusiasm and motivation.

The two components are likely to have different influences at different stages of an individual's career, leading to skill that varies over time. For any individual with varying skill, information ratio, or average historical skill, is likely to be different from actual skill.

To illustrate this, consider an investment professional with very simple gain and loss components such that his skill varies over time in a way determined by (A6.44). Then (A6.45) determines his career average skill. Figure 9.1 plots his actual skill at any time and the average skill he has demonstrated over his career to date.

Such an individual learns rapidly, as his skill is positive after only one year's training. It then rises to a peak after nine years, falling off thereafter and becoming negative after 25 years. After 36 years, his skill is back where it started. Now consider his career average skill. This rises much more slowly and only peaks after 16 years, at which point actual skill crosses it on the way down. But the average also falls much more slowly. In this case, its level when actual skill becomes negative is the same as its level when actual skill peaks.

Calculating the confidence interval that skill exists from historical data gives even more perverse results. For example, the confidence interval when actual skill peaks is only 60% of the confidence interval when actual skill goes negative again.

---

* This mechanism may give rise to a vicious circle, where declining confidence in active management skill makes investors and their advisors tighten up on active management flexibility, leading to lower active risk relative to policy risk, leading in turn to lower confidence and so on.

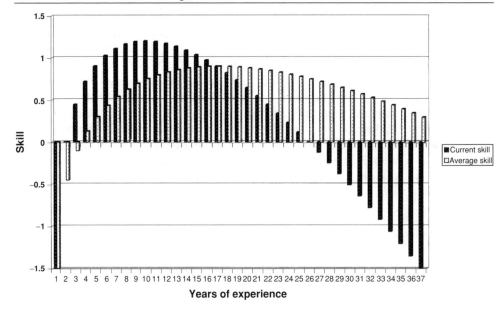

Figure 9.1   Skill over time

For an investment professional whose skill follows this kind of pattern, the assumption that skill is constant is likely to be particularly misleading during the early part of his career and during the latter stages of his career. Because he improves during the early part of his career, the information ratio will consistently underestimate his skill. In addition, confidence that skill exists at all will be low because of the shortness of his track record. Because his skill deteriorates in the latter stages of his career, the information ratio will consistently overestimate his skill. In addition, confidence that skill exists will be high as his personal track record will by then be long.

9.4   ADVISORS AND SKILL

The degree of discretion and therefore the degree of responsibility taken by advisors searching for skill is linked to product type. Advisors specialising in the task of finding skill in traditional products have preferred to present their conclusions as recommended shortlists of products from which the investor makes the final choice. Advisors specialising in the task of finding skill in hedge funds have been more ready to act as discretionary managers of managers, taking full responsibility for the performance of their selections.

9.4.1   Traditional products

Investment manager search consultants specialising in traditional product research need to demonstrate that their research can confidently identify skilfully managed products. Their reluctance to publish their results underlines the difficulty of the task.

A rare publicly available study[15] calculates the information ratios of the average quarterly excess returns before fees of products, with the investment manager search consultant's highest research ratings in each of the 48 categories monitored, since the research ratings started in July 1995. They range between −0.4 and 2.1 with an average of 0.5. The confidence interval of the average is 0.5 multiplied by the square root of 7.25, or 1.35. This would be somewhat less for average product skill, or skill after deducting fees.

As suggested in Chapter 8, a search consultant, who is confident that he can continue to identify skill in traditional products with reasonable precision, has an economic incentive to reformat his product as a discretionary one. We are therefore likely to see investment manager search consultants, with high confidence that they can find skill, launching manager of manager products.[*]

9.4.2   Hedge funds

Advisors, who specialise in selecting products from among the 6000 hedge funds[†] controlling US$0.5 trillion[16] that are currently available, usually act as managers of managers.

They do this because, while mutual funds as a whole do not demonstrate skill, there is growing evidence that hedge funds do, making skill easier to find in these products. The CSFB Tremont index has now been going for nine years and includes two features designed to make it a realistic proxy for hedge fund industry experience. First, it is capitalisation weighted rather than equal weighted. It attempts to capture the results of at least 85% of the assets under management of each type of fund monitored. Second, the designers have taken specific steps to minimise survivorship bias.

At 1 January 2003, the CSFB Tremont index[17] had achieved an annualised excess return over the nine years since 1 January 1994 of 6.17%, with standard deviation of 8.86%. Over the same period, the excess return of the S&P 500 index was 2.84%, with standard deviation of 16.45%. The beta of the CSFB Tremont relative to the S&P was 0.27 and the correlation was 0.49.

Comparing the characteristics of this distribution with the characteristics of the distributions of annual stock returns analysed in Chapter 6, we find a similar degree of abnormality.[‡] However, the annualised volatility using four-month data periods is some 10% greater than the annualised volatility using one-month data periods. This suggests that market memory for hedge funds takes a different form. Unlike the stock distributions, where good years have a tendency to be followed by poor years and vice versa, there is a tendency in this distribution for good months to be followed by good months and poor months by poor months. This is probably because many hedge funds use appraised prices rather than market quotes for their more complicated, illiquid or unusual positions. Valuations of these funds will have a tendency to lag reality in the short term.

I will define the independent return of the CSFB Tremont index as that component of its return that is independent of the S&P 500.[§] From (A5.19), the independent component of the return on the index is therefore 6.17 less 2.84 multiplied by 0.27, or 5.40%, which is also the MPT alpha (A5.19).

---

[*] This trend started in 1980 when the Frank Russell Company first offered a manager of manager product. The trend's slow development since then underlines the difficulty of the task.

[†] Most hedge fund products are offered in two or more formats. For example, there may be an onshore US limited partnership and an offshore Bermuda registered open-ended fund. The true number of distinct hedge fund products is probably half the total number of funds, or approximately 3000.

[‡] The distribution's t values (A1.16) are 0 for skewness and 3 for kurtosis, suggesting a tendency towards having fat tails. The abnormality of this distribution is thus no worse than the abnormality of stock returns. We saw in Chapter 6 that the t values for skewness and kurtosis were 1.4, 12.6 and 2.7, 1.5 for the UK and USA respectively.

[§] This conforms to the convention, often adopted by financial economists, that the S&P index is a good proxy for the market portfolio.

The independent standard deviation is 7.67%, so that product skill is 0.70. Multiplying this by three, or the square root of the life of the index, gives a confidence interval of 2.1 that skill is positive.* From (A6.46), unless product skill suddenly falls to below 0.35, this confidence interval will continue to grow.

The index return is net of fees. One way to estimate fees is to assume that the fees deducted from the index conform to the standard hedge fund formula of a flat 1% plus 20% of the excess return. Reversing this formula, it is easy to see that a fee of 2.54% is consistent with an after-fee excess return of 6.17%. Adding this fee estimate to the independent return gives 7.94%. Dividing this grossed up independent return by 7.67 gives an estimate of skill before deducting fees of 1.04.† This in turn leads to an estimate of the confidence level that skill is being shown before fees of 3.12.

Consistent with the notion that skill is easier to identify for hedge funds than it is for traditional products, there is also evidence that the process of elimination is much more active for hedge funds than it is for mutual funds. "Last year, a fifth of all hedge funds closed, according to Tremont Advisers, the research group. And Tremont estimates that this year up to 1,000 of the remaining 6,000 will fail."[18] Consistent with this, researchers find drop-out rates for hedge funds of 15–20% per annum (depending on database) as compared with a drop-out rate for mutual funds of 5% per annum.[19]

One interpretation of this is that investors are actively discriminating between superior and inferior products, bringing a virtuous circle into existence. Inferior products are eliminated,‡ raising the average, while survivors and new entrants have extra motivation to demonstrate superiority, raising the average still further.

9.5   CONCLUSION

In order to justify using actively managed investment products, investors have to believe that this will reliably result in better risk-adjusted returns for them. Investors therefore look for two things from their active managers: the ability to generate risk-adjusted active overlay returns that exceed expenses; the ability to manage risk so that the active overlay returns are reliably positive. Skill is a combination of these two qualities. Its measure is simply the expected risk-adjusted active overlay return divided by the expected active risk.

Opinion is divided as to whether investment skill is an illusion or just elusive. The former school of thought doubts that skill exists or, if it does, can be found. Despite such scepticism, the majority of investors belong to the latter school of thought as they use actively managed products, which they believe to be skilfully managed either by individuals or by teams. Advisors' efforts to identify skill concentrate on the past performance, experience and teamwork of the investment professionals involved in making investment decisions.

Short manager tenure, ambiguous benchmarks and changing manager skill make it hard to identify either superior or inferior traditional products with confidence. This inhibits the elimination of inferior products. Hedge funds seem more prone than traditional products to

---

* Confidence that hedge funds have skill is thus similar to confidence that stocks beat cash. It is also similar to confidence that traditional products do not have skill. From the data presented in the UK unit trust study quoted earlier, the confidence interval that product skill is negative for an equally weighted portfolio of UK unit trusts can be inferred to be 2.3.

† If the true index volatility is 10% higher than the annualised volatility, the independent standard deviation will be 15% higher and the skill estimates 13% lower.

‡ The evidence is therefore that average manager tenure for hedge funds is no more than five years. It will be less to the extent that manager changes have occurred without fund closure.

elimination from poor performance. Empirical analysis suggests that, on average, hedge funds demonstrate skill while traditional products do not.

ENDNOTES

1. Pattie Dunn, Chairman of BGI, a leading index fund provider, quoted in the *Financial Times*, 21 May 1999.
2. 1995 *Pensions and Investments* magazine Top 1000 US Money Managers.
3. 1995 ICI US Mutual Fund Factbook.
4. Posted on www.trustnet.com as at December 2002.
5. Myners, p. 143.
6. D. Smith, *How to Select and Evaluate Investment Managers*, Frank Russell Company, p. 7.
7. Malkiel, p. 391.
8. Myners, p. 83.
9. Myners, p. 80.
10. J. Chevalier, and G. Ellison, "Career concerns of mutual fund managers", *Quarterly Journal of Economics*, 14(2).
11. The UK Fund Industry Review and Directory 2002, quoted in *Sunday Telegraph*, 4 August 2002.
12. Sourced from www.hedgeindex.com.
13. T.H. Goodwin, "The Information Ratio", *Financial Analysts Journal*, July/August 1998.
14. Brinson.
15. "Summary of value added through Mercer manager research recommendations as at 30 September 2002", additional private material quoted with permission from Mercer Investment Consulting.
16. *Economist*, 13 April, 2002.
17. CSFB Tremont Hedge Index Report, published on website on 15.1.03.
18. *Sunday Times*, 12 January 2003.
19. Fung and Hsieh.

10

Using Style

Every man will have his own style which will distinguish him as much as his gait.[1]

As noted in the previous chapter, the second problem an investor has to solve when using active managers is to decide both how much to allocate and what asset or combination of assets currently in the portfolio should be sold to fund the allocation. This problem forms the subject of the rest of this chapter. As also noted in the previous chapter, there are a very large number of actively managed products to choose from, which makes the problem harder. The industry has evolved the concept of product style to help investors and their advisors to find solutions.

10.1 ACTIVE PRODUCT WEIGHTS

In principle, Modern Portfolio Theory should allow an investor to calculate his optimal weights in active products without going through the intermediate step of designing an investment policy. In practice, the industry has found models based on MPT to be inaccurate tools for determining the weights of active products that best meet an investor's objectives.

10.1.1 The MPT solution

Dividing up his wealth between active products is straightforward for a mean variance investor, if he has accurate estimates of the excess returns and covariances of all the products that he is trying to fit into his portfolio. He merely solves (A5.6), the expression for optimal weights in risky assets for such an investor. This is the basis of the commercial optimiser technology that has been available since the 1980s and is widely used for active asset allocation.

In addition, he can work out the rate at which risk-adjusted return is added to his portfolio by adding a new product. Product alpha (A5.19) is the excess return on a product less the excess return on an index multiplied by the product's beta against that index.

Alpha equals risk-adjusted overlay return for the investor (A5.18) when the index is a component of the investor's policy. Thus beta is a risk adjustment parameter. When efficient markets apply so that alpha is zero, beta determines return (A5.20).

The difficulty with using mean variance analysis of this kind to assemble a portfolio of investment products is that the best possible forecasts of product excess returns, variances and covariances are too imprecise.* For example, (A5.12) shows that the weights in a solution to a two asset problem are very sensitive to a small change in the forecast of one of the two returns. As there are thousands of products available, many with very similar characteristics, a small amount of extra information leading to modest changes in estimated excess returns and covariances can trigger dramatic changes in the MPT solution for the weights of a product portfolio. In a world where substituting one product for another results in substantial transaction

---

* Similar imprecision in short-term judgemental forecasts of asset returns limits the effectiveness of optimisers as tools for determining actively managed asset allocation overlays.

costs, this procedure will generate costs which are likely to swamp any benefits from active management.

10.1.2 Accuracy

Equation (A3.7) proves that the more data upon which an estimate is based, the more accurate the estimates. Individual products have invariably been in existence for shorter periods than the asset classes they invest in. This means that estimates of risk and return based on historical data are much more accurate for asset classes than they are for products. This is why the MPT approach embodied in (A5.6) is much more successful and consequently much more widely used to calculate the policy mix between asset classes and components of asset classes, as presented in Chapter 8, than it is to calculate the weights of a portfolio of actively managed products. The trick is therefore to find benchmarks with long historical track records that are closely related to both the active products selected and the asset allocation policy selected.

10.1.3 The industry solution

The steps practitioners take to decide what weight to assign to an actively managed product are then simple in principle. First, find a benchmark portfolio that is both closely related to the product and forms a component of investor policy. Second, satisfy yourself that the product is skilfully managed so that it can be confidently expected to beat the benchmark. Third, substitute* the active for the passive. The product weight then only needs to be changed either if new information changes the estimate of skill or if policy is changed to eliminate or reduce the benchmark weighting.

The link between demand for a product and its benchmark is thus straightforward. It depends on the degree to which the benchmark forms part of investors' policies. Investment management firms will try to deploy skilful investment professionals to manage products with benchmarks in demand but with limited competition. A firm offering an actively managed balanced product will be forced to create a product† if a new asset class appears in its clients' policies. Traditional actively managed products have therefore evolved to deliver both policy and active management.

10.2 STYLE DEFINITION

The industry shorthand for a benchmark portfolio that aligns the measurement of product skill with investor policy is style. A useful style is therefore one that is adequately correlated both with a large number of products and with elements of the policies of a large number of investors. Chapter 6 noted that when active risk is small relative to risk from style, the correlation between style and a product's true passive portfolio has to be very high in order for the style benchmark to be a useful tool in identifying skill. The difficulty in finding styles of practical use means that advisors have adopted a wide variety of approaches to style definition including basing them on asset classes, categories within asset classes and product universes.

---

* In practice, depending on what is available, the passive can be partially replaced or replaced by more than one suitable active product.
† When material allocations to overseas bonds appeared in UK pension fund policies from 1989 onwards, those balanced managers who did not have an actively managed product of this type had to set one up.

10.2.1   Asset classes

One approach is to use the indices that reflect the various asset classes in the investor's policy. The advantage of this is that there is an obvious fit with policy. However, these asset class benchmarks often have high noise factors when used to assess the performance of active portfolios that belong to the asset class but specialise in a small part of it. For example, portfolios that concentrate on small capitalisation stocks will not correlate very closely with a broad equity index.

10.2.2   Specialised categories

Another approach is to sort products into specialised categories within the asset class, each with its own benchmark. The advantage of this approach is that products in appropriately defined categories will have lower noise factors with the category benchmarks than they have with the asset class benchmark. In addition, classifying products into categories can be verified by cross-checking* their contents against the contents of the category benchmarks that seem to match them. Thus a product that correlates closely with a large capitalisation value benchmark and turns out to contain mostly large capitalisation value stocks can be confidently expected to continue to correlate closely unless something dramatic happens to the way its investment decisions are made. In the USA, the 3×3 scheme of product categories described in Chapter 1 is widely used, although even here it has to be supplemented by industry categories to reflect the range of products available.

   The disadvantage of this approach is that categories that fit well with large numbers of products are very hard to find. For example, no dominant style system has emerged for equities outside the USA. Advisors are still debating the relative merits of classifying securities by industry or country, or some other scheme.

10.2.3   Universe medians

If suitable categories cannot be found, an alternative approach is to assemble universes of products and measure performance relative to the universe median, which effectively becomes the style benchmark. The great advantage of universes is that they give a relatively unambiguous answer to the question: how has the portfolio or subportfolio done against its competition? Another way of putting this is that they eliminate the risk of selecting an inappropriate index to judge performance against.

   However, universes suffer from some substantial disadvantages. Two have already been presented in Chapters 4 and 8. But there are others.

   One is that there is some uncertainty as to how well they reflect the competitive environment. They probably do for UK pension funds, where the products are fairly uniform and the universe assemblers also calculate the performance. But they may not be so representative in the USA, where the investment firms themselves calculate performance. This has the effect of making US universes self-selecting and self-reporting.[†]

---

* Cross-checking also acts as a restraint on data mining or selecting, in arrears, the benchmark that presents the product in the most favourable light.

[†] This has occasionally resulted in abuses. Representative portfolios have sometimes been anything but. In one case, a competitor told the advisor assembling the universe that, for reasons of confidentiality, he had to give a code name for his representative portfolio. What he did not say was that he changed the code-named portfolio each quarter to conform to whichever was his best performing portfolio. To eliminate such behaviour, advisors try to track weighted average rather than representative performance.

Another is when a style or asset class benchmark is used to calculate the weighting of the style or asset class in policy. If manager value added is calculated relative to a universe median and policy value added is calculated by reference to benchmarks, who is accountable for a shortfall between median and benchmark return? As we saw in Chapter 6, average mutual fund active overlay returns are negative when the overlay is defined by a benchmark.* This means that for most mutual fund universes, index funds representing the benchmarks perform better than the universe medians. Does this mean that the index funds are skilfully managed?

10.3   PORTFOLIO CONSTRUCTION

Investors and their advisors have to construct portfolios of products that achieve a compromise between getting the best fit with desired policy and getting the best possible consolidated active overlay.

10.3.1   Specialist portfolios

Advisors follow two schools of thought when constructing portfolios out of specialist products, or products provided by different investment management firms. One favours a core/satellite approach while the other favours a multi-style/multi-manager approach. What these two approaches mean is summarised in the following advisor statement.

> Two distinct approaches are emerging:
>
> – The core/satellite approach uses a passive, or moderately active core, around which are placed a number of active specialists who take much larger active positions. This has the benefit that the core reduces tracking error relative to a passive benchmark, permitting the satellite managers to be aggressive in seeking return.
> – The multistyle/multimanager approach reflects a philosophical dissatisfaction with core/satellite, which does not attempt to control risk selectively. Core/satellite assumes that all risk is bad and scales all risks back in a portion – the core – of the portfolio. This also reduces the potential to add value in the core. Multistyle seeks a more efficient risk reduction, distinguishing between less reliable bets (market timing, sector and style bets, and the like) and more reliable bets (security selection). Multistyle seeks to reduce the less reliable type of risk and emphasise the more reliable type, by blending managers with complementary styles.[2]

The two approaches have evolved because products currently available can be sorted into those with high, medium and low active risk. High active risk corresponds to the alternative products such as hedge funds from which satellite products are chosen. Medium active risk corresponds to the traditional products from which multi-style products are chosen. Low active risk corresponds to the index and enhanced index[†] products from which core products are chosen.

If all products are managed with the same skill, high active risk products will have low optimal weights and low active risk products will have high optimal weights (A6.3). Thus a portfolio can be made up either by medium active risk products as in multi-style or by a combination of low and high active risk products as in core/satellite.

An advisor's decision to adopt either approach depends on two factors: his comparative advantage in finding skill in any or all of the three product categories and his view on whether

---

* They are, by definition, close to zero when the overlay is defined by the median.
† The name comes because a skilled product with low active risk will have a high probability of beating its index but will only do so by a small margin.

skill is more prevalent in some categories than in others. Ultimately, the core/satellite approach will prove superior if, for structural reasons, skill is easier to find in both high and low active risk products than it is in medium active risk products.

While CSFB Tremont supplies data on hedge funds, enhanced index product performance is harder to identify. However, consultants favouring the core/satellite approach clearly believe that skilful products of this type can be found:

> Enhanced index tracker managers say they can achieve consistent information ratios that may be as high as 1.0. This is far higher than the information ratios achieved by most [traditional] active managers, which are around 0.3. So, although regular active managers will outperform more than enhanced index trackers, they will take a lot more risk to do so. This is why Irwin [global head of investment consulting at Watson Wyatt, an advisory firm that favours the core/satellite approach] finds enhanced index tracking attractive.[3]

10.3.2 Balanced portfolios

Balanced or multi-asset portfolios are products where one investment management firm is providing a comprehensive solution to the investor's objectives. Such products differ from specialist portfolios in two ways. First, investment professionals working for the same firm manage the active overlays for all the asset classes. Second, they usually include an actively managed policy overlay. In order to get the best result for the investor, the asset allocator has to balance his views on asset classes with his views on the relative skills of the various asset class managers.

Consider such an allocator who has to decide how much of his investor's risky asset portfolio to allocate to domestic equities and how much to overseas equities. He has high confidence views about the distribution of both asset classes' excess returns.

However, he also knows that his domestic equity manager is more skilled than his overseas equity manager. The optimal allocation between the active products will be different from the optimal allocation between the asset classes as he will put more into domestic equities, the more skilfully managed product, and less into overseas equities, the less skilfully managed product.

This explains why, anecdotally, balanced allocators have a tendency to allocate assets to the asset class where the manager is in form. Another approach would be to give the more skilled manager more freedom and the less skilled manager less freedom.* In the extreme, if the less skilled manager's skill is zero or negative, this implies indexation of his asset class.

10.4   FREESTANDING OVERLAYS

We have seen that the industry convention of delivering policy and active management as a package creates difficulties for investors seeking both to implement their policies and to gain an optimal exposure to skilfully managed active overlays. These difficulties would be greatly reduced if the excess returns from active management processes became available as freestanding active overlays. Decisions on the right mix of styles and asset classes are then completely separated from decisions on the right mix of active overlays.

---

* If the active overlays are independent (A6.9) shows that, for each overlay, the optimal active risk exposure is proportional to the quantitative definition of skill.

As presented in Chapter 2, a freestanding overlay is viable as long as it has minimum capital and investor restrictions that are consistent with the liquidity of its positions. We have already seen some examples of the product genre. Hedge funds are one although, as we shall see in Chapter 13, they tend both to contain residual style portfolios and to be overcapitalised. Currency overlay products and TAA products provide two further examples.

However, these cases are the exception rather than the rule. Given the advantages it has for investors, one might ask why the freestanding active overlay format has made such little progress in displacing the traditional product format. Hype about losses, vested interest, regulation and borrowing costs collectively provide an explanation.

Any discussion of hedge fund risk usually includes a topical list of well-publicised failures. For example, a recent article[4] gives the following list of "hedge-fund catastrophes":

> Sep 1998, near collapse of Long-Term Capital Management. Jan 2000, Manhattan Investment Fund goes bust with losses of more than $400 m. Feb 2002, Lipper & Co. admits that one of its hedge funds had lost about 40% of its value, $315 m, in 2001. It had previously reported a gain. Lipper is liquidating all its hedge funds and mutual funds. Oct 2002, Beacon Hill Asset Management admits that its two hedge funds lost 50% of their value, or $400 m.

But as we have already seen, there are a thousand or so hedge fund closures a year. If only one or two of these experience losses of more than 40% in their last year of operations, this suggests that large losses are a rather rare event. As we will see later in Chapter 13, they are probably too rare for investors who diversify. This is because limited liability is particularly valuable when the size of the active overlay is a multiple of the capital committed. For then, the investor effectively owns a stop loss. When the LTCM overlay was in freefall, there was never any question of the investors paying losses* over and above their investment.

A large vested interest has built up in the status quo. Many thousands of careers and a vast sum of capital tied up in investment management firms providing traditional products have been committed to products in the traditional format.

Freestanding overlays involve short positions and leverage, or supporting capital that is a fraction of the gross size of the active overlay. Both short positions and leverage introduce the possibility of product bankruptcy. As we have seen with LTCM, this is not necessarily a bad thing for investors, provided they are not expected to cover losses over and above their investments. However, as we saw in Chapter 2, preventing product bankruptcy has become a priority for regulators, which has biased them against leverage and short positions. Regulators are also prone to being influenced by lobbying from investment firms offering traditional products.

> David Prosser, chief executive of Legal & General, one of Britain's biggest life and pension funds, has called for a regulatory review of the way hedge funds are influencing stock markets. Prosser believes a new tax should be introduced to make it less attractive for hedge funds to sell stocks short.[5]

Freestanding overlays have to borrow stock from external lenders, who charge a spread that reflects the market rate for lending that class of security. Figure 10.1 shows the average gross margin achieved from lending various asset classes by the California Public Employees Retirement System in the first quarter of 2001.[6] In contrast, in a traditional product, the style portfolio lends the stock without charge.† The figure thus gives an indication of the cost advantage that linked overlays currently have over freestanding overlays.

---

* If firms begin to guarantee minimum levels of performance relative to benchmark, this will have the effect of isolating the capital supporting their active overlays as the maximum attainable loss.

† In theory, the style portfolio suffers an opportunity cost as it could lend the stock at a commercial rate to someone else.

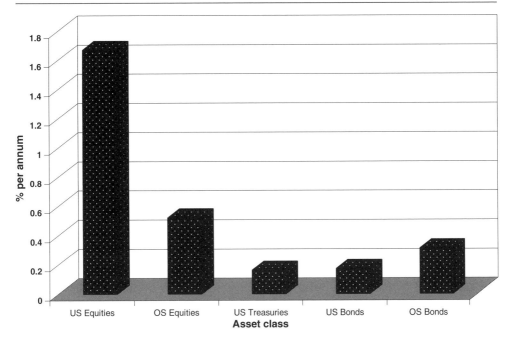

Figure 10.1   Security lending revenue
Source: California Public Employees Retirement System

It is no coincidence that LTCM principally dealt in bonds, which are relatively cheap to borrow, and that one of their key skills was the ability to borrow cheaply. Rather than employing a specialist hedge fund custodian known as a prime broker, they did much of the work themselves, playing off brokers and security lenders against each other to minimise both the margins they had to deposit and the spreads they had to pay.[7] Thus, the lower borrowing costs get, the more practical actively managed freestanding overlays will become.

10.5   CONCLUSION

Once he has identified skilfully managed products, an investor's next problem is to decide what weights they should have in his portfolio. Because of the number of products available and the uncertainties involved, these weights are closely related to his investment policy.

The tool that has been developed to connect actively managed investment products with investors' policies is called style. A style is a portfolio that is both a component of policy and a benchmark for assessing the performance of an actively managed product. The greater the cumulative weight a style has in a group of investors' policies, the more demand these investors will have for products with that style.

In practice, because of the difficulty in finding skilfully managed products, investors have to compromise between expected skill and the degree to which the styles of these products match policy. Different advisors have different views about how to go about making this compromise, resulting in different approaches to constructing portfolios of products to match a given policy. The compromise would be unnecessary if the two component parts of actively managed products, the style portfolio and the active overlay, were separately available.

ENDNOTES

1. "Of style", *Manaductio ad Ministerium*, Cotton Mather.
2. K. Ayers and D. Ezra, "A new age dawns", *Professional Pensions*, 6.4.2000. Ayers and Ezra were both then employed by the Frank Russell Company, which favours the multi-style approach.
3. *Financial News*, 18 June 2000.
4. *Economist*, 11 January 2003.
5. *Sunday Times*, 7 July 2002.
6. *Financial News*, 9 July 2001.
7. Lowenstein, pp. 45–48.

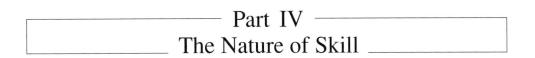

Part IV
The Nature of Skill

11

Firms and Professionals

An outstanding performance record usually indicates that the manager was successful in determining which was the best risk to take, then took a lot of it.[1]

Chapter 9 noted that sometimes the investment industry behaves as though product skill is an attribute of the investment management firm that sponsors the product, or a team within it, while sometimes it behaves as though product skill is an attribute of an individual investment professional working within the firm. The question is an important one. First, as already noted in Chapter 9, it affects which track records investors should use to analyse skill and whom they should hold accountable for performance. Second, as presented later in Chapter 12, it affects the way product risk is managed. Third, as presented later in Chapter 14, it affects how investment professionals are paid and how investment firms are valued.

Although investment professionals adopt a wide variety of approaches, all ultimately either decide what investment risks to take or participate in such decisions. The way they do this is either skilful if the risk is rewarded or not if the risk is unrewarded.*

Active management is thus the industry term for taking investment risk. It is worth pointing out that the term is somewhat misleading. Once the initial positions of the active overlay have been set up, risk taking need not involve much, if any, activity.

11.1 EXCEPTIONAL TALENTS

Some outstanding investors such as Warren Buffett have held the same stocks in their portfolios for decades. It is useful at this stage to look at Buffett and two investors of similar distinction from the generation before, Benjamin Graham and Phillip Fisher.

11.1.1 Benjamin Graham

Graham was an early Wall Street prodigy. In 1919, at the age of 25, his compensation totalled US$600,000. Ruined by the crash of 1929, he was subsequently successful in rebuilding his fortune and his investment firm† continued until 1956. He also taught investment and his thoughts are set out in his book.[2] Its key recommendations were: reduce risk by diversification, a ground-breaking concept at the time; maintain a margin of safety by paying less than intrinsic value; calculate intrinsic value by making use of the facts.

He found that these principles could be implemented by paying less than liquidation value per share for a security or less than fair value for earnings calculated by reference to other publicly available facts. He was therefore the first person to articulate the principles or decision rules used by value investors. An important feature of Graham's approach was that he did not

---

* Managing index funds, while requiring a great deal of technical competence, only needs investment skill at the margin. The managers have limited discretion over both the timing of buying and selling stocks entering and leaving the index and the response they make to corporate actions such as takeovers.

† Buffett entered Graham's class at Columbia in 1951 and later served an apprenticeship with his firm.

need special knowledge about either the management teams or the underlying businesses of his investments.

11.1.2   Phillip Fisher

Fisher came slightly later to the scene. He established his investment company in 1931, after three years of double digit losses for the US stock market. With hindsight, his timing was brilliant. Fisher focused on companies able to grow sales and profits faster than the average of their competitors and classified such companies as either fortunate and able or fortunate because they were able.

In uncovering such superior companies with confidence, Fisher found that the accounting data was not enough. He had to arrive at a deep understanding of the quality of the business and the quality of the management. This involved gathering information that was not generally known, which he called scuttlebutt. Collecting scuttlebutt was extremely time consuming and Fisher had to concentrate his investments, sacrificing diversification for confidence in individual ideas. His portfolio often had four or fewer companies accounting for 75% or more of the total. His book[3] was one of the first to articulate the principles of concentrated growth investment using judgements about the quality of management and the underlying business based on private sources of information.

11.1.3   Warren Buffett

After his apprenticeship with Graham, Buffett set up an investment partnership, which performed exceptionally well. It acquired a depressed textiles business called Berkshire Hathaway, at one time responsible for 25% of textile production in the USA,[4] in 1965. In 1969, the partnership disbanded. Buffett and some of the partners invested their proportional interests in the company; Buffett acquiring a majority stake in what effectively became a closed-end investment company.

As is widely known, the performance of Berkshire Hathaway has also been exceptional.[*] From 1968 to 2002,[5] the outperformance relative to the S&P 500 has been such that the historical information ratio is 0.87. This understates the skill demonstrated as the active overlay return has a negative correlation with the index. The distribution of annual outperformance is close to normal with skewness and kurtosis t factors both less than one.

Making the conservative assumption that Berkshire's active overlay is actually independent of the index, the confidence interval in skill is 5.15 and the probability that the performance has been achieved by luck is effectively zero. The main risk for Buffett's investors, as it is for products managed by any other exceptional investment professional with an outstanding long-term track record, is the chance that his current skill is significantly less than his career average skill.

Over most of the period, Buffett has adopted a highly concentrated approach to investment. Figure 11.1 summarises the annual presentation of Berkshire Hathaway's investments in equity securities by year.[6] The percentage of the portfolio represented by the largest holding varies from 19.7 to 49.7. The percentage of the portfolio in the top four or fewer stocks ranges from 50.7 to 100, with an average of 74.6.

---

[*] Making Berkshire Hathaway an outstanding example of a business that, in Fisher's terminology, was lucky because it was able.

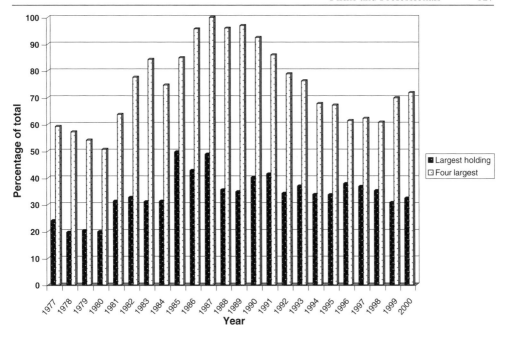

Figure 11.1   Berkshire concentration

While Buffett continues to pay tribute[7] to the ideas of Graham, the concentration figures suggest that his own thinking has moved on. He also pays tribute to the ideas of Fisher,[8] has developed an extensive business network[9] and quotes Keynes approvingly:[10]

> As time goes on, I get more and more convinced that the right method in investments is to put fairly large sums into enterprises which one thinks one knows something about and in management of which one thoroughly believes. It is a mistake to think that one limits one's risk by spreading too much between enterprises about which one knows little and has no special reason for special confidence. . . . One's knowledge and experience is definitely limited and there are seldom more than two or three enterprises at any given time [in] which I personally feel myself entitled to put full confidence.

Perhaps most significantly, he has evolved the concept of permanent holdings.[11] These are stocks where his appreciation of the quality of management and the underlying business is such that he will continue to hold them even if price appreciation eliminates the margin of safety over intrinsic value. For these stocks, his judgement overrules any signal from Graham-type analysis, however strong.

11.2   PUBLIC AND PRIVATE INFORMATION

I was fortunate enough to participate in Professor Jack McDonald's Investment Seminar at Stanford Business School in the spring of 1978. We were familiar with the ideas of both Graham and Fisher but particularly with those of Fisher, a Stanford alumnus. Buffett led one of the sessions. His presentation was designed to demonstrate how attractive investments could be found in the unlikeliest places. To illustrate his point, he took us through an opportunity to invest in a duck-shooting club. However, the discussion soon turned to how to hear of such opportunities and in particular how the scope for collecting information about businesses that was not already discounted in the market was greater in Omaha than on Wall Street.

11.2.1   Graham and Fisher

An important difference between the Graham approach and the Fisher approach is the information needed to drive investment decisions. Graham focused on converting publicly available security prices, annual reports and public filings into investment strategy. All this information is relatively easy and cheap to uncover. The advent of computers and financial research databases has taken much of the drudgery out of this approach. Nowadays a Graham would get most of what he needed by acquiring the CRSP and COMPUSTAT tapes.

Fisher focused on collecting scuttlebutt and his main tool was what is now called business networking: talking to customers, competitors and company management. In order to assess the likely impact of private information* on prices, Fisher also needed to be aware of what information was in the public domain. But the collection of public information was a secondary part of his process.

11.2.2   Market anomalies

By the 1970s, wider knowledge of techniques of analysing accounting data meant that the Graham approach was harder to apply. According to Buffett, the last time it was easy to profit from Graham's methodology was in 1973–1974.[12] In addition, the Efficient Market Hypothesis called into question the ability of investors to generate superior returns from public information. Financial economists and investment advisors became receptive to the notion that a credible actively managed product had to be able to demonstrate access to private information sources. The vast majority of all active managers conformed (and still conform) to this stereotype.

But then in the 1980s, with the availability of CRSP and COMPUSTAT data in machine-readable form, financial economists were able to test some of the systematic effects whose assumed presence had influenced the behaviour of market practitioners for years. These included the small versus large effect and the growth versus value effect discussed in Chapter 1 and the forward foreign exchange effect discussed in Chapter 5. Other effects tested successfully were momentum or persistence effects and various seasonal effects such as the propensity of stocks to go up in January. The resulting excess returns exceeded the returns predicted by the EMH with very high degrees of confidence. It appeared that risk taking based on analysis and interpretation of publicly available historical data could add value after all.

11.2.3   Size and value effects

An example of this kind of analysis, which has been put to work in developing investment strategy, is the work on value and size carried out by the financial economists Eugene Fama and Kenneth French. They ranked stocks within each time period by the two criteria noted in Chapter 1: the ratio of book value to market value and market capitalisation. They then formed

---

* Private information should not be confused with inside information, or information that it is illegal to use in making investment decisions. The definition of inside information varies from jurisdiction to jurisdiction, so what is legal in one country may be against the law in another. One of my colleagues attended an internal presentation on the way the new UK Financial Services Act defined insider information. At the end of it a visiting client from a country with a Mediterranean littoral turned to him in some puzzlement and said "In my country, what you call insider trading, we call investment management".

Table 11.1

Portfolio	Alpha	Confidence interval	Beta	Confidence interval
SMB	0.19	1.32	0.21	6.54
HML	0.56	4.42	−0.21	7.53

two overlays. High book to market stocks financed by short sales of low book to market stocks comprised the first. Small stocks financed by short sales of large stocks comprised the second. They called the first portfolio HML (High Minus Low) and the second portfolio SMB (Small Minus Big). Because of accounting data limitations, the time series used originally started in 1963.

They then regressed the monthly HML and SMB excess returns against the market excess return. The results[13] are shown in Table 11.1.

Both overlay returns had significant betas, so neither overlay was independent. The alphas represent the independent components of the overlay returns. Both alphas were positive, although the significance of the HML alpha was almost three times that of the SMB alpha.

The SMB overlay corresponds to an active equity strategy of investing in small stocks. Its positive beta means that it benefits from an equity bull market. As the HML overlay has a negative beta, an LMH overlay, corresponding to an active equity strategy of investing in growth stocks, will have a positive beta and will benefit from an equity bull market. Thus, as foreshadowed in chapter 1, small stock strategies and growth stock strategies are both implicitly bullish.

The development of the anomaly literature of financial economics was paralleled by the development of investment management firms adopting a quantitative approach.* This entails identifying models based on historical data anomalies, which can then be used to construct portfolio risk positions. These firms have achieved some success, particularly in the USA. However, their products are still very much in the minority, both in numbers and in weight of assets.

This should not be surprising. Using statistical methods to make decisions on investment strategy relies on a large number of historical observations and a review period that is long enough to generate confidence that the strategy has been both successful in the past and is likely to be successful in the future.

11.3   INTUITIVE AND SYSTEMATIC APPROACHES

As presented in Chapter 9, there are tens of thousands of investment professionals and products in the global investment management industry. In addition, most investment banks have proprietary trading operations. There are consequently many thousands of different approaches to investment risk taking. Analysing these and the active return track records they generate to predict skill in the future represents a major challenge for investors and their advisors.

The approaches of all investment professionals engaged in active management involve gathering information, forming conclusions from the information and, if satisfied that competitors

---

* In addition to their academic activities, Fama and French work for Dimensional Fund Advisors, the third largest such quant shop. Its profile states that "Dimensional focuses on capturing the size (small capitalisation) and value (high book-to-market) premiums worldwide in a low cost, efficient manner".

have not already discounted the conclusions in the price,* taking the largest risk position that is consistent with conviction and risk tolerance.

All approaches face the problem that there is an almost infinite amount of information available. Virtually all of this information is either irrelevant or already discounted in the price. Information not discounted in the price is information that still has the potential to move prices. This means that the information is either not known or has been dismissed by the bulk of market participants.

11.3.1   Keynes's metaphor

Keynes provides a vivid and much cited[14] metaphor of active investment management, which is sometimes interpreted, particularly by sceptics about active management, as a coded statement that successful active management is impossibly difficult.

> Professional investment may be likened to those newspaper competitions in which the competitors have to pick out the six prettiest faces from a hundred photographs, the prize being awarded to the competitor whose choice most nearly corresponds to the average preferences of the competitors as a whole; so that each competitor has to pick, not those faces which he himself finds prettiest, but those which he thinks likeliest to catch the fancy of the other competitors, all of whom are looking at the problem from the same point of view. It is not a case of choosing those which, to the best of one's judgement, are really the prettiest, nor even those which average opinion genuinely thinks the prettiest. We have reached the third degree where we devote our intelligences to anticipating what average opinion expects the average opinion to be.

But we know from Keynes's behaviour that he believed in active management and was rather good at it. We also know from the quotation earlier in the chapter that he came to base his active management decisions on research, albeit of the concentrated, private kind. Rather than dismissing active management as impossible, the metaphor therefore tells us that it is difficult and that the frame of reference for active investment decisions should be relative to other active managers' decisions rather than absolute. To illustrate the relative nature of investment decisions, the metaphor can be extended to show how successful active management can be based on either a Graham-style approach using public information or a Fisher-style approach using private information.

Let us suppose that one of the competitors is a follower of Graham. He starts by collecting all the winning and losing photographs from previous editions of the paper. Let us further suppose that careful analysis of these photographs leads him to the conclusion that photographs where the face is symmetrical are highly correlated with winning photographs. He naturally chooses the most symmetrical photographs for his entries. Notice that he makes no attempt to identify and apply an absolute standard of beauty. If he found that there was a high correlation between past winners and photographs he found ugly, he would choose the photographs he found most ugly for his entries.

Let us introduce another competitor who is a follower of Fisher. He also reviews the historical evidence. But in addition, he has a series of private conversations with a representative sample of the other competitors† before each competition. He is skilled at deducing which photographs

---

* There is a saying from poker that if you cannot spot the sucker at the table when you sit down, you are he. This also applies to investment management. An active manager has to find counterparties who are prepared to buy from him at prices he considers too high and sell to him at prices he considers too low. If they are equally diversified and well-informed competitors, his chance of success is low.

† Note that collecting private information by doing work that other competitors could do but don't is very different from collecting inside information. In this case, inside information would be a clandestine report before the competition deadline, from the newspaper staff collating the entries, as to which six photographs were most popular based on the competition entries to date.

they have picked from what they say and do not say. If he is aware of the symmetry insight, he will not hesitate to override it if his instinct, or intuitive judgement about the other evidence he has, tells him to. Notice that, like the follower of Graham, the follower of Fisher is trying to pick winners rather than identify and apply an absolute standard of beauty.

The Graham disciple has the advantage that, having arrived at his insight, he can pick winners with very little extra work. Also, he can easily articulate a consistent explanation of why he picked the entries he did. But this can also be self-defeating if it becomes generally known that symmetrical photographs win. The Fisher disciple has to work hard all the time. In addition, he finds it harder to explain what he is doing. But as long as he does the work and retains his skill, he will retain his edge and continue to pick winning photographs.

11.3.2   Information and strategy

Extending the metaphor in this way illustrates that there are two contrasting focused research strategies with the potential to lead to successful active management. The first, following Fisher, is to concentrate on private information, which can come from private research or private networking, which usually involves the exchange of private research. Also following Fisher, this strategy requires the collection of such public information as is necessary to evaluate the private information. Some investors and investment professionals outsource the collection of private information to the research departments of financial intermediaries such as investment banks. But the investment banks will also be distributing the information to other clients and their own proprietary trading departments. This exacerbates the fundamental problem of private information, which is that it only has to be known and acted on by a relatively small circle of investors to be fully discounted or reflected in security prices.

Private information has several characteristics that influence the behaviour of the investment professionals who use it. It is expensive and/or time consuming to gather. It is fragmentary – the number of securities or markets about which even the best-informed investment professional has current private information will be small – so risk positions are concentrated. The judgement as to how the private information will affect the price may be informed by analysis but is ultimately based on instinct. This in turn makes research and decision making hard to separate.

Finally, any intuitive decision maker will have difficulty explaining why he made the choices he did. The Macmillan Committee of Enquiry into finance and industry, set up by the Chancellor of the Exchequer, interrogated Montagu Norman, the Governor of the Bank of England, in 1930. The members included Keynes, Bevin and Brand. Norman struggled.

> In large part his problem had been, as he had conceded rather disarmingly to Bevin, that of artic-
> ulating what was essentially instinctive behaviour. The secretary of the committee would recall
> how at one point, asked how he knew something, Norman simply replied by tapping his nose three
> times. Another moment not recorded in the minutes, but recalled by Brand, was when Macmillan
> told Norman that his committee would be very interested to hear the Governor's reasons for
> forming BIDC; to which Norman replied "Reasons, Mr Chairman, I don't have reasons. I have
> instincts."[15]

A decision-making approach of this kind will depend primarily on the individual making the decisions. George Soros of Quantum Fund, a leading contemporary hedge fund firm, describes his decisions as follows:[16] "So my decisions are really made using a combination of theory and instinct. If you like, you may call it intuition." Soros contrasts his role with that of Jim Rogers, an early colleague, by describing himself as the trigger puller, or decision maker, while Rogers was the researcher: "I did the investing while he did the investigating."[17]

Louis Bacon of Moore Capital, another leading contemporary hedge fund firm, "Relies on an obsessive attention to detail – and ultimately instinct. 'He is like an animal in his ability to sense the market', says one long term investor."[18] Bacon has other attributes of an intuitive investor. First he acquired a noteworthy private network early in his career. "Trading on behalf of some of the biggest names in the hedge fund world . . . Bacon deployed a powerful Rolodex . . . Louis was very fortunate to be right in the middle of that network."[19] Second, he keeps close personal control of investment risk taking: "Very few people at the firm are allowed to take serious risk, says one source. There's a lot of people there, but they are mostly in support, research or administrative positions."[20]

Teams using this kind of research strategy divide into those who are allowed to make independent investment decisions and those who support them. Such decision makers often call themselves risk takers to distinguish their roles from those of the other members of the team. More often than not, a product has only one risk taker. Jesse Livermore (1877–1940) was perhaps the most successful market speculator of his time in the USA. At his peak, he employed a team of statisticians to gather data but his investment decisions were based on intuition or what he called hunches. Like Bacon, his attention to markets bordered on the obsessive and he had little time for anything else. "He liked to tell a story of a stock trader who was asked, 'What do you think of Balzac? and replied, I never trade in them curb stocks'."[21]

The second focused strategy, following Graham, is to concentrate on unearthing conclusions from public information that others have failed to draw or act upon. Public information comes from all sources, whether written, electronic or some other medium, that are sufficiently widely available to be accessible to the average market participant. In contrast to private information, which is scarce, perishable and expensive, public information is abundant, cheap and forms part of the permanent record.

The volume of data available favours a systematic approach to processing information. A systematic approach leads to a decision-making model that does not depend on individual judgement, such as Graham's rules for calculating intrinsic value or the SMB/HML model that drives Dimensional's core product. A systematically applied model in turn means that changes in relevant information lead directly to changes in the active portfolio. It is logical with such a process to separate research, or model development based on analysing historical data, from portfolio construction, or model implementation, and to appoint different people responsible for each phase.

Investment approaches can thus be divided into those where the same information and analytical methodology result in the same investment decisions even if the people change and those where this is not the case. The former have been systematised and can be carried out by teams of changing composition while the latter depend on the intuition of specific individuals. The connection with public and private information is the degree to which an intuitive approach is better adapted to dealing with private information while a systematic approach is better adapted to dealing with public information.

For the rest of this and subsequent chapters, I will use "intuitive process" as shorthand for a process using individual flair and subjective judgement to create an investment strategy based on private information. I will also use "systematic process" as shorthand for a process using proprietary models, or rules based on experience or analysis of historical data, to create an investment strategy from public information.*

---

* One pointer as to whether a firm is systematic or intuitive is the performance it considers when deciding compensation. If individual performance is more important than collective performance, the firm is likely to be intuitive.

11.3.3   Demonstrating skill

The track records that give the best predictions of skill are different. For an intuitive process, the length of this track record is the period that the investment professional has been making the decisions, provided that the analyst believes that his skill has been stable over the period. The estimate of skill is therefore an estimate of his personal skill.

For a systematic process, the relevant track record is either performance since inception or a reconstruction of performance using all available data. If you know that the process is driven by a model but do not know what the model is,* you can only look at the performance that has actually been achieved. Thus looking at performance since inception suggests both an assumption that the model has been consistently applied and an inability to reconstruct the effect of the model.

If you know what the model is, you can reconstruct performance over the entire period for which security price data is available. This allows an advisor to build his confidence further by checking modelled performance against realised performance to verify that the process is actually sticking to the model. The dilemma for an investment management firm is that, if it opens the box by disclosing the model, it maximises advisors' confidence. However, it also gives competitors the opportunity to replicate the model.

The tendency for systematic track records to be longer has two consequences. First, the skill needed to generate a given level of confidence is lower for systematic processes than it is for intuitive processes. Second, estimates of abnormality and covariances with other excess returns can be made with greater precision for systematic processes than is possible for intuitive processes. The SMB/HML results quoted earlier illustrate this feature of systematic models. The confidence intervals on beta and therefore dependence were both substantially higher than the confidence intervals on alpha and therefore skill.

11.3.4   Portfolio manager autonomy

An intuitive investment professional creates judgements about security prices and markets while a systematic investment professional creates models, which make the judgements as long as they are followed. Historical data is used to evaluate systematic models before they are introduced to the investment process, at which point they become the property of the firm. The only way to evaluate intuitive judgements is to give the investment professional the ability to create a track record by making them. This ability is sometimes known as portfolio manager autonomy, or the freedom to take whatever active positions he judges appropriate, subject to investor guidelines and regulatory constraints.

Chapter 9 explained that only the independent component of an active overlay is of any value to an investor. This factor sets bounds on the degree of cooperation that is possible between intuitive traders even if they are working on the same product or working for the same firm. They can share and debate ideas but the need to retain and demonstrate an ability to create positive and independent excess returns means that they cannot let all their positions and consequently their personal track records become dependent on others' views or positions.

It took Buffett 18 years[22] to formalise his relationship with his partner and heir apparent, Charles Munger. Even now, Munger maintains a personal track record in the form of the results of Wesco Financial Corporation.

---

* Such products are known as black box products. When the rules for a product are set out, quant firms like Dimensional Fund Advisors show simulated performance as far back as they have data. When the rules are undisclosed, they show actual performance since inception.

When a firm adopts an intuitive approach its investment role is not entirely eliminated. We have already seen in Chapter 9 that mutual fund manager departures are much more frequent than liquidations and mergers of mutual funds themselves. The main investment role of an intuitive investment management firm is therefore to appoint and replace the designated managers of its funds. Mutual fund companies are usually frank about the autonomy they give individual portfolio managers and the role of senior management:

> The key factors have been attracting and keeping talented people, making sure one person is closely associated with the performance of a fund and still providing a team environment so that those talented individuals can discuss ideas constantly.[23]

11.4 FAULT LINES

Hedge funds and quant shops both appear to demonstrate higher skill than traditional products. Hedge funds predominantly adopt an intuitive approach involving a single decision maker. Quant shops have to adopt a systematic approach, although even they sometimes make intuitive judgements.

Interestingly, while hedge funds cannot be accommodated within a traditional product format, many quant products can. An intuitive active overlay has concentrated risk positions and therefore needs net short positions* to manage its risk efficiently. Provided that the size of a systematic overlay is small, its diversification means that individual short positions will be small enough to be generated by selling components of the index portfolio. This probably explains the popularity of presenting quant products in an enhanced index format.

As well-executed intuitive and systematic processes both create investment value, it is not obvious why polarisation should be associated with superior demonstrated skill. An investment management firm will improve the demonstrated skill of a product by using both approaches, provided they are skilfully managed. The problem is that intuitive investment professionals only maximise their personal ability to add investment value when they have maximum freedom to make independent investment decisions. Listed below are some examples of the fault lines that arise when a firm tries to integrate the work of intuitive individuals with systematic processes.

11.4.1 Institutional processes

The more an investment process is perceived to be embedded in an investment management firm rather than in the thought processes of an individual, the more value it adds to the firm. This is not just because such a process protects the firm against any one individual's departure. It is also because the relevant time period for assessing the track record is not the tenure of an individual but the life of the firm, or at least the period since the process was introduced. Advisors favour firms with embedded processes for two reasons. First, because an investment process that extends the longevity of a track record also extends the confidence that investors have in its skill. This confidence is therefore an important ingredient of a firm's reputation. Second, because their task is simplified: rather than having to make judgements about the skill of individuals they have to make judgements about the skill of firms or teams within

---

* Anecdotally, proprietary traders and commodity trading advisors (CTAs) seem to find it easier to make the transition to hedge funds than managers of traditional products, perhaps because of their familiarity with the disciplines of short selling and daily marking to market. Bacon started as a CTA while Soros and the LTCM team started as proprietary traders.

firms. There are other advantages: Chapter 5 gave an example of how embedded skill creates comparative advantage for firms entering new markets.

A process that is embedded in a firm rather than dependent on an individual starts to take on systematic characteristics. Information becomes more public because it is shared more widely. The individuals taking part have to agree on strategy. To achieve this without coercion requires a shared philosophy about how the market works and a common response to new research.

Because of the commercial attractiveness of having a long-term track record and because most talented investment professionals are intuitive, investment management firms have devoted enormous ingenuity to trying to fit intuitive individuals into processes that have systematic characteristics. But this results in conflict because the intuitive investment professionals want to maximise their individual freedom or autonomy while the investment management firm wants them to work within a collective approach. This collective approach has to provide sufficient discipline to allow advisors and investors to accept the longest possible track record, ideally the product's performance since inception, as the relevant time series for evaluating future skill. An example[24] of such a framework is set out below:

- Identifiable person with whom "the buck stops" at each decision-making stage.
- Smooth communication flow between research and portfolio management.
- Responsive and timely decision-making process.
- Adequate controls in place to ensure performance commonality.
- Clearly identifiable and understood roles of research and portfolio management.
- Identifiable portfolio manager latitude, which is used in individuals' appraisals.

This boils down to a common investment strategy with a defined tolerance for individuals to deviate from it that is limited by the requirement for performance commonality. For such a process, the compromises required to get team members to work together in this way can lead to sluggish decision making and benchmark hugging. Responsibility for performance results can become diffuse and intuitive investment professionals demotivated or disaffected.

11.4.2   LTCM

We were introduced to LTCM in Chapters 2 and 3. It had many systematic characteristics. Much of the information it had access to, while not necessarily publicly available, was widely known in the community of hedge fund managers and proprietary traders.[25] Models using historical financial data supported its investment process. The risk aggregator,[26] a model summarising the portfolio's exposure to the 40 different strategies or types of position it recognised, was at the centre. Decisions to introduce, change the scale of or modify trades, the LTCM term for a package of long and short positions designed to isolate a profitable factor, were taken by a weekly risk committee meeting of partners chaired by Meriwether. All ideas, including those of the more senior partners, were subject to extensive scrutiny and debate. There was no attempt to calculate individual traders' profit and loss accounts.[27] The total number of individual positions was approximately 60 000.[28]

But the process also had some intuitive characteristics. One was internal information asymmetry. Only a few people at LTCM had access to the risk aggregator and were thus able fully to relate their ideas to the investment process. Another was the degree of subjectivity applied to decisions about what scale should be used for trades. The two hitherto most successful traders seem to have used this subjectivity to dominate these decisions, particularly in the latter stages of the life of the fund.[29] The fault lines in LTCM's approach appear to have created tensions among the traders and between the financial economists and the traders.[30]

11.4.3   MAM fixed interest

The hedged bond opportunity described in Chapter 5 was a systematic strategy. However, most of our active overlays were intuitive. Even with the hedged bond product, we superimposed an intuitively managed overlay in order to increase its appeal to investors and advisors. In the event, although the hedged strategy achieved an annual excess return over gilts of more than 4% over the first four years, the intuitive overlay was disappointing. It had a negative return over the same period, despite shorting sterling successfully in September 1992.

This gave rise to a later irony. In the early 1990s, some UK pension funds began to include hedged foreign bonds in their policies and to make appointments of managers to handle actively traded portfolios with hedged bond benchmarks. Despite having pioneered the concept, MAM was unable to compete for the business because our track record gave advisors no confidence that we could handle an active overlay against a hedged bond benchmark.

In this case, the relative contributions of the systematic strategy of owning synthetic spreads when they were positive against gilts and the intuitive opportunistic trading strategy were easy to distinguish. In general, this was more difficult. Our systems were too unsophisticated to capture accurately the relative contributions of different elements to the same portfolio. The only way to link excess return to individual skill and accountability was to make each portfolio the responsibility of a single designated investment professional.

A number of the team's more skilled investment professionals argued strongly for maximum portfolio manager autonomy. This directly conflicted with the leading investment manager search consultants' criteria for an acceptable investment process (compare with the criteria listed earlier). Failure to satisfy these criteria meant that they would not recommend us to their investors. We resolved this conflict by developing an investment process that was specifically designed to maximise autonomy while still being acceptable to the consultants who advised our investors.*

In order to minimise performance dispersion, we grouped client portfolios with similar objectives into products. As far as possible, we assigned each group to one investment professional with proven skill.

The common investment strategy required by the consultants consisted of a series of views on the various sectors, such as UK bonds and US bonds, of the global bond and currency markets. Each view was positive, neutral or negative. Where only one product used the asset class, the view was that of the investment professional responsible for the product. Where more than one product used the asset class, the view was a composite of the views of the relevant investment professionals. If they were all either positive or neutral, the collective view was positive. If they were all either negative or neutral, the collective view was negative. If they were all neutral or all three, the collective view was neutral. As our process allowed active overlays to be neutral if the collective view was positive or negative and positive or negative

---

* While the consultants accepted this process, they were not entirely happy with it, pointing out that most of our competitors advertised processes that gave much less freedom to the individual. The conflict between internal pressure from investment professionals for increased autonomy and external pressure from advisors for increased commonality led to inconsistencies between the processes some competitors described to consultants and the processes we were aware that they actually operated. One former colleague described such processes as marketing fig leaves.

within certain limits if the collective view was neutral, the effect was to give an almost entirely free hand to a limited number* of the team's investment professionals.

11.5 CONCLUSION

Skilful investment managers use information to identify the best risk to take and then construct portfolios that take as much risk as their investors' risk appetite allows. A useful distinction can be made between private information, which is more accurate but more expensive, and public information, which is less accurate but cheaper to acquire. Intuition is required to transform private information into a successful investment strategy while a systematic approach is required to transform public information into a successful investment strategy.

Intuitive investment decision-making processes depend on individuals while systematic investment decision-making processes depend on firms. For the former, the relevant track record is performance since the individual was appointed. For the latter, it is the performance either since product inception or since data became available. While the firm owns a systematic process, the individual owns an intuitive process.

In order to maximise his potential to add value, an investment professional using an intuitive approach needs scope for independent decision making. This creates conflicts between investment professionals of this type when they are required to agree on strategy. A systematic investment process with a limited intuitive overlay has commercial advantages but creates further conflicts. The difficulty of combining intuitive and systematic approaches gives an incentive to firms to use either an intuitive approach, or a systematic approach but not both.

ENDNOTES

1. Smith, p. 8.
2. B. Graham and D. Dodd, *Security Analysis*. New York: McGraw-Hill, 1951.
3. *Common Stocks and Uncommon Profits*. New York: Harper, 1958.
4. R.G. Hagstrom, *The Warren Buffett Way*, New York: John Wiley, 1994, p. 5.
5. Figures taken from the Berkshire Hathaway 2000 Annual Report, which compares changes in book value against the S&P 500. 1968 was the first year on a calendar basis. As Berkshire is effectively a closed-end investment company, a shareholder would experience lower information and Sharpe ratios owing to the volatility of Berkshire's market to book value ratio.
6. Copywright Berkshire Hathaway material used with permission of the author.
7. Hagstrom, p. 44.
8. Hagstrom, p. 27.
9. Hagstrom, p. 47.
10. Letter from Keynes to F.C. Scott, quoted in Berkshire Hathaway 1991 Annual Report.
11. Hagstrom, p. 100.
12. Hagstrom, p. 47.
13. Fama and French.
14. *The General Theory of Employment, Interest and Money*, 1936, p. 155. [quoted in Myners, frontispiece; Malkiel, p. 32, Siegel, p. 75].
15. D. Kynaston, *Illusions of Gold*. London: Chatto, 1999, pp. 201, 202.
16. G. Soros, *Soros on Soros*. New York: John Wiley, 1995, p. 10.
17. Soros, pp. 48, 49.
18. *Institutional Investor*, International Edition, 1 July 2000.

---

* The more people who have a say in such a process, the more chance that two have opposing views on a sector and the more views that are neutral. If every member of a large group has an independent say, all views are likely to be permanently stuck in neutral.

19. *Institutional Investor*.
20. *Institutional Investor*.
21. Brooks, pp. 76–77.
22. Hagstrom, p. 18.
23. Edward Bonham Carter, Investment Director of Jupiter Asset Management, *Money Observer*, March 2000.
24. Smith, p. 12.
25. Author interview with Eric Rosenfeld.
26. Lowenstein, pp. 187, 188.
27. Author interview with Eric Rosenfeld.
28. Lowenstein, p. 155.
29. Lowenstein, pp. 58, 128, 129.
30. Lowenstein, p. 119.

12

Active Overlay Risk

As presented in Chapter 6, one of the foundations of modern financial economics is the proposition that the risk of a portfolio of financial investments is accurately defined by the annualised variance or standard deviation of its return distribution. This is because the annualised variance can be converted to the variance of return to any time horizon by multiplying it by the time horizon itself. The probability of losing more than a specified amount at that time horizon is then precisely defined by the normal probability distribution. Chapter 9 introduced active risk, or the standard deviation of active overlay return. If standard deviation equals risk, active risk equals active overlay risk.

The proposition takes practical form in the shape of risk management systems that calculate active risk and then use this to calculate the probability of achieving a given level of underperformance against benchmark over a given time horizon, usually one year. The theoretical difficulty with this procedure is that, as also pointed out in Chapter 6, if active returns are normally distributed, they should average out to zero, thus negating the point of active management and systems designed to manage its risk. The practical difficulty with this procedure is that the probabilities of achieving given levels of underperformance deduced from active risk seem consistently to underestimate the frequency of such unwelcome events.

There is only one plausible explanation for this discrepancy, if one discounts the suggestion that we are going through a particularly unlucky period for active management. This is that active risk is an inaccurate measure of true risk. As Chapter 6 makes clear, this happens when excess returns are not normally distributed.

12.1 LTCM

To illustrate how active risk seems to underestimate the probability of unwelcome events, it is helpful to review how such estimates compared with experience for LTCM. Fortunately, the estimates are easy to calculate, as we know that LTCM maintained a daily active risk that was approximately constant[1] throughout the period.

At the beginning of 1998, LTCM's capital was US$4.7 billion and its daily active risk was approximately US$45 million. As discussed in Chapter 2, there was a US$1.9 billion cushion before the liquidation threshold was reached.

If LTCM's active returns were normally distributed, the confidence interval that capital would not fall to liquidation cost in one year was just this cushion divided by annualised active risk, or 2.6. The probability of liquidation occurring was therefore 0.5%. It consequently appeared to be a very unlikely event.

Sadly, a series of unwelcome events occurred. By close of business on Thursday 20 August 1998, the fund had lost US$1.25 billion over the year to date, an event with a calculated probability of 1.5%. The following day the fund lost US$552 million,[2] an event with a calculated probability of zero. It could be argued that the pricing of many of LTCM's less liquid positions had lagged reality, so the huge move on August 21 reflected a great deal of catch up. Even if this were the case, the calculated probability of the year to date losses of US$1.8 billion at the close on August 21 was 0.1%, or one in a thousand. Taken individually and together, these probabilities are so low that it is virtually certain that LTCM's active returns were not normally distributed.

12.2   ACTIVE RETURN DISTRIBUTIONS

The likelihood that active returns are not normally distributed should not be surprising. Many common strategies and trading disciplines used by active managers have abnormal pay-off distributions. For example, several common ways to create negative skewness through active strategies and trading rules are described below.

12.2.1   Active strategies

Writing options gives a negatively skewed pay-off pattern as the downside is unlimited and the upside is limited to the premium collected. LTCM's option writing activity thus implied negative skewness. Similarly, writing an insurance policy gives a negatively skewed pay-off distribution. Because of unlimited liability, membership of Lloyds of London provided individual names with a very negatively skewed distribution of returns.

Most spread strategies are negatively skewed. Lending to risky borrowers is negatively skewed as the lender captures a spread over risk-free instruments of identical maturity profile. However, he loses all or a fraction of the loan if the borrower experiences financial distress. A strategy that is short governments and long mortgages is also negatively skewed as if rates do not move, the investor collects the spread while if rates do move, the variable effective life of the mortgage position can create substantial downside. LTCM's spread position in Italian governments versus lira swaps was negatively skewed. As long as the Italian government did not default, they would collect the spread. If the government defaulted they would lose their principal. In order to protect against this, they took out credit risk insurance.[3]

Merger arbitrage is a strategy involving equity securities that do not themselves necessarily have strongly skewed excess return distributions but which itself has a strongly negatively skewed return distribution. To see why, consider what happens when company A offers $1.3x$ worth of its own shares for each share in company B which was trading at x prior to the offer. Unless another offer is thought likely (B is considered "in play"), B's shares will rise in price to a level that is significantly above x but lower than A's offer. This is because some of the original shareholders of B, when presented with a windfall profit, are inclined to cash in at a modest discount rather than waiting for the transaction to go through.

The buyers are the merger arbitrageurs who pay, say, $1.25x$ cash in anticipation of receiving $1.3x$ in value. In order to protect themselves from a fall in the market price of A, they simultaneously short the number of A shares that they expect to receive. Thus, when the transaction goes through, they will receive a profit before transaction and security borrowing costs of $0.05x$ for each B share they originally bought. The net profit can be leveraged up.

Of course, if the merger fails to go through, the price of B will fall, perhaps back to its original level of x. Even if the price of A is unaffected by this, the arbitrageurs will take a loss, in this case of $0.25x$ before costs for every share of B they originally bought. Thus a merger arbitrage trading record will be negatively skewed as it will consist of a series of profits punctuated by the occasional large loss. These losses can be very large:

Table 12.1

Position	Price movements	Position trading	Net profit
1	Up x	Cut	y
2	Down x, up x	Doubled, cut	$2y - y = y$
3	Down x, down x, up x	Doubled, doubled, cut	$4y - 2y - y = y$

Shares in General Electric and Honeywell, whose $42 billion (£30 billion) merger is being blocked by the European Commission on competition grounds, are set to come under further pressure this week as hedge funds start to unwind positions in the two companies. Losses of $3 billion would put GE/Honeywell second only behind Ciena/Tellabs in the league of the world's costliest failed arbitrage trades. That deal, the proposed 1998 merger between two US technology companies is understood to have lost hedge funds between $4 billion and $5 billion [including $150 million by LTCM].[4] It would also eclipse losses sustained on the aborted 1997 takeover of MCI by British Telecom. The unravelling of that deal – the hit from which is put at between $1 billion and $2 billion led to the eventual demise of some hedge funds.[5]

12.2.2   Trading rules

Trading rules, even applied to securities with normal excess return distributions, can create abnormality. The following example demonstrates how profit targets and doubling up creates negative skewness. Consider a trader who does the following:

1. He sets himself a profit target for the position of $x\%$ to reflect the fact that, if this level of profit is reached, the mispricing upon which the position was based has diminished and the economic justification for the position is therefore less compelling.
2. If the position initially goes against him by $x\%$, the security mispricing becomes even more pronounced and he doubles the position. This is a form of trading strategy known as averaging in. Many traders, including those at LTCM,[6] use versions of this strategy.

A stylised version of his profit and trading record will look as in Table 12.1. As long as he is in a position to keep on doubling up when prices go against him, his positions will generate a constant stream of profits. The problem comes when he hits a constraint like a liquidation threshold and cannot double up any more. He is then forced to cut the position and record a large loss. His trading record will thus show a large number of profits with the occasional large and painful loss. This pay-off profile is obviously negatively skewed.

12.3   DIFFERENT PROCESSES

There is nothing intrinsically wrong with an investor having exposure to active products with abnormally distributed active returns. This is because, according to the Central Limit Theorem (A1.13), the abnormality of the active return of his consolidated active overlay is both less than that of the individual products and can be reduced further by more diversification. There is thus a trade-off. The fewer products used, the more selective the investor can be and the higher his confidence that the products he uses are skilfully managed. But the fewer products he uses, the greater the abnormality of his consolidated overlay and, from equation (A4.11), the greater the risk adjustment he has to apply.

In order to evaluate this trade-off, he has to make accurate assessments of not only product skill but also product skewness and kurtosis. The accuracy of these assessments depends on the type of active process that drives the overlay.

12.3.1   Systematic

The parameters of the distribution of a systematic process are easy to assess in principle. The active returns are merely reconstructed using past data and the parameters calculated. Where several systematic processes are used, the consolidated active return has to be reconstructed and the parameters calculated.

In practice, this can be difficult if there are large numbers of systematic strategies, each with a different length track record. Practitioners often assume the problem away by taking the view that there is sufficient diversification in place to justify estimating both skewness and excess kurtosis as zero. The LTCM episode, where a portfolio diversified across tens of thousands of positions turned out to have a high degree of abnormality, has highlighted the weakness of this assumption. Another problem highlighted by LTCM was shortage of data. Their record of swap spreads did not even go back as far as 1992, so the risk aggregator did not adequately incorporate the experience of the market crises of that year and 1987.[7]

12.3.2   Combined

The previous chapter pointed out that institutional processes tend to be a combination of the intuitive and the systematic. Because of this, advisors do not accept reconstructions. Rather, they look at actual performance since the institutional process started. Because of their relative shortness and survivorship bias, these track records may not be fully representative of the distributions of the underlying active returns. Short periods of poor performance can radically alter advisors' perceptions of such products. An example is the recent change of heart in the UK over balanced products.

For a long time, UK advisors recommended both specialist mandates and balanced or multi-asset mandates to their UK pension fund clients. The arguments in favour of balanced management are that: it offers the convenience of one-stop shopping; it is usually cheaper; and it provides active policy management, or tactical asset allocation, as an add-on. The argument against it has always been that no single investment management firm will have both skilled active asset allocation and the best active managers in all the asset classes. Of a 1999 sample of 273 UK pension funds totalling £407 billion, 50% by number and 30% by assets were managed as balanced funds.[8]

However, the argument has now swung decisively in favour of the specialist structures introduced in Chapter 10. This is because there has been "growing dissatisfaction with the investment performance of a number of leading balanced managers".[9] In 1997, some balanced managers achieved active returns that lagged their benchmarks by three times active risk or more. This highlighted the awkward fact that the active overlays that comprise a balanced process are not well diversified as they share a common or house investment policy. In addition, diversifying across balanced managers turned out to be disappointing because competitive pressures had caused active balanced strategies to converge. In contrast, it was believed that, because investment professionals in different firms handle the different asset class overlays for a specialist structure, they are likely to be more independent.

A typical advisor recommendation[10] of a core/satellite specialist structure put these arguments as follows:

> Future investment structures will pay more attention to the allocation of manager risk. Ideally a fully specialist structure should include a satellite layer of half a dozen or more aggressive portfolios managed according to different styles or approaches so that at the total fund level a reasonable degree of outperformance can be captured with a relatively low chance of serious disappointment. In contrast, the current approach for many funds of using two or three balanced managers with perhaps quite similar styles is almost bound to lead to periods of significant underperformance.

"Periods of significant underperformance" suggests that the consolidated active overlay of a balanced structure is prone to negative skewness. "A relatively low chance of serious disappointment" suggests that the consolidated active overlay of a specialist structure is not. "Managed according to different styles or approaches" suggests that individual active overlays in a specialist structure are independent while "with perhaps quite similar styles" suggests that those in a balanced structure are not. Interestingly, the advisor recommends a minimum of only six high active risk products. This suggests either that his investors are relatively risk tolerant, so he believes that residual abnormality is less important, or that the abnormality can be predicted and dealt with by selecting the right combination of products.

12.3.3 Intuitive

The parameters of the distribution of the active returns resulting from an intuitive process are very hard to assess. First, the track record will be short and second, survivorship bias means that the track records of individuals still active will under-represent periods of substantial underperformance.

One practical response to this problem is to force the consolidated overlay towards normal by diversifying across products so much that the risk adjustment attributable to abnormality becomes negligible. This may explain why some manager of manager products contain 30 or more product positions, even when they represent an asset class that is only a small part of policy.

12.4 CONCLUSION

Risk management systems that assume normally distributed active returns have a propensity to underestimate the chance of an active product blowing up, or experiencing a period of exceptionally poor returns. This is because active strategies tend to have abnormally distributed returns.

This in itself is not a good reason for discarding quantitative risk measurement. Unless they are solely relying on instinct, investment professionals have to have a quantitative way to estimate the risk of complicated portfolios. Standard deviation-based measures of risk such as active risk are prone to inaccuracy. The more abnormal a consolidated active return distribution is, the greater the inaccuracy.

Provided that the historical return distribution is representative of the future return distribution, back-testing, or reconstructing the impact of historical market movements on the current portfolio, can measure its risk. As data builds up about new financial instruments and their behaviour during times of market stress, the historical record will allow more and more sophisticated back-testing of systematic strategies leading to more accurate estimates of their degrees of abnormality and the chances that they will suffer unacceptable losses. Back-testing is not an option for intuitive strategies.

ENDNOTES

1. Author interview with Eric Rosenfeld.
2. Lowenstein, p. 147.
3. Lowenstein, p. 57.
4. Lowenstein, p. 146.
5. *Times*, 28 June 2001.
6. Lowenstein, pp. 21, 126.
7. Lowenstein, p. 146.
8. Myners, p. 53.
9. Myners, p. 54.
10. 1999 Watson Wyatt conference presentation.

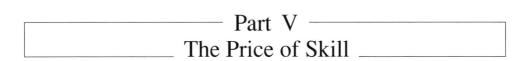

Part V
The Price of Skill

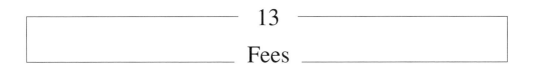

13

Fees

Troilus: "What's aught but as 'tis valued?"

Hector: "But value dwells not in particular will: it holds his estimate and dignity as well wherein 'tis precious of itself as in the prizer.[1]

This chapter looks at: different types of fee charging arrangement; demand for active products; fee rates and research costs. It also looks at how these factors relate to each other and to product skill.

13.1 TYPES OF FEE

Because active products are made up of a combination of an active overlay and a passive portfolio, which in turn is made up by a combination of index funds and cash, the fee for an active overlay can be inferred by subtracting the index fund or money fund management fee from the total product fee. In practice, these deductions are small, so it is a reasonable approximation to equate active overlay fee to product fee. There are three types of fee.

13.1.1 Flat fees

A flat fee, or ad valorem fee, is where the investor pays the investment firm a fixed percentage of the value of the assets committed to the product. The origin of this charge comes from the notion that the investment firm has stewardship of the assets and should be compensated in proportion to the responsibility it bears. The simplest way to measure responsibility is volume of assets. As a percentage of volume of assets, a flat fee is simple to calculate. It is therefore an advantage for pooled products where fees are accrued daily. Its predictability also makes it an advantage for investment firm budgeting purposes. This is fine for an index fund. The disadvantage, when applied to active management, is that the investor is paying the same fee for good and bad performance alike.

Table 13.1 shows the management fees in basis points charged in different countries for a £100 million institutional mandate to manage domestic stocks (E) or bonds (B).[2] Not only are these fees tightly grouped within countries, they are also tightly grouped across countries, although bond management in the USA seems relatively expensive and equity management in Canada seems relatively cheap.

Even when products are managed in the same asset class with the same skill, reconciling flat fees with investment value added is difficult as different overlays have different constraints and therefore different levels of active risk. The definition of skill (A5.21) shows that two overlays, each managed with the same skill and linked to benchmark portfolios of the same size, will have different expected profits if their expected active risks are different. The consequence of this, as sketched in Figure 13.1, is that reducing active risk increases fees as a proportion of active return.

Table 13.1

Basis points per annum	Canada		UK		Australia		USA	
	E	B	E	B	E	B	E	B
Upper quartile	28	22	48	23	47	22	50	30
Median	24	18	40	18	44	19	42	26
Lower quartile	21	16	30	17	40	18	33	23

Source: Frank Russell Company

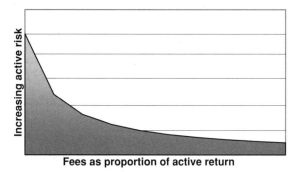

Figure 13.1   Flat fees and active risk

The objection to closet index products, or products with very low active risk, is not that they are necessarily unskilfully managed but that their active returns are low relative to their fees. Advisors sometimes correct for this by including an active risk target in the active mandate.

13.1.2   Performance fees

These are calculated as a percentage of the outperformance achieved against benchmark or cash. This links pay directly to investment value added. While payment by results is intuitively appealing, there is a potential problem. This is that as the investor underwrites any downside, the investment firm has an incentive to play double or quits* with the investor's money.

The solution to the problem proposed by some financial economists[3] is a structure known as symmetric performance fees. Performance fees of this type require the investor and the investment firm to share equally in both profits and losses. The only performance fees allowed for regulated funds in the USA are symmetric.† The UK regulator takes a different line: "The Financial Services Authority (FSA) allows fund managers to discount their fees when they post a poor performance, but they cannot increase charges when they outperform."[4]

Symmetric performance fees have proved unpopular in practice so that virtually all traditional products have flat fee formulae. Performance fees are almost exclusively used, in

---

* A rational strategy for a proprietary trader nursing a large loss is to double his position. If it goes against him, he is no worse off as he would have been fired anyway. If it goes in his favour, he makes a profit, keeps his job and gets a bonus. This behaviour is sufficiently common to have a name: putting on a trader's hedge.

† A 1970 modification to the 1940 Investment Advisors Act prohibits a US registered investment advisor from receiving compensation "on the basis of a share of capital gains upon or capital appreciation of the funds or any portion of the funds of the client". The SEC makes an exception to this for fulcrum or symmetric fee formulae.

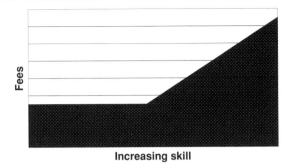

Figure 13.2 Hedge fund fees

conjunction with flat fees, by alternative products such as hedge funds. Because the flat fee is charged regardless, the relationship between fees and demonstrated skill follows the pattern sketched in Figure 13.2.

There is a limited degree of symmetry. This comes from clawback features, which require the product to recover any underperformance since its last high water mark, or highest level of cumulative performance to date, before receiving further performance fees.

While preventing excessive fees relative to cumulative outperformance,* the symmetry introduced by clawback is incomplete. First, the firm never has to write a cheque to its investors; at worst it suffers an opportunity cost. Second, it can close the product and return their money to investors with performance arrears still unpaid. Third, the flat fee means that the investor still pays for underperformance. The only exposure the firm has to real loss comes from its own investment in the product.

The problem with symmetric performance fees is that only when there are positive scale effects do they provide any benefit to investment firms. The argument runs as follows.

Consider a process that has no scale effects so that skill is the same whatever the size of the overlay. Let us suppose that the only fee is a symmetric performance fee where the firm takes a proportion f of the profits and refunds a proportion f of any losses. Let us also suppose that without clients, the firm's risk preferences are such that the optimal size of its active overlay it would choose to expose itself to has an active risk of O dollars. Then the expected profit P equals SO, where S is the skill with which the overlay is managed.

The firm can achieve an identical result by having clients who participate in an expanded overlay with active risk of O/f dollars and pay (receive) a symmetrical fee of a proportion f of their profits (losses). For then the expected profit on the overlay equals SO/f and the expected fee is just this multiplied by f or SO. But this is the best it can do. If it takes on greater client participation, the active risk becomes greater than O/f and the effect for the firm is that it owns a greater than optimal sized overlay. If it takes on less client participation, it ends up with a less than optimal sized overlay. The maximum incremental benefit from having clients over that from taking an optimal amount of risk on its own account is thus zero.

Things are even worse when scale effects are negative so that S falls with increasing active risk. For then, the expected fee to the firm on an overlay managed for clients with standard

---

* Without clawback, the investor pays a fee for each accounting period for which there is outperformance, regardless of intervening accounting periods of underperformance. Cumulative fees are thus an excessive proportion of cumulative performance. The shorter the accounting period, the more chance that underperformance will occur even for skilfully managed products and the worse this effect is.

deviation O/f is sO, where s is smaller than S because the overlay is bigger. When scale effects are negative, the maximum incremental benefit to a firm from having clients over taking an optimal amount of risk for its own account is always negative. Only when scale effects are positive does the same logic suggest that, with the right client participation, a firm can do better with clients than it can by investing on its own.

Unfortunately, there are few economies of scale in active management so scale effects are at best neutral. This explains why there has been very little take-up by regulated mutual funds of the opportunity to have a symmetrical performance fee formula.

The good news is that, despite the fears of regulators and financial economists, there is little evidence that investment professionals managing unregulated products systematically abuse their asymmetric fee formulae by playing double or quits with their investors' money. One study[5] finds that: "Contract provisions would suggest that hedge fund managers have a strong incentive to take on extreme risk, particularly when their incentive contract is out of the money. The interesting fact is that they do not behave as this simple theory would suggest."

There are likely to be two reasons for this enlightened behaviour. First, hedge fund managers invest their own money in their products. Second, they have their reputations to worry about. Word about this kind of behaviour gets around and would damage or eliminate their ability to attract or retain investors in the future.

13.1.3   Transaction charges

The third form of fee structure is a charge on turnover, or the value of transactions. This has its origins in arrangements where a stockbroker also acts as portfolio manager. As the standard form of paying a broker is by commission, or as a percentage of turnover, it seemed natural to extend the system to compensation for investment management. The perceived advantages are threefold. First, the investor only pays for work done. Second, for some products, there is a tax advantage as fees attract value added tax while transaction charges do not. Third, turnover charges allow investment firms to reduce flat fees to very competitive levels. The main disadvantage is that, as with flat fees, turnover charges are paid whether performance is good or bad. Another disadvantage is that the investment firm has a perverse incentive to execute an excessive volume of transactions.*

Transaction charges were surprisingly popular even with UK pension funds where the standard fee formula in the 1970s and 1980s was a combination of a flat fee and two charges related to turnover: continuation and foreign security charges. Continuation was a by-product of cartelised UK equity commissions, which reduced with increasing volume according to a set formula. A firm executing a large transaction for several investors would be charged the commission rate for the full size of the transaction by the broker but would charge its investors the higher commission rates appropriate to their shares of the transaction. This went out with Big Bang in 1986. Foreign charges were a straight add-on to foreign security transaction costs. MAM charged its clients 0.5%, known internally as the "half-up". Fee formulae including such charges were known as dirty fees and phased out with a shift to clean, or excluding transaction charges, fee formulae in the 1990s.†

---

* Commonly known by the pastoral metaphor of churning the portfolio.
† It has been suggested that one reason why these charges lasted as long as they did was a common arrangement whereby the sponsoring firm paid fees while the fund paid transaction charges. The finance director of the sponsoring firm was reluctant to see his expense budget increased by a shift from charges to fees.

13.2   DEMAND AND SKILL

Increasing a product's fees reduces the return to investors and the skill that is relevant to them, or active overlay return after expenses divided by standard deviation of active overlay return after expenses. Reducing fees increases return and product skill. An investment management firm only has an economic incentive to reduce fees if this increases demand so much that revenues increase. Similarly, a firm only has an economic incentive not to increase fees if this reduces demand so much that revenues decrease.

Understanding the link between demand and product skill is therefore essential to understanding fee setting. It also provides a good lead indicator as to which investment products are bought and which are sold. If product skill drives demand, investors are more likely to buy or seek out skilfully managed products. If product skill does not drive demand, investment management firms will need to work harder at selling their products to investors.

One of the conclusions of Chapter 10 is that the relationship between style and demand is straightforward: the greater weight a particular style has in investors' policies, the more demand there will be for products with that style. The relationship between skill and demand is more complex. The relative demand for two products with the same style will depend on skill and a whole range of other factors.

Anecdotally, three factors beside skill seem particularly important: first, skilful promotion of selected short-term performance, star fund managers and fashionable concepts to get investors in; second, product switching costs including skilful structuring of charges to penalise withdrawal; third, the problem that, in some tax regimes such as the UK, withdrawing from a product crystallises capital gains and tax payments. The tax problem comes from the practice in traditional products of linking the style portfolio with the active overlay. A combination of a strongly performing style and a poorly performing active overlay can still result in taxable gains.

13.2.1   The evidence

If product skill determines demand, one would expect three things. First, for two products with the same style, the more skilfully managed product will be in greater demand than the less skilfully managed product. Second, there will be zero demand for products with negative skill. Third, investors or their advisors have to have skill on average in predicting skill. At the very least, any product for which they predict positive skill has to have more than a 50% chance of demonstrating positive skill. Combining the three expectations gives us a simple test as to whether product skill determines demand. For then investors will choose skilfully managed products and assign greater weights to the more skilful. Thus if weighted average historical overlay returns are positive, it does. If they are not, it does not.

As we have seen in Chapter 6, studies by advisors and academics of actively managed traditional products conclude that there is now a high level of confidence that average* active overlay returns after expenses are negative. Thus traditional products probably fail the test.

We have also seen in Chapter 9 that there is a similar level of confidence that weighted average active overlay returns on hedge funds are positive. Thus hedge fund products probably pass the test. The relative importance of skill in determining demand and revenues for

---

* The studies cited use equal weights rather than actual weights in calculating average excess returns, leaving open the theoretical possibility that large funds perform consistently better than small funds so that the weighted average excess return is positive. As, anecdotally, the opposite appears to be the case, analysts have tended to dismiss this possibility.

traditional products and hedge funds should not be surprising. The corollary to the difficulty experienced in finding skilfully managed traditional products with confidence is that much of the active return in this sector is quite likely to have been achieved by chance rather than by skill.

Because it is hard to tell between active return achieved by chance and active return achieved by skill, both forms of active return will be equally useful in attracting assets. Assets attracted by luck or skilful marketing will, through the flat fee system, generate exactly as much revenue as assets attracted by skill. The retail fund star system tacitly recognises that good promotion is at least as important as good performance in attracting new assets. Investment firms offering traditional products, where marketing skill is at least as important as investment skill in creating demand, have a natural incentive to organise around distribution channels rather than investment teams.*

Because skill is easier to identify with confidence in the hedge fund sector, active return achieved by chance is now less likely than active return achieved by skill to attract new assets. In addition, assets attracted by luck or skilful marketing will, because of performance fees, generate less return than assets attracted by skill. While marketing and access to clients will continue to play a part, it is thus plausible to assume that skill will have a significant influence on both the demand for hedge funds and the fees they generate.

13.2.2   Skill-driven demand

The demand for an active overlay that is attributable to skill is slightly different depending on whether the overlay is freestanding or whether it is attached to a style portfolio. Equation (A6.4) shows demand for a freestanding active overlay. This depends on two factors. The first is the active return divided by the square of the active risk. The second is a factor depending on the financial position and risk tolerance of the product's investors. As this is constant for different overlays, demand for an overlay is thus proportional to the overlay's active return divided by its active variance.

Expression (A6.11)[†] shows that the demand for an actively managed product with style depends on three factors. The first, as before, is the active return divided by the square of the active risk of the product. The second is the total demand for the style of the product. The third is the inverse of the same function of the active returns and active risks of all the competing products. As the second factor is constant and the third factor is approximately constant, when there are a large number of skilled competitors, demand is once again proportional to active return divided by active variance, but with a different constant of proportionality.

Similarly, from (A6.5) and (A6.9), demand for product active risk is proportional to skill for both types of product. The closer the relationship between demand and skill, the more accurate the model will be in explaining real behaviour.

Figure 13.3 sketches the relationship between demand for active risk and skill for products where the two depend on each other in this way and for products where the two are independent.

---

* Regulation often requires the incorporation of a subsidiary, such as an SEC registered entity for US pension funds, to access certain investors. The decision is then whether the subsidiary has its own investment team or outsources investment to other parts of the firm. At MAM, we finally adopted a matrix structure, which compromised between the two organisational approaches.

† These results assume that skill seeking investors are also mean variance investors. Their accuracy and the accuracy of results depending on them are subject to the usual caveats about the accuracy of MPT.

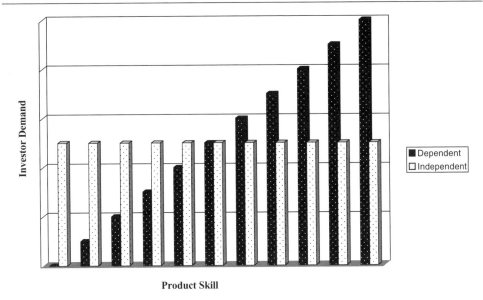

Figure 13.3   Demand and increasing skill

13.3   FEE RATES AND SKILL

If demand depends on skill and investment firms have the flexibility to adjust fee rates to maximise their revenues, they will. Technically, they will seek to maximise their risk-adjusted revenues. However, an investment firm, which always receives a fee that is greater than or equal to zero, experiences little risk from the fee, so fees and risk-adjusted fees are close to being the same thing.

13.3.1   Revenue maximising

The fee charged by an investment firm can be expressed as a fraction f of the valuable or independent component of the profit on the overlay.* For products whose demand is dependent on product skill, the higher f, the lower product skill and the less of the product investors will wish to own. (A6.4) and (A6.11) give the demand function for the product; (A6.12) gives the revenue to the firm with a fee rate of f.

Figure 13.4 sketches the relationship between revenues and fee rate for dependent and independent products. There is no economic incentive for an investment firm with an independent product to reduce fees and every incentive to increase them.

The situation is different for firms with dependent products. From (A6.13), they maximise their revenues when the fee equals half the active overlay profit. This sounds excessive until one recalls that much of the return on both traditional and alternative products is dependent as it comes from style, so that we are only talking about half the excess return over cash for a truly uncorrelated product. From (A6.14), the maximum economic value of the active overlay

---

* One way of pricing an overlay is to get investors to underwrite a share l of the loss of the overlay in return for a smaller share p of the profit of the overlay. This means the firm takes a proportion $(1 - p/l)$ of the investors' profit and leaves them with any loss. Such a formula has to include a clawback provision, or alternatively an arrangement where investors pay the fees owed to date only when they withdraw, as otherwise the ratio of p/l will be affected by the length of the overlay accounting period.

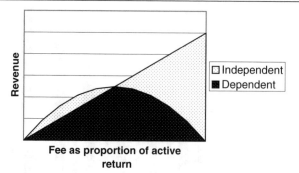

Figure 13.4   Revenues and fee rate

to the firm is proportional to the square of S so that a small difference in skill gives rise to a much greater difference in profitability.

13.3.2   Paying for information

Intuitive investment professionals rely on private information, which is expensive to acquire. The custom has grown up of paying for much of this information through bundled transaction charges. These extra payments to brokers are either for private information the broker provides or for private information provided by other people, which the broker then pays for.* There is a school of thought that investment firms should pay for information directly and that softing should be outlawed. For example:

> The review recommends that it is good practice for institutional investment management mandates to incorporate a management fee inclusive of any external research, information or transaction services acquired or used by the fund manager rather than these costs being passed on to the client.[6]

When skill drives demand and fee setting is flexible, the controversy resolves itself. (A6.22) shows that if the costs of information are charged directly to the product, the optimal fee will be the active overlay profit less the information cost divided by two.

Expression (A6.25) shows that if the costs of information are charged to the investment firm, the optimal fee will be the active overlay profit plus the cost of information divided by two. In either case, expression (A6.26) gives the maximum revenue from the product for the firm so the firm should be completely indifferent† between the two mechanisms for paying for information when it believes it has achieved an optimal fee rate.

Subtracting (A6.21) from (A6.23) gives (A6.24), or the revenue effect to the manager of a dependent product of paying for research directly rather than charging it to the product. Figure 13.5 sketches how this varies with fee rate for both types of demand pattern.

For dependent products, when the fee is more than the optimal rate, charging the manager rather than the product actually increases the revenues because the fee is so high that the increased product demand generated more than compensates for increased cost. When the fee

---

* The latter form of payment is called softing. Payments for information through this mechanism are called soft payments to contrast them with direct or hard payments by investment management firms.
† This analysis ignores the broker's mark-up. When converting soft commissions into payments to third-party vendors, the broker applies a discount of between 10% and 50%. All other things being equal, this cost might incline people to make hard payments.

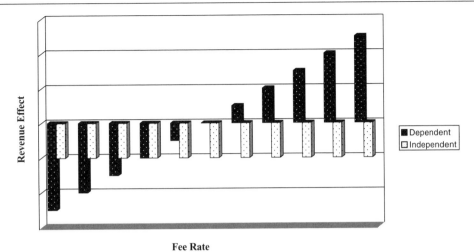

Figure 13.5   Cost of charging information to manager as fee rate increases

is less than the optimal rate, the increased product demand generated no longer compensates for increased cost because the fee is too low.

Thus the importance of the issue for investment firms running dependent products depends on where the fee rate is relative to optimal. If it is too low, they have an incentive to charge the product. If it is too high, they have an incentive to pay for information themselves. The closer the firm believes the fee is to optimal, the less heated the issue becomes.

13.4   FEE-SETTING BEHAVIOUR

The different linkage between product skill and demand explains most of the differences in fee setting and other pricing behaviour between firms offering traditional products and firms offering hedge fund products. Interestingly, fee-setting behaviour for manager of manager hedge fund products is more similar to that of traditional products than it is to directly managed hedge fund products.

13.4.1   Traditional products

As skill has only a marginal effect on demand, there is little incentive to tailor the fees charged on a product to the skill the product demonstrates. There is therefore no disadvantage to using types of fee that have no connection with demonstrated skill, such as flat fees and transaction charges. In addition, as presented in Figure 13.5, traditional investment firms are always worse off if they have to pay for information costs rather than charging them to their funds. They are thus always likely to oppose unbundling information costs from transaction charges.

13.4.2   Funds of hedge funds

Research shows that manager of manager hedge fund products have average returns that are lower than the average returns of directly managed hedge funds.[7] This suggests that fees exceed average value added from product selection skill and that product skill does not therefore drive demand for such products.

Rather, the value proposition of manager of manager hedge fund products appears to be based on access rather than skill. One of the things that differentiates hedge funds from mutual funds and traded securities is that they are not easy to gain access to. They usually have large minimum investments and hedge funds that are performing well often close themselves to new investors. Part of the reason for this is that, in order to maintain their lightly regulated status, they are frequently required to accept restrictions on the number of investors they accept. But we have already seen that the abnormal distributions of active overlays make diversification essential for investors. Thus there is an opportunity for investment intermediaries to add value by allowing investors to take positions that they could not take directly.

The market assigns a different value to access than it does to skill. In contrast to directly managed hedge fund products, manager of manager hedge fund products charge flat fees. One study[8] finds that the most common fee rates for manager of manager products are 1–2% flat fees but zero performance fees. If access was unrestricted, hedge fund index products would emerge, the value of access would be competed to zero and the fee of a manager of manager product would become half the independent excess return the manager could generate above the index.

13.4.3 Hedge funds

As skill has a stronger effect on demand, one would expect evidence that hedge fund firms tailored fees to skill. As described earlier, hedge funds do indeed use performance fees, the type of fee that has the closest connection to demonstrated skill. However, they also make flat charges and the rates for both flat and performance fees are relatively fixed.

Because of these rigidities the hedge fund industry as a whole charges its investors fees that are lower than those that would maximise revenues. As presented in Chapter 9, an excess return net of fees of 6.17% implies fees of 2.54% and an independent return before fees of 7.94%. Thus fees as a proportion of active return are only 32% rather than the 50% suggested by (A6.13).*

Hedge fund firms do have the opportunity to adjust their fees by manipulating style and active risk. Because outperformance contributing to performance fees includes the excess returns from any product style, the more style the product has, the higher the fee as a proportion of independent return. Because the flat fee is charged on assets, the lower the product's active risk, the higher the fee as a proportion of independent return.

Introducing style into a hedge fund can also have the benefit of improving the Sharpe ratio, as long as the style has a positive Sharpe ratio and not too much is introduced. Equation (A6.36) shows the relationship between the Sharpe ratio of a product and both the skill of the independent active overlay and the Sharpe ratio of the style benchmark when these are combined with optimal weights. The higher the ratio of the style Sharpe ratio to active overlay skill, the more incorporating style will improve the product Sharpe ratio and the higher the correlation between the product and the style will be, as shown in (A6.37).

---

* The 2.54% estimate is understated to the extent that some funds charge more than 1% flat fees and some charge more than 20% performance fees. In addition, there will be some unpaid clawback when funds exit the index. however, all these effects together are most unlikely to total the 2.86% needed to raise the fee rate to 50%.

Let us suppose that the hedge fund industry estimates the Sharpe ratio of US equities to be the long-term ratio of 0.28. Let us also suppose that the industry estimates its collective skill to be 1.04, as calculated in Chapter 9. Then (A6.37) gives the optimal correlation between the hedge fund index and the S&P as 0.26. This is only just over half the actual correlation of 0.49, suggesting that the industry tends to introduce more style into hedge fund products than necessary to maximise their Sharpe ratios. The excess style benefits hedge funds by increasing their fees as a proportion of their independent returns.

Similarly, the low volatility of the CSFB Tremont index,* which is only 54% of the volatility of the S&P index measured over the same period, also increases fees as a proportion of independent return by increasing the relative importance of the flat fees charged. But a volatility as low as this is not ideal for most investors. This can be illustrated in two ways.

First, consider an investor who puts all his wealth into a portfolio with identical characteristics to the CSFB Tremont index. Rearranging (A6.32), the optimal volatility of a risky asset portfolio, as a proportion of an investor's wealth, is equal to its Sharpe ratio divided by his risk aversion. As the Sharpe ratio of the index is 0.70 and its volatility is 8.86%, an investor would need a risk aversion of 7.9 to want a weight in the CSFB Tremont index that was precisely equal to his total wealth. But 7.9 is the risk-aversion of a highly risk averse investor.†

Second, consider an investor who wishes to impose an absolute limit on the losses he is exposed to from active management. As the losses from investing in hedge funds are only limited by the investment itself, such an investor investing in the CSFB Tremont index will incur one dollar of potential loss for every 5.4 cents of expected active overlay return. If he wants to limit losses from active management to an absolute 3% of his portfolio, he could invest no more than this in the index and could therefore expect no more than a rather modest 0.16% return from active management.

Restructuring the active overlay of the CSFB Tremont index as a freestanding overlay provides more interesting alternatives. Suppose the overlay is designed to experience a one in 20 chance of failure each year. As the overlay distribution is close to normal, this corresponds to a 1.64 sigma event. Suppose also that the liquidation threshold of the overlay is zero. The backing capital needed for the overlay reduces to 1.64 sigma from the 11.29 sigma of the index, and the expected return on the backing capital rises to 37.16%. In return for risking 3% of his capital, our investor's expected annualised return after fees from active management is now 1.11%.

Some advisors argue that the way ahead for liquid security investment is for traditional products to cease to offer active management and become index funds. At the same time, all skilful active managers migrate to hedge funds, which become the only products offering active overlays. This argument has its attractive features.

As noted first in Chapter 9, hedge funds demonstrate skill on average while traditional products do not. The structural advantages that help them to demonstrate skill are: their ability to charge performance fees, which helps them to attract both skilled investment professionals and discriminating investors who force the closure of failing products; their freedom from investment constraints, particularly their ability to go short, which helps them to manage risk more efficiently; their low style weightings relative to the sizes of their active overlays, which make it

---

* Following (A6.20), the weighted average active risk of the component funds is likely to be higher than the active risk of the index.
† If such an investor expected the future return pattern on US stocks to match the long-term historical return pattern, from (A5.7), he would only invest 17% in the market, retaining the balance of 83% in cash.

easier for investors to identify skill. In addition, the evidence noted earlier in this chapter suggests that a diversified portfolio of hedge funds such as that represented by the CSFB Tremont index has an excess return distribution that is, if anything, more normal than the broadly diversified equity indices on the Barcap database.

But hedge funds also have problems. The chief ones are that they have too much style and that they require excessive capital. Style that an investor does not want, either because he has his desired weight in it already or because it does not form part of his policy, can be cancelled by shorting the appropriate index fund or index future, but this is onerous, expensive and inconvenient. Capital can be released from low active risk products by borrowing against them, but again this is onerous, expensive and inconvenient. These problems would be eliminated if hedge funds were reformatted as freestanding active overlays.

13.5   CONCLUSION

There are three different types of fee: flat fees, transaction charges and performance fees. Industry convention fixes the type of fee and the rate charged for different types of product. Flat fees and transaction charges, which are the normal method of charging for traditional products, bear little relation to demonstrated skill. Performance fees, which are almost exclusively applied to hedge funds, are closely linked to demonstrated skill.

If demand is driven by product skill, investment firms maximise their revenues when fees are equal to half the independent component of active overlay return. If demand for a product is driven by other factors, there is no reason for a link between fees and skill. Thus, the traditional product sector as a whole does not demonstrate positive product skill but still charges substantial fees. Without a link between skill and demand, there is no incentive for sponsoring firms to absorb costs, such as those for research, which they can charge to their products.

Although successful on average at demonstrating skill, hedge funds have disadvantages as vehicles for delivering active management to investors. Because there is limited scope to change fee rates, hedge fund management firms improve the revenue-generating potential of their products by manipulating active risk and style. The active risk and style that have evolved for the hedge fund industry as a whole provide a poor fit with the needs of risk-tolerant investors with low cash allocations in their policies.

ENDNOTES

1. William Shakespeare, *Troilus and Cressida*, Act 2 Scene 2.
2. Myners, p. 82.
3. For example: L.T. Starks, "Performance incentive fees, an agency theoretic approach", *Journal of Financial and Quantitative Analysis*, XII, 1987.
4. *Sunday Times*, 12 January 2003.
5. W.N. Goetzmann, S.J. Brown and J. Park, "Careers and survival: competition and risk in the hedge fund and CTA industry", *Journal of Finance*, 53(5), 2001.
6. Myners, p. 96.
7. Fung and Hsieh.
8. Fung and Hsieh.

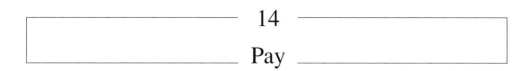

14

Pay

The labourer is worthy of his hire.[1]

Pay, or the compensation investment professionals receive for their efforts, is linked to fees. Without fees, there cannot be pay. Where the investment management firm has one product and one investment professional, who also owns the firm, fees and pay are only separated by business expenses.

However, the link between investment professional pay and fees can be quite tenuous. Large, complex investment management businesses have outside shareholders and many employees who are not acting as investment professionals but need to be compensated for their contributions in the areas of management, sales, marketing, finance, administration, etc.

Pay can come in other forms than cash. Traditional investment firms conventionally deliver part of employee compensation as shares in the business or options on shares in the business. In contrast to this, hedge fund managers conventionally receive their bonuses in the form of cash, which they often reinvest in the products they manage. We will see later that there are good reasons for this difference.

Chapter 11 makes a distinction between those who use an intuitive and those who use a systematic approach. From the point of view of analysing pay, the key difference is that the models underlying a systematic approach become the property of the firm. This suggests that systematic investment professionals should receive incremental profit shares or equity participations when they deliver their models. The value of these will of course be linked to the success of the models.

As most of the arguments in the rest of this chapter assume that an individual can take his skill with him when he leaves his firm, they are mainly about individuals using an intuitive approach. Through knock-on effects, their pay indirectly affects the pay of analysts and traders, whose role is to support and execute decisions rather than to make them, and people performing other roles, including those with backgrounds as investment professionals.

14.1 PAY AND SKILL

We have seen in Chapter 13 that the link between skill and fees depends on the link between skill and demand and is weaker for traditional funds than it is for hedge funds. The link between skill and pay is therefore weaker for traditional funds than it is for hedge funds. This notwithstanding, the link between pay and skill for investment professionals managing traditional funds has been strengthened by the development of the hedge fund sector.

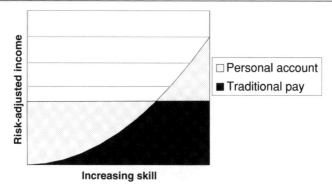

Figure 14.1   Before hedge funds

14.1.1   Before hedge funds

Because of concerns about front running,* the regulations governing traditional investment management firms have the effect of severely inhibiting trading for personal account. Because the investment strategies of traditional products are also restricted by regulation, they seldom reflect their portfolio managers' preferred investment strategies and are thus unattractive vehicles for personal account investing. The restrictions on trading for personal account therefore create a real opportunity cost for a skilled investment professional. He is always able to go out on his own and concentrate on managing his own money. Expression (A6.33)† gives the maximum risk-adjusted return he is able to achieve by doing this. It represents the floor under the compensation a traditional firm has to pay to retain his services.

This floor is proportional to the product of three factors: the square of his investment skill, his risk tolerance and his personal wealth. This has the following implications: small differences in skill result in large differences in pay; risk takers get more than risk-averse people with the same skill; wealthy people get more than poor people with the same skill. In addition, the effect of multiplying the factors together makes it harder for a risk-averse individual, however skilled, to accumulate wealth.‡ The direct effect of increasing skill on both the pay from a traditional investment firm and the risk-adjusted profit from personal trading is sketched in Figure 14.1. Figure 14.2 shows the relationship between personal net worth and the compensation packages traditional firms have to provide to retain individuals with the same skill but different levels of wealth.

14.1.2   After hedge funds

In recent years, skilled investment professionals have had the opportunity to leave their investment banks or traditional investment management firms and run hedge funds. As discussed in Chapter 13, hedge funds have two useful characteristics: demand depends on skill so that higher skill usually leads to higher revenues and the riskiness of fees is low. In addition, front running

---

* An investment professional behaving unethically by putting attractive securities into his or his firm's portfolio before putting them into his clients' portfolios.

† This result depends on investment professionals being mean variance investors. Its accuracy and the accuracy of results depending on it are subject to the usual caveats about the accuracy of MPT.

‡ Investment professionals working for traditional firms thus have good reasons for behaviour that exaggerates their tolerance for risk and their personal net worth, particularly to people who might be in a position to influence their compensation.

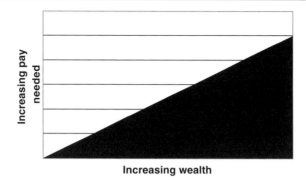

Figure 14.2   Constant skill

is no longer a problem because their investment flexibility is such that they can incorporate their investment professionals' preferred investment strategies. An investment professional's maximum risk-adjusted return from managing a hedge fund is consequently arrived at by adding the maximum he can get from outside investors to the maximum he can achieve by following the same strategy for himself (A6.34). This is sketched in Figure 14.3, where the fees he gets from running money for other people are superimposed on the risk-adjusted profits he gets from running his own money in the product.

This leads to two conclusions. First, he will always do better from running a hedge fund than from investing on his own as any external investors will always produce a net gain for him. Second, his total gain is still proportional to the square of his skill but it is no longer proportional to his wealth and risk tolerance. It now depends not only on his wealth and risk tolerance but also on an external demand factor, common to all competing products, that in turn depends on the wealth and risk tolerance of the skill-driven external investors who can access these products. Thus the relevance of his wealth and risk tolerance to his compensation falls as the external demand factor grows.

As the risk-adjusted profit they could achieve from running a hedge fund increasingly reflects the floor compensation for skilled investment professionals rather than the risk-adjusted profit from investing their own personal net worth, the hedge fund opportunity has put sustained upward pressure on compensation for skilled investment professionals across the industry.

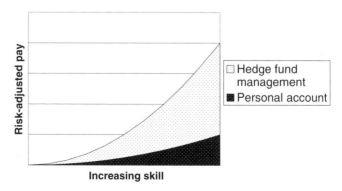

Figure 14.3   After hedge funds

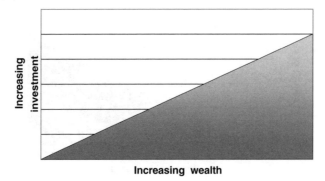

Figure 14.4 Manager investment in product

14.1.3 Hedge fund self-investing

Expression (A6.34) also equals risk-adjusted compensation for an individual managing a single hedge fund product for a firm where he is the sole proprietor. Expression (A6.35) gives the amount of the product the investment professional will wish to own as a proportion of the amount owned by outside investors. This is independent of his skill and equal to twice his wealth divided by his risk aversion, divided by the external demand factor. Figure 14.4 sketches this relationship.

Thus for two products competing in the same market, so that the external demand factor is effectively* the same, the ratio of two managers' investments in their own products equals the ratio of wealth multiplied by risk tolerence.

Older managers will naturally own more of their products than younger managers. This is because the richer and more risk tolerant an investment professional is, the more he will want to own of the product he manages. For a successful product, the wealth of the manager will automatically increase over time through the performance fees he is paid.[†]

Advisors conventionally pay great attention to the percentage of a product an investment professional owns. If it looks low after taking external demand, his wealth and his risk aversion into account, it suggests that the investment professional has less confidence in the product than he should, an obvious danger signal. There is thus an incentive for investment professionals with confidence in their own skill to invest a substantial proportion of their bonuses in units of the funds they manage. If the percentage owned by the investment professional looks high, it suggests that his process has negative scale effects.

14.2 DIVIDING THE SPOILS

Chapter 11 noted that intuitive investment professionals need autonomy to function effectively. However, because active overlays are self-financed, it is possible to combine an unlimited number of independent active overlays into one product provided the systems are available to keep track of each individual's decisions. Although many investment professionals act as

---

* The external demand factor for product A differs slightly from the external demand factor for product B as it excludes demand from manager a and includes demand from manager b.
[†] As LTCM kept active risk constant throughout the life of the fund, the only way the management team could keep their own participation optimal was by increasing their share at the expense of their outside investors.

sole investment decision makers for the products they manage, many products are managed by groups of autonomous decision makers. The challenge for the investment firms sponsoring such products is not only to maximise product skill but also to compensate the investment professionals appropriately.

14.2.1 Prima donnas

At first sight, the reason for working together is obvious. Combining independent overlays results in a superior product with higher skill than the skill of any of the individual overlays. This is shown in (A6.18), where the square of the skill of an optimal combination of independent overlays is equal to the sum of the squares of the skills of the individual overlays.

But we can also see from (A6.14) that the maximum revenue that can be attained from an active overlay is proportional to the square of the skill of the active overlay. As the same constant of proportionality applies whether the overlays are sold separately or combined as one product, we come to an interesting conclusion.

From equations (A6.14) and (A6.18), it is clear that the maximum revenue possible from combining overlays into one product is equal to the sum of the maximum revenues possible on each overlay if marketed as separate products. Worse, while you only have to get the fee right to get the maximum revenue on separate overlays, you have both to get the fee right and to combine the overlays in the right proportions to get the maximum revenue on the overlays combined.

Anecdotally, it is hard to combine two exceptionally skilful investment professionals with independent approaches to create a product with an even higher skill rating. This is conventionally explained by the supposed tendency of talented individuals to behave like "prima donnas". In fact, they have no economic incentive to work together.* Indeed in order to avoid cutting their total compensation, they have to set each other exactly the right position limits, which in practice is hard to do as it depends on the two individuals making and agreeing on the right assessments of each other's skills.

14.2.2 Threshold skill

One reason why investment professionals work together on the same product is that there appears to be a minimum skill necessary before a product is acceptable to the market place. Investment professionals with skills below this critical level do not have the option to go off and set up their own products. This minimum skill depends on the relationship between what revenues are expected and what the product will cost to set up and run. A prospective hedge fund manager currently has to demonstrate quite a high level of skill before he can get sufficient outside investor interest to make his product viable.

A threshold skill level introduces the opportunity to make money by organising managers with subcritical skill. Figure 14.5 shows this schematically, with the vertical line representing critical skill and the triangle to the left of this representing the organiser's profit opportunity.

There are various different types of economically viable combinations of independent overlays. All share the characteristic that all or some of the investment professionals have skill

---

* They have a modest incentive if their excess return distributions have negative skewness and excess kurtosis as they can diversify some of this abnormality away by combining.

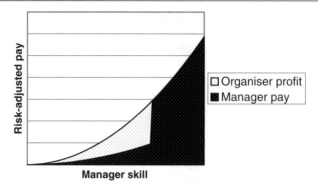

Figure 14.5   Critical skill

that is below the critical level. The prima donna problem only comes when more than one investment professional has greater skill than the critical level.

In the numerical examples that follow, I have assumed, for illustrative purposes, a critical level for skill of 0.7, equal to that shown by the CSFB Tremont index after deduction of fees, and high enough to create high confidence levels from short track records.*

Thus, from (A6.18), two investment professionals with skill of 0.5 each can band together to create a product with a combined skill of just over 0.7, or 0.5 multiplied by the square root of two. They would share the benefits of doing this. The opportunity for an investment professional whose skills are just below the threshold to take on a partner with a similar skill level is a good one and often taken in practice, as evidenced by the hedge fund start-ups with two names on the letterhead.

Similarly, an investment professional with a skill of 0.5 could recruit two investment professionals with skills of 0.35 and combine with them to create a product with a combined skill rating of just over 0.7 (A6.18). The profitable opportunity to collect investment professionals with skills that could be significantly below the threshold but with independent excess returns and put them together into a strong product with a profit margin for the organiser is also often taken in practice. This is what happens when senior hedge fund figures move from trading securities to trading investment professionals.

A variant of this is where the dominant investment professional has the threshold skill of 0.7 but recruits four others, each with half his skill. By giving himself and the others appropriate limits he enhances the combined skill rating of his product to 1, or 0.7 multiplied by the square root of two (A6.18). Because he has to make judgements about the skills of the lesser individuals and the correct limits to set, this is a difficult investment process to optimise. The upside for the dominant investment professional is that because the lesser traders are so far below the critical level and because they know they are not essential for the product to reach the threshold, he will only have to pay them a modest uplift on the certainty equivalent that they would get from trading on their own and thus capture much of the value they add for himself.

The opportunity for firms to exploit investment professionals with skills lower than the critical level ultimately depends on information asymmetry. With perfect information, each

---

* Within a year, the probability that skill is being shown has risen above 75%. Consistent with this, hedge fund product selection decisions are made with much shorter performance time series. Also consistent with this, managers of groups of traders find it useful to look at individual trader profit and loss on a daily basis.

investment professional would be able to capture most or all of the revenue he creates as, if the firm sponsoring his current product does not pay it to him, he can always leave and find a product where the organiser will. If only he and the firm know about his skill, his bargaining position is much worse. In practice, investment professionals working for a firm seem to be able to capture about half the value added, leaving half for the owner or owners. Soros[2] takes half the profits on his products and divides the rest among his traders. From an earlier era, JP Morgan took half the profits of the eponymous partnership and divided the rest among the other partners. Although it was formally a partnership, Morgan controlled the business as he had the right at any time to dissolve the partnership or to compel any partner to withdraw.[3]

14.2.3 Position limits

In addition, it can be shown that allowing one investment professional in a group working on a product to set the limits for the group introduces potential conflicts when investment professionals are rewarded on the profits they generate. This is because such an investment professional will have an incentive to award himself higher limits than his skill justifies (A6.42). Although doing this reduces the overall fee generating potential of the product [(A6.42), (A6.43)], the effect is small relative to the enhancement to his overlay profit and therefore his compensation [(A6.39), (A6.41)]. In practice, the limit setter is often the most skilled trader: "Bacon has been increasingly willing to delegate responsibility for specific sector investments, once he has set the appropriate asset allocation."[4] Alternatively, the limit setter can be an individual who does not trade and therefore does not have a potential conflict. Other combinations are possible but industry behaviour is generally consistent with conflict minimisation. Soros, while not investing on a day-to-day basis himself, delegates limit setting to his senior investment professional while retaining control over the allocation of compensation.[5] Morgan kept the final say on which deals to do and partners' pay.[6]

14.3 VALUING INVESTMENT MANAGEMENT FIRMS

Industry convention is to value firms at a higher multiple of earnings when the link between skill and demand is weak than when the link is strong. Taking stock or options rather than cash is thus more attractive for investment professionals working for firms where the link between skill and demand is weak.* This explains why investment professionals working for traditional investment management firms are usually prepared to accept at least part of their pay in the form of stock or options on stock in the firm.

14.3.1 Traditional firms

The convention for valuing traditional firms is well established. Table 14.1 shows an analysis of the prices paid in 30 separate acquisitions of traditional US investment management firms between 31 December 1992 and 31 December 1996. The prices are shown as multiples of operating profits, multiples of recurring revenues and percentages of assets under management. The margin is the pre-acquisition operating profit expressed as a percentage of

---

* If the multiple of pre-tax earnings is 10, giving up a dollar of pay creates an extra 10 dollars of shareholder value and, without reducing shareholder value, the company can grant up to 10 dollars worth of stock or options, which currently attract special accounting advantages in the USA, to employees as compensation for forgoing the cash. The lower the multiple, the less potential there is for enhancing earnings in this way.

Table 14.1

	Profit ×	Revenue ×	Margin %	Assets %
Mean	10.5	4.1	38	2.1
Median	10	4	39	2.1
High	20.8	7.7	62	4
Low	6.3	1.6	20	0.3
Standard deviation	2.7	1.1	10	1.1

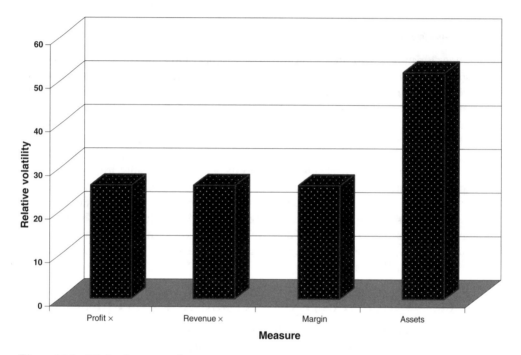

Figure 14.6   Valuing investment firms

recurring revenue. The mean, median, high and low are shown together with the standard deviations of the four measures commonly used as criteria for assessing the capital values of investment firms.

The more stable acquisition prices are when they are expressed in terms of each criterion, the more useful the criterion. Figure 14.6 shows the standard deviations expressed as a percentage of the mean for each criterion.

The figure shows that, because of the stability of margins, or profits as a percentage of revenues, acquisition prices are a relatively stable multiple of profits and revenues. They are less stable as a percentage of assets. This is because different firms have different combinations between high-fee business, such as equities and mutual funds, and low-fee business, such as bonds and institutional clients.

The stability of margins suggests that traditional investment management firms, or at least those that had a chance of being acquired between 1992 and 1996, organise their finances so that they have a profit margin of approximately 40%. Skilled investment professionals, who are also shareholders and holders of options on the shares, have an incentive to forgo some of the compensation they could otherwise extract in order to fatten up the margin, if they expect capital gains from so doing.

The evidence implies that such investment management firms are assumed to have stable profit margins, stable revenues and stable shares of investor assets. For some products, this assumption does not depend on stable skill. As discussed in Chapter 13, flat fee formulae predominate in traditional product pricing. This automatically creates a stable link between revenues and assets that is independent of skill. As also discussed in Chapter 13, skill only has a minor role in determining product demand for traditional products.

14.3.2 Hedge fund firms

When skill becomes the dominant factor driving product demand, the traditional method of valuing investment management firms as a percentage of assets under management or as a multiple of revenues or profits becomes heavily dependent on assuming stable skill. While this may be true for a systematic firm with an inventory of proven models, there are two reasons why the assumption is questionable if the underlying investment processes are intuitive and rely on the subjective judgement of talented individuals.

The first is that, as discussed in Chapter 11, skill depends on the current group of decision makers and the stages they have reached in their careers. The skill of such a firm is therefore likely to be a lot less stable than the acquirer expects.

The second is that the profit margin will be hard to maintain after the acquisition has been consummated. This is because any individual with skill above the critical level should be able to extract most or all of the value of his investment skill in compensation. The net value of his investment skill to the firm will therefore be close to zero. Even though his skill will attract assets generating revenues that are proportional to the square of his skill, the profits from these assets will accrue to him rather than the firm.

Such a firm, consisting of one or more highly skilled investment professionals, will have substantial assets under management but a purchasing institution would be unwise to pay a percentage of those assets without locking these professionals in at below market rates of compensation. If it does this, it will have a problem with motivating them. If it does not do this, they will either demand the full market rate, in which case there is no profit, or they will leave, in which case there are no assets. This difficulty in securing a worthwhile premium explains why the conventional exit for proprietors of hedge fund firms seems to be to liquidate and return the money to investors rather than to sell the business.*

14.3.3 Fund of hedge fund firms

Chapter 13 pointed out that product skill does not appear to drive demand for manager of manager hedge fund products. Consistent with this, businesses sponsoring such products do change hands, often at generous multiples. A recent example[7] was the acquisition by Man Group of RMF, a hedge fund of funds business, for a price that was 21 times earnings and 10% of funds under management.

---

* A high-profile example was the decision by proprietor Julian Robertson in March 2000 to close Tiger Management, after 20 years of operation, and return the money to investors. Eighteen months before this, Tiger had US$22.8 billion in assets, making it the largest hedge fund group in the world. Although assets since then had been much reduced by US$7.7 billion of withdrawals and absolute performance of −43%, the capital returned still amounted to US$6 billion.
[*Source*: contemporary press comment.]

Chapter 13 also pointed out that if access became open, the value of access would be competed to zero and manager of manager hedge fund products would have to compete on skill. This in turn would have positive consequences for the pay of their more skilled investment professionals and adverse consequences for the capital values of their sponsoring businesses.

14.4   CONCLUSION

In the absence of products where demand depends on skill, an intuitive investment professional's pay will depend on the product of his personal net worth, risk tolerance and the square of his skill. Thus highly skilled investment professionals who are risk averse or poor may be paid little. When intuitive investment professionals work on products whose demand depends on skill, pay will be largely independent of net worth and risk tolerance but a greater multiple of the square of skill. As competition bids up pay across the board, the growth of the hedge fund industry has resulted in higher pay and a more direct relationship between skill and pay, where small differences in skill can result in large differences in pay.

Because the link between pay and skill requires independent investment decisions, the degree of cooperation between intuitive investment professionals is limited by economic self-interest. Because it increases the ability of skilled investment professionals to extract the value they create, an enhanced link between skill and pay weakens the link between the client assets and the capital value of an intuitive investment management firm.

ENDNOTES

1. *Luke*, Chapter 10, Verse 18.
2. Soros, p. 62.
3. JP Morgan 1933 testimony to Senate Currency and Banking Committee, Brooks, p. 184.
4. *Institutional Investor*.
5. Soros, pp. 61, 62.
6. Brooks, p. 184.
7. *Times*, 24 May 2002.

Afterword

The old order changeth, yielding place to new.[1]

In contemplating the future, one thing is clear. The investment industry has to change. Meeting investor expectations of superior active performance has to become the rule rather than, as now, the exception. Efficient market theorists, and other sceptics about active management, argue that the way ahead is also clear. Investors should only buy index products. But the Efficient Market Hypothesis leads to a paradox. The more it influences investor behaviour, the less accurately it will describe the world. For if all active overlays are shut down, the securities industry implodes and security prices are set far less efficiently than they are at present.

Alternatively, the industry can change to make active overlays available in a way that better meets investor needs. The scenario that follows draws together some of the themes already touched upon in earlier chapters.

It starts with investors refusing to accept from their advisors any portfolios of active overlays except portfolios that they can confidently expect will provide them with positive risk-adjusted returns after expenses. It amounts to the same thing if investors only pay their advisors for advice when it has resulted in profitable active management.

Advisors will need to improve their estimates of the skill of every active overlay they consider. They will also need to improve their knowledge of the distribution of returns of these overlays to ensure that the portfolio of overlays they choose is adequately diversified. They will then have to negotiate mandates with the investment firms supplying their chosen products that incorporate two features. The first feature is customised active risk, or an active risk target and tolerance that ensures the weight the active overlay has in the portfolio of active overlays assembled for each investor closely corresponds to their estimates of product skill. The second feature is a performance fee formula so that fees are only deducted when the overlay is profitable.

Investment firms offering traditional active products will be faced with demand for: a higher standard of proof that product skill is positive; performance fees rather than flat fees; customised rather than standard active overlays. They will respond to the first demand by pressing for loosened guideline constraints on their active overlays in general and the ability to go short in particular. They will resist the latter two demands. Shifting from flat to performance fees will reduce the values of their businesses. Customised active overlays will complicate their activities. However, competitive pressures will ensure that even these demands are met in time.

Investment firms offering hedge funds will be faced with the same demands but will respond differently. They do not have the same problems with guideline restrictions and are under less pressure collectively to prove that they have skill. They already offer performance fees. However, if they wish to attract investors with limited cash in their policies, they will have to offer versions of their products with active overlays customised to deliver higher active risk. These customised versions will have a greater emphasis on performance fees relative to flat fees.

The active overlays of both traditional products and hedge funds will thus converge into a form which gives both their investment professionals the maximum chance to demonstrate skill and their investors the maximum assurance that they will receive a positive risk-adjusted return from their participation. Skill will become of increasing importance in determining demand.

At the same time, the growing prevalence of fees tied to active overlay results rather than assets and exposures based on active risk rather than assets will weaken the commercial link between active overlays and their style portfolios. At some stage in this process, investment firms will detach the active overlays from their underlying style portfolios and offer them separately.

Investors will then be able to make their decisions on active management and investment policy completely separately. Assets will no longer be needed to supply the raw material for active overlays. The demand for an active overlay will depend entirely on the skill with which it is managed and the fees charged.

Fees will be defined by the relationship between the investor's share of overlay profit and his share of overlay loss and can be changed for each investor holding period to take supply, or desire of the investment firm to expand or contract the overlay, and demand into account. However, investors who renew will be protected from overpaying due to subsequent underperformance either by clawback or by only paying for net performance when they withdraw.

His judgement of the extent to which the overlay profit correlates with his policy and the rest of his portfolio of active overlays will influence the fee an investor is prepared to pay. When he expects the correlation to be negligible, he will be prepared to accept a share of profit as low as half the share of loss he underwrites. He may even be prepared to accept less than half, either if the investment firm pays for information or if the overlay is known to suffer from negative economies of scale.

The combination of skill-driven demand and flexible fee setting will take the sting out of the information cost issue. The closer firms feel their fees are to the optimal level, the less strongly they will feel about paying separately for information. The consequent unbundling of information costs from execution costs will improve efficiency and reduce conflicts of interest.

Recognising the differences between products using intuitive and systematic approaches will lead to a more customised approach towards using historical return information to form expectations of investment skill.

The length of the time series used for analysis will depend on the type of process in question. For intuitive processes, the length of the investment professional's career will limit it, while for systematic processes, the availability of historical price data will limit it.

The periodicity of the time series used for analysis will also depend on the type of process. For a systematic process, it will be annually or quarterly as it usually takes decades for systematic skill to become apparent. For an intuitive professional, it will be weekly or even daily as intuitive skill both can become apparent in less than a year and can change over time.

The covariance of active overlay returns with the excess returns of either style portfolios or other active overlay returns will no longer automatically be assumed to be zero, particularly for those using a systematic approach. If it is significant, explicit adjustments will be made.

The skills of industry participants will become more focused and specialised. Investment management firms will need to have excellence in at least one specialist function to survive. However, because of the increasing opportunities to outsource investment decision making, a firm with specialist skills in index management, administration, marketing or finance could be profitable without any investment skill at all, as long as it recognised this and took the appropriate action.

Advisors will divide into two types. One will specialise in setting policy and one will specialise in constructing portfolios of skilfully managed active overlays. Both types will have discretion and both will be paid on the basis of the skill they demonstrate.

The investment function of a policy-setting advisor will be to create appropriate policies for his clients which take into account their risk preferences, locality and liabilities. He will work closely with index designers and index fund providers to provide this service. A passive investor will not need to use any other investment decision-making service.

As access to skilfully managed active overlays becomes easier, access alone will no longer attract a premium fee. Active overlay index funds will become both commodities and benchmarks for manager of manager products. The investment decision makers of such products will need skill both in identifying the skill with which active overlays are being managed and in constructing portfolios of the active overlays selected.

A systematic process of this kind would primarily depend on the publicly available overlay performance data. An intuitive process of this kind would, in addition to the public information, use private information about investment professional behaviour and skill. It would have some similarity to the task of compensating traders and setting limits for today's proprietary trading activities and multi-trader hedge fund products. The active manager selection services of investment consultants will develop into manager of manager services as they increasingly accept the economic consequences of their judgements of manager skill.

As information about skill becomes more transparent, the ability of firms to provide training that enhances investment skill will become essential to maintaining profit margins. Investment professionals with below threshold skill will increasingly only accept compensation below their full value if they judge that this gives them the opportunity to improve.

Actively managed overlays will polarise into two types, each serviced by a very different type of investment professional. Good systematic processes will eventually become styles, while good intuitive processes will eventually retire.

Systematic investment professionals will naturally coalesce into groups. They share the same need for historical data and processing power to test their hypotheses. Different rules can be combined easily to form diversified processes.

The ability to find and use private information to make independent investment decisions will be a *sine qua non* for an intuitive investment professional. Such people will move between three categories. Some, usually the most skilled, will act as sole or lead decision maker for investment products. Some, usually less skilled than the first group, will act as members of teams of investment professionals working independently on products. Some, usually the least skilled, will support other investment professionals by providing ideas and execution. They may work exclusively for one investment professional or they may choose to leverage their ideas by working for a broker with a group of investment professionals as clients. All intuitive investment professionals will maintain personal track records to validate their skill.

Detaching active overlays from their style benchmarks will create a symbiotic relationship between active investment management and passive investment management that is far removed from today's mutual antipathy. With their highly predictable security holding patterns, index funds will become dominant in security lending. Volumes of security lending will rise and margins will fall as freestanding overlays grow. There will also be opportunities to sell derivatives reflecting long-term short positions in established style benchmarks to support overlay managers who only want to manage the long side of their positions.*

Index fund providers will have a very similar function to the one they carry out today. However, the passive style portfolios they administer will comprise the vast bulk rather than the minority of institutional portfolios. In addition they will have the opportunity to provide active overlay index funds. They will be measured on the accuracy with which their products track the relevant indices and their compensation will be kept low by competition.

Marketing managers will continue to determine the optimal marketing mix of styles, overlays, service, promotion and price for their channels but now they will no longer be locked into in-house investment skill as styles and freestanding overlays can be bought in or discarded at will. This will greatly increase their flexibility.

Some products will be structured, as now, as a combination of a style and an active overlay but the overlay no longer has to relate to the style. If the most attractive active overlay is based on small capitalisation stocks and the style in demand is large capitalisation stocks, there would no longer be any need for conflict.

Some marketing managers will decide to market individual freestanding active overlays. Others will buy in manager of manager skills and market portfolios of freestanding active overlays either on their own, to meet investor requirements for active management alone, or in combination with policy portfolios to meet investors' complete investment needs.

In addition to taking a share of the profit in return for a larger share of the loss, there will be other opportunities to invest in overlay businesses. For example, there will be demand for guarantees that freestanding active overlays will lose no more than a specified amount. There will also be demand for a whole range of financial products based on active overlays and style benchmarks including forward positions, short positions and options.

Like today's custodians and prime brokers, administrators will continue to provide settlement services, cash collateral administration and record keeping services. As overlay administrators they will also have to arrange for competitive security lending. In addition, they will monitor active risk limits and liquidation thresholds, calculate the performance and fees of freestanding overlays and calculate the performance of overlays attributable to individual investment professionals. Another function they could take on would be to act as information middlemen. For example, they would be in a good position to provide reconstructed performance information on systematic processes to advisors, where the investment firms did not want to put the details of the decision process into the public domain for competitive reasons.

In a world such as that outlined so far in this scenario, investors and their advisors will find it sufficiently easy to locate and make use of skill that they will make it the chief determinant of active product demand, active product fees and investment professional pay. The process of moving to such a world can be helped or retarded by government policy.

Government can help by taking steps to make index funds and active overlays more efficient at delivering value to investors. Such steps might include giving index funds special privileges in making non-competitive applications for IPOs, large secondary offerings and perhaps even

---

* For a given index, if investor style portfolios totalled X and overlay manager short positions totalled Y, the index fund manager would only need to maintain a volume Z at the custodian where $X - Y = Z$.

active overlays themselves. They might also include giving systematic investment professionals special privileges to help them collect the largest and most accurate possible historical data sets. In addition, governments should frame insider trading regulations in a way that does not preclude or excessively impede legitimate efforts to gather private information. One way to do this would be to recognise, with appropriate safeguards, the relationship intuitive investment professionals specialising in a stock need to have with its management team.

As we have seen in Chapters 10 and 13, regulation of traditional products, designed to eliminate the possibility of product bankruptcy and excessive active risk taking, has helped make skill hard to find in such products. This in turn has hampered their ability to add value. If freestanding active overlay products are discriminated against by government policy, they will remain in lightly regulated centres with limited access and the onshore and offshore investment management worlds will diverge still further.

The stakes are high. Unless regulated actively managed products are encouraged to develop to the point where, on average, they enrich their investors as well as their sponsoring firms, their credibility with investors will continue to seep away. Regulated investment will shift to index funds and active management will only be available to those able to access the unregulated sector.

In summary, the root cause of the current discontent with active investment management is that investment skill is elusive, making it hard for investors to find and put to work. The problem is particularly acute for traditional products, whose style portfolios dwarf the corresponding active overlays and whose fees reward assets rather than skill. Hedge funds partially address these structural difficulties, but not completely. Both types of product need to evolve so that investors and their advisors find it easier to locate skill and make use of it. When this happens, skill will drive demand for active products and pay for investment professionals. This in turn will change the way investment firms are organised and valued.

The simplest way to make skill more accessible is to detach active overlays from their style portfolios and make them separately available. Investors and their advisors will find skill easier to assess and will no longer have to juggle skill and style in fitting active products into investment policy. Three developments are needed to make this possible. First, short positions need to be cheaper and more accepted, as without them freestanding overlays cannot exist. Second, leverage, or having less supporting capital than the gross size of the active overlay, also needs to be more accepted, as otherwise freestanding overlays will require excessive capital. Third, fees must be based on active overlay performance rather than assets, as otherwise investment firms will be reluctant to detach one from the other.

All this may sound strange, but no stranger than the investment world of today would seem to an investor from 1900. The way the investment industry is organised and paid, the products available, the competences required, will all change and evolve.

But some things will be as familiar to an investor at the end of the twenty-first century as they would have been to an investor in 1900 and before. I shall finish with an old story[2] about an investor who divides his wealth between three managers, one of whom is neither able to deal with investment risk nor capable of handling the resultant passive portfolio to the investor's satisfaction.

> ...A man travelling into a far country...called his own servants, and delivered unto them his goods. And unto one he gave five talents, to another two, and to another one; to every man according to his several ability; and straightway took his journey.
>
> Then he that had received the five talents went and traded with the same, and made [an]other five talents. And likewise he that had received two, he also gained [an]other two. But he that had received one went and digged in the earth and hid his lord's money.

And after a long time the lord of these servants cometh and reckoneth with them. And so he that had received five talents came and brought [an]other five talents, saying, Lord, thou deliveredst unto me five talents: behold, I have gained beside them five talents more. His lord said unto him, Well done thou good and faithful servant; thou hast been faithful over a few things, I will make thee ruler over many things: enter thou into the joy of thy lord.

He also that had received two talents came and said, Lord, thou deliveredst unto me two talents: behold I have gained two other talents beside them. His lord said unto him, Well done, good and faithful servant; thou hast been faithful over a few things, I will make thee ruler over many things: enter thou into the joy of thy lord.

Then he that had received the one talent came and said, Lord, I knew thee that thou art a hard man, reaping where thou hast not sown and gathering where thou hast not strawed: and I was afraid, and went and hid thy talent in the earth: lo, there thou hast that is thine.

His lord answered and said unto him, Thou wicked and slothful servant, thou knewest that I reap where I sowed not, and gather where I have not strawed: thou oughtest to have put my money to the exchangers, and then at my coming I should have received my own with usury. Take therefore the talent from him, and give it unto him which hath ten talents.

ENDNOTES

1. Alfred, Lord Tennyson, "The Passing of Arthur", *Idylls of the King*.
2. *Matthew* XXV, v. 14–28.

Technical Appendix

A.1 BASIC MODELLING TOOLS

Most of the mathematical basis of models used to analyse relationships between variables such as time, risk and return was developed from the late seventeenth century onwards. There are three main elements: calculus, natural logarithms and ways to analyse a probability distribution or density function. The key concepts of the latter are the normal distribution and higher moments, or the degree of abnormality of a given distribution.

A.1.1 Calculus

The first important set of results comes from calculus, which was invented independently by Isaac Newton and Gottfried Leibniz.* The idea is as follows. Suppose that two variables are related in a well-behaved way so that plotting one against the other gives a smooth curve. Suppose also that one, the dependent variable, can be expressed as a function, or in terms of, the other or independent variable. Following tradition, I will call the dependent variable y and the independent variable x. Then differentiating, or performing a special algebraic manipulation on, the function with respect to the independent variable can find the gradient of the curve. The expression for the gradient is dy/dx. As the gradient can be found at any point, it also forms a curve, which can be differentiated itself to give the gradient of the gradient d^2y/dx^2, and so on. In addition, the whole process can be reversed. The gradient can be integrated to give the original function: $\int (dy/dx)dx = y$.

Because a curve has a gradient of zero at a peak or trough, differentiating a function and setting the differential equal to zero can be used to find at what values of the independent variable the function is at its maximum or minimum.[†] Finding maxima and minima is the main use of calculus in this appendix. The actual manipulation required can be highly complex but, with a few exceptions, all the integrals and differentials in this appendix can be found using the following three properties.

The first property is that, if a function consists of a number of components added together, the differential of the function is equal to the sum of the differentials of the

---

* Newton did his work between 1664 and 1666, communicated his results privately, but did not publish. Leibniz did publish between 1684 and 1686. This led to a furious row as to who deserved the credit for the discovery.

† From the geometry of any curve, if the second differential is positive it is a minimum while if the second differential is negative it is a maximum. They are usually styled local maxima and minima because a curve may have more than one of each.

components:

$$\frac{d(y+z)}{dx} = \frac{dy}{dx} + \frac{dz}{dx} \tag{A1.1}$$

The second property is that, if a function can be expressed as a power of the independent variable, the differential of the function is given by the expression:

$$\frac{d(x^n)}{dx} = nx^{n-1} \tag{A1.2}$$

The third property is that the differential of function y, which can be expressed as a function of an intermediate variable z, which itself is a function of x, can be expanded as follows:

$$\frac{dy}{dx} = \frac{dy}{dz}\frac{dz}{dx} \tag{A1.3}$$

Finally, if x is given a small increment h, the function of x and the function of $x + h$ can be related by the following expression, which is called Taylor's* theorem:

$$f(x+h) = f(x) + h\frac{df(x)}{dx} + \frac{h^2}{2!}\frac{d^2f(x)}{(dx)^2} + \cdots + \frac{h^n}{n!}\frac{d^nf(x)}{(dx)^n} \tag{A1.4}$$

A.1.2 Natural logarithms

Some integrals and differentials use the special properties of the base of the natural logarithm e, which was defined by Leonhard Euler in 1748 as:

$$e : e^x = 1 + x + \frac{x^2}{2!} + \frac{x^3}{3!} + \frac{x^4}{4!} + \cdots \tag{A1.5}$$

Then, from (A1.1) and (A1.2):

$$\frac{de^x}{dx} = e^x \tag{A1.6}$$

The natural logarithm, ln, of (A1.5) is x. Using this, (A1.1) and (A1.3):

$$W : W = e^u$$
$$\frac{dW}{du} = W, \quad \ln W = u \tag{A1.7}$$
$$\frac{d(\ln W)}{dW} = \frac{d(\ln W)}{du}\frac{du}{dW} = \frac{1}{W}$$

As Bernoulli's proposition can be expressed mathematically as:

$$du = \frac{dW}{W} \tag{A1.8}$$

the mathematical form of his utility function from (A1.7) is:

$$u = \ln W \tag{A1.9}$$

---

* First published by Brook Taylor in 1717.

A.1.3   Normal distribution

The third important set of results are those related to the Central Limit Theorem and the normal distribution which was discovered by Abraham de Moivre in 1733. The formulation of the probability density function (PDF) of the normal distribution uses e and had to wait for Carl Friedrich Gauss, who used it to refine measurements of the curvature of the earth:[1]

$$PDF = \frac{1}{\sigma\sqrt{2\pi}}e^{-(x-\mu)^2/2\sigma^2} \qquad (A1.10)$$

The mean μ and standard deviation σ are given by the following expressions:

$$\mu = \sum_{i=1}^{n} \frac{x_i}{n} = \int xf(x)dx \qquad (A1.11)$$

The first formulation of (A1.11) gives the mean of n observations while the second gives the mean of a population with a PDF of $f(x)$.

$$\sigma^2 = \sum_{i=1}^{n} \frac{(x_i - \mu)^2}{n} = \int (x - \mu)^2 f(x)dx \qquad (A1.12)$$

The first formulation of (A1.12) gives the variance (standard deviation squared) of n observations while the second gives the variance of a population with a PDF of $f(x)$.

A.1.4   Central Limit Theorem

The Central Limit Theorem, which places the normal distribution at the heart of statistics, can be stated as follows:

> The distribution of sample means follows a normal curve. More precisely, if a number of random samples of size n are drawn from a given population, their means tend to form a normal distribution provided that the size of the sample is large and the population is not unduly skewed. If the population is skewed, the distribution of sample means will be much less skewed, in inverse proportion to the size of the sample.[2]   (A1.13)

Thus, even if the population from which the samples are drawn is not normally distributed, the sample means will be provided that the sample is large enough.

A.1.5   Higher moments

The third moment, skewness, is given by the formula:

$$\Sigma = \sum_{i=1}^{n} \frac{(x_i - \mu)^3}{n\sigma^3} = \int \frac{(x - \mu)^3 f(x)}{\sigma^3}dx \qquad (A1.14)$$

While a fourth moment, kurtosis, is given by the formula:

$$K = \sum_{i=1}^{n} \frac{(x_i - \mu)^4}{n\sigma^4} = \int \frac{(x - \mu)^4 f(x)}{\sigma^4}dx \qquad (A1.15)$$

For large samples of normally distributed data, the expected values of skewness and kurtosis are zero and three with variances $6/n$ and $24/n$.[3] The t values of sample skewness and the excess of kurtosis over three are the sample values divided by standard deviation. The higher the t values, the less chance that the sample is normally distributed. (A1.16)

A.2 INVESTMENT ALGEBRA

A.2.1 Time value of money

In assessing money market investments, investors find it convenient to relate the payment they make now M, to the payment they will receive back a fraction t of a year in the future P, to an annualised interest rate r^* by the formula:

$$M(1 + rt) = P \qquad (A2.1)$$

This allows them to compare the returns they get from different investments yielding different sums at different times in the future on a like-for-like basis.[†] In addition, the formula can be adapted to calculate the discount that needs to be applied to a payment in the future to compensate for the delay:

$$M = P/(1 + rt) \qquad (A2.2)$$

The continuously compounded version of this is:

$$M = Pe^{-\rho t} \qquad (A2.3)$$

Equating the two and taking natural logarithms gives:

$$\rho t = \ln(1 + rt) \qquad (A2.4)$$

which gives the relationship between the continuously compounded rate of interest ρ and the periodic rate of interest r.

A.2.2 Time versus money-weighted performance measurement

For n cash flows C occurring at times t where the final cash flow leaves a net asset position of zero, the continuously compounded internal or money-weighted rate of return is the ρ that solves the equation:

$$\sum_{i=1}^{n} C_i e^{-\rho t_i} = 0 \qquad (A2.5)$$

The time-weighted rate of return requires the portfolio to be valued V before each cash flow C. The continuously compounded time-weighted rate of return is the ρ that solves the equation below where T is the elapsed time from the first cash flow to the last cash flow:

$$\prod_{i=2}^{n} \left(\frac{V_i}{V_{i-1} + C_{i-1}} \right) = e^{\rho T} \qquad (A2.6)$$

---

[*] r is assumed to be positive. Switzerland did introduce negative interest rates in 1979 to curb the rise of the Swiss franc but this was only for a brief period.
[†] Assuming they use the same method to calculate t. This is not always the case. Different types of fixed interest security have different day count methods which lead to slightly different results.

A.2.3   Bond prices

Fixed income investors chiefly consider three different types of cash flow pattern. These are: a bond, which pays an annual coupon of C and repays 100 on maturity at the end of n years; a terminable annuity which makes n annual payments of a fixed amount C; a zero coupon bond which makes no interim payments but pays 100 at the end of n years. A bond can be thought of as a combination of the other two when all three have the same life.

Fixed income investors are interested in the internal rate of return that they will earn from investing in such instruments. For a bond, this is the r in the following equation* where P is the price and t is the time to the next coupon payment:

$$P = \frac{1}{(1+rt)} \left(\sum_{i=1}^{n} \frac{C}{(1+r)^{i-1}} + \frac{100}{(1+r)^{n-1}} \right) \tag{A2.7}$$

where the expression outside the brackets is the discount factor that accounts for the delay before the first payment, the first expression inside the brackets is due to the periodic payments and the second expression is due to the repayment. The expression can be adapted to deal with annuities by setting the repayment to zero and zeros by setting the periodic payments to zero. To simplify further, assume going forwards that t equals one. This expression is a special case of the internal rate of return equation as r is the internal rate of return that equates P to the present value of the cash flows on the bond.[†]

As the life of the bond gets longer and longer, the price tends towards C/r (A2.8), which is the price of a perpetual bond such as a UK consol. This can be proved by remembering that:

$$\sum_{i=1}^{\infty} \frac{C}{(1+r)^i} = \frac{C}{\left(1 - \frac{1}{(1+r)}\right)} = \frac{C(1+r)}{r} \tag{A2.9}$$

and substituting in (A2.7).

The consol yield r equals the consol price P divided by 100 when:

$$r = \frac{P}{100} = \sqrt{\frac{C}{100}} = \sqrt{0.025} = 0.1581 \tag{A2.10}$$

A.2.4   On and off the run

When $C/100$ equals r, P equals 100. This can be proved by substituting $100r$ for C in (A2.7) and solving for P. You have to use (A2.11) but the answer is intuitively obvious:

$$\sum_{i=1}^{n} \frac{r}{(1+r)^i} = \frac{r\left(1 - \frac{1}{(1+r)^{n+1}}\right)}{\left(1 - \frac{1}{(1+r)}\right)} = 1 - \frac{1}{(1+r)^n} \tag{A2.11}$$

Thus for a "par" bond (one trading at par), the coupon equals the yield to maturity. The cash flows from premium bonds (those trading at above par) and discount bonds (those trading below par) can be converted to the cash flows from a par bond by adding or subtracting zero coupon

---

* Before the advent of electronic yield calculators, this equation was solved by hand for all the combinations of periodicity, day count method, r, C and n that were thought likely and tabulated in yield books, unwieldy volumes over an inch thick. During the early 1980s, when yields reached levels never thought possible these became useless, accelerating the conversion to yield calculators.
† The periodicity of payments varies from instrument to instrument but is normally once, twice or four times a year.

bonds with the same final maturity. This calculation is useful in arbitraging between on-the-run bonds (which typically trade at or close to par) and off-the-run bonds (which typically trade at discounts or premia). To see this, consider the cash flows from a hundred dollars nominal of any bond, where the subscripts refer to timing:

$$CF = \sum_{i=1}^{n} C_i + 100_n$$

$$CF = \frac{C}{r} \left(\sum_{i=1}^{n} r_i + 1_n \right) + \left(100 - \frac{C}{r} \right)_n \tag{A2.12}$$

which are of course the cash flows arising from C/r nominal of par bonds and $(100 - C/r)$ nominal of zero coupon bonds maturing at the same time as the bonds mature. When C/r is greater than 100, the position in zeros is short (negative).   (A2.13)

   This expression can be extended to express any lower coupon bond as a combination of a higher coupon bond and a zero of the same maturity. One dollar nominal of the lower coupon bond has exactly the same cash flows as a combination of p nominal of the higher coupon bond and q nominal of the zero where p equals the lower coupon divided by the higher coupon and q equals $1 - p$.   (A2.14)

   The proof comes from considering what happens when the par bond yield equals the lower coupon and remembering that the proportions are independent of market yields.

A.2.5 Seventeenth century Dutch annuities

The seventeenth century Dutch method of valuing annuities set the yield on an annuity at twice the yield r on a perpetual bond. Thus the value of the annuity was equal to the value of a perpetual bond with half the yield. Equating (A2.8) and (A2.11) to find the breakeven life L leads to the equation:

$$2 - \frac{2}{(1+r)^L} = 1$$

$$(1+r)^L = 2 \tag{A2.15}$$

$$L \ln(1+r) = \ln 2$$

$$L \approx (\ln 2)/r$$

Thus the longevity L required to break even is inversely proportional to the market rate for perpetual annuities. The Dutch could not have performed this calculation because natural logarithms had not yet been invented.

A.2.6 Duration

The rate of change of price with changing yield is the expression for price (A2.7) differentiated with respect to yield:

$$\frac{dP}{dr} = -\left(\sum_{i=1}^{n} \frac{iC}{(1+r)^{i+1}} + \frac{100n}{(1+r)^{n+1}} \right) \tag{A2.16}$$

Rearranging (A2.16) to get the fractional change in price for a given change in yield, we have:

$$\frac{dP}{P} = -\left[\frac{1}{P}\left(\sum_{i=1}^{n}\frac{iC}{(1+r)^{i+1}} + \frac{100n}{(1+r)^{n+1}}\right)\right]dr \qquad (A2.17)$$

As r and C are always positive, this expression is always negative. Thus if yield rises, price falls and vice versa. The expression in square brackets is known as adjusted duration to distinguish it from Macaulay duration, which is given by the expression below and is equal to adjusted duration multiplied by $(1 + r)$. If r is the same for both portfolios, equalising Macaulay duration is the same as equalising adjusted duration:

$$\text{Macaulay} = \frac{1}{P}\left(\sum_{i=1}^{n}\frac{iC}{(1+r)^{i}} + \frac{100n}{(1+r)^{n}}\right) \qquad (A2.18)$$

As can be seen from the expression for Macaulay duration, duration can be interpreted as the average life of the cash flows of the instrument weighted by their present values. This explains why the duration of a portfolio equals the average duration of the instruments in the portfolio weighted by their present values. The Macaulay duration of a zero coupon bond is equal to the term to final maturity (n in the equation). While a perpetual instrument has an infinite average life, it has a finite adjusted duration equal to $1/r$ (A2.19). Differentiating (A2.8) with respect to r can easily prove this.

A.2.7 Bond attribution

In attribution, one is comparing the return on an actual portfolio P with that of a benchmark portfolio B:

$$R_p = y_p - dy_p D_p$$
$$R_b = y_b - dy_b D_b$$
$$\Rightarrow R_p - R_b = (y_p - y_b) + (dy_b D_b - dy_p D_p)$$

But:

$$D_p = D_b + (D_p - D_b)$$
$$\Rightarrow R_p - R_b = (y_p - y_b) + D_b(dy_b - dy_p) + dy_p(D_b - D_p) \qquad (A2.20)$$

The first term in the expression is just the yield spread between the portfolio P and the benchmark B. The second term in the expression is the impact of any change in the spread. If the spread widens, it will be negative and if the spread compresses, it will be positive. The third term in the expression reflects the impact of the duration positioning of the portfolio. If the portfolio yield rises the impact will be positive if the duration of the portfolio is less than the duration of the benchmark.

A.2.8 Constant growth model

This assumes that the price of an equity security is given by the present value of its dividends, which are growing at $g\%$ per annum discounted back at a rate of $r\%$ per annum. Then price is given by the following equation:

$$P = \sum_{i=1}^{\infty} \frac{D(1+g)^i}{(1+r)^i} = \frac{D}{\left(1 - \frac{(1+g)}{(1+r)}\right)} = \frac{D(1+r)}{(r-g)} \tag{A2.21}$$

Equation (A2.21) can be rearranged to give the equally useful expression:

$$r = D(1+r)/P + g \tag{A2.22}$$

A.2.9 Purchasing Power Parity

Purchasing Power Parity states that the equilibrium exchange rate between two countries is such that prices are equalised. Formally:

$$x_{ij} = k \frac{P_i}{P_j} \tag{A2.23}$$

where x is the exchange rate and the two P's represent the domestic price level in countries I and J.

A.2.10 Covered interest arbitrage

Covered interest arbitrage sets the forward rate on a currency in the following way. Consider a bank which has a certain amount of currency j. It can place a deposit in currency j. It can also sell the currency into currency k at the spot rate of x, place a deposit in currency k and sell the proceeds back into j. Ignoring transaction costs, the two strategies should realise equal amounts of j as otherwise an easy arbitrage would be possible. This equality sets the forward rate:

$$\frac{(1+r_k)x}{x_f} = 1 + r_j \Rightarrow x_f = \frac{x(1+r_k)}{(1+r_j)} \tag{A2.24}$$

If the k interest rate is higher than the j interest rate, the forward rate must be at a discount to (weaker than) the spot rate and vice versa.

A.3 TIME SERIES ANALYSIS

A.3.1 Standard approach

The standard approach underlying the analysis of historical returns on assets is that the compounded excess return (also known as a return relative) E on asset P over a historical period T years can be given by the expression:

$$E = \exp \int_0^T f(t)dt \tag{A3.1}$$

where $f(t)$ is the difference between the return on the asset $R(t)$ and the risk-free rate $F(t)$ at time t. Both R and F vary with t. Formally: $f(t) = R(t) - F(t)$. This can be broken up into subperiods, each with its own return relative:

$$E = \exp \int_0^{t_1} f(t)dt \exp \int_{t_1}^{t_2} f(t)dt \cdots \exp \int_{t_{(n-1)}}^{t_n} f(t)dt \tag{A3.2}$$

Let us assume that the time series is chopped up into n equal intervals of length t so that nt equals T. Taking natural logarithms of both sides allows (A3.2) to be re-expressed as follows:

$$\ln E = \sum_{j=1}^{n} \int_{t_{(j-1)}}^{t_j} f(t)dt \tag{A3.3}$$

Let us now define the annualised return on the asset and the risk-free asset in period j in the following way:

$$\int_{t_{(j-1)}}^{t_j} f(t)dt = (R - F)_j t \tag{A3.4}$$

Then (A3.3) can be rearranged. Dividing one side by T and the other by nt gives:

$$\frac{\ln E}{T} = \sum_{j=1}^{n} \frac{(R - F)_j}{n} \tag{A3.5}$$

Equation (A3.5) is the expression for the geometric mean excess return, or annualised excess return that compounds up to E over the period T, which we shall call $(r - f)$.

A.3.2 Confidence interval

If the subperiod returns are independently and identically distributed, we can use a standard statistical result to arrive at a confidence interval (CI) that the excess return of the wider population of which these returns are samples is greater than zero:

$$CI = \frac{(R - F)\sqrt{n}}{\sigma_t} \tag{A3.6}$$

The sigma term is the standard deviation of the n subperiod excess returns. If the future excess returns on this asset also form part of the same wider population, then this CI also measures the confidence that an analyst can have that the asset will generate excess returns in the future.

From this equation, it would appear that the CI can be affected by choosing the interval because the shorter the interval, the greater n becomes and, all other things being equal, the greater the CI. Assuming Brownian motion deals with this problem because with this assumption, the variance of the subperiod excess returns is proportional to the interval, t. If $(r - f)$ and σ represent the distribution's annualised mean excess return and standard deviation, then:

$$CI = \frac{(R - F)\sqrt{n}}{\sigma_t} = \frac{t(r - f)\sqrt{T/t}}{\sigma\sqrt{t}} = \frac{(r - f)\sqrt{T}}{\sigma} \tag{A3.7}$$

A.4   UTILITY THEORY

The following argument follows the standard literature in relating the utility hypothesis to variance and introduces the concept of certainty equivalent. The same argument is then extended to include the effects of skewness and kurtosis.

A.4.1   Certainty equivalent

Consider an investor with wealth level W facing a fair gamble f with expected return of 0 which is uncertain, so that its variance is greater than 0. The certainty equivalent is driven by the fraction of wealth ρ the investor would be prepared to give up to avoid the risk of f.

$$\widetilde{W} = (1+f)W, \qquad W_c = (1-\rho)W \tag{A4.1}$$

A.4.2   Expected utility

Next, consider the first five terms of a Taylor expansion (A1.4) of the utility of wealth:

$$E[U(\widetilde{W})] = E\left[U(W) + U'(W)fW + \frac{U''(W)f^2W^2}{2!} + \frac{U'''(W)f^3W^3}{3!} + \frac{U'''(W)f^4W^4}{4!}\right] \tag{A4.2}$$

As the expected value of f is zero, the second term is also zero. From (A1.12), the expectation of f squared in the third term is the variance of f. From (A1.14), the expectation of f cubed in the fourth term is skewness times the third power of the standard deviation of f. From (A1.15), the expectation of the fourth power of f in the fifth term is kurtosis times the fourth power of the standard deviation of f. The expected utility of uncertain wealth is thus:

$$E[U(\widetilde{W})] = U(W) + \frac{U''(W)\sigma_f^2W^2}{2} + \frac{U'''(W)\sigma_f^3W^3\Sigma}{6} + \frac{U'''(W)\sigma_f^4W^4K}{24} \tag{A4.3}$$

where Σ represents skewness and K represents kurtosis.

A.4.3   Risk adjustment

Next, consider the first two terms of a Taylor expansion (A1.4) of certainty equivalent utility:

$$U(W_c) = U[(1-\rho)W] \approx U(W) - U'(W)\rho W \tag{A4.4}$$

As the utility of certainty equivalent equals the expected utility of wealth (A4.4) equals (A4.3). The resulting equality can be solved for ρ. Discounting the terms containing skewness and kurtosis simplifies the expression for ρ to:

$$\rho \approx -\frac{\sigma^2 W U''(W)}{2U'(W)} \tag{A4.5}$$

For constant relative risk aversion investors we will see from (A4.16) that the utility function takes the form $U = \left[W^{1-\gamma}/(1-\gamma)\right] + A$. The first and second differentials of U with respect to W are easy to calculate using (A1.2):

$$U'(W) = W^{-\gamma}, \qquad U''(W) = -\gamma W^{-(\gamma+1)} \tag{A4.6}$$

The expression for ρ reduces to:

$$\rho \approx \frac{\gamma \sigma^2}{2} \qquad (A4.7)$$

A.4.4   Abnormal distributions

Where skewness and excess kurtosis are large enough to matter, the full expression for ρ is:

$$\rho \approx -\frac{\sigma_f^2 W U''(W)}{2U'(W)} - \frac{\sigma_f^3 \Sigma W^2 U'''(W)}{6U'(W)} - \frac{\sigma_f^4 K W^3 U''''(W)}{24U'(W)} \qquad (A4.8)$$

From (A1.2), the third differential of the utility function is:

$$U'''(W) = \gamma(\gamma + 1)W^{-(\gamma+2)} \qquad (A4.9)$$

and the fourth differential is:

$$-U''''(W) = \gamma(\gamma + 1)(\gamma + 2)W^{-(\gamma+3)} \qquad (A4.10)$$

Substituting these back into (A4.8), the expression for ρ reduces to:

$$\rho \approx \frac{\gamma \sigma^2}{2} - \frac{\gamma(\gamma + 1)\sigma^3 \Sigma}{6} + \frac{\gamma(\gamma + 1)(\gamma + 2)\sigma^4 K}{24} \qquad (A4.11)$$

Dividing the second term of the right-hand side of (A4.11) by the first term, the ratio of the skewness term of the risk adjustment to the variance term is:

$$-\frac{(\gamma + 1)\sigma \Sigma}{3} \qquad (A4.12)$$

A.4.5   Constant relative risk aversion

The utility function U that has constant relative risk aversion is a solution to the differential equation where γ is a positive constant number.

$$-\frac{U''(W)W}{U'(W)} = \gamma \qquad (A4.13)$$

From (A1.3) and (A1.7), (A4.13) can be rearranged and integrated:

$$\frac{d \ln U'(W)}{dW} = \frac{U''(W)}{U'(W)} = -\frac{\gamma}{W}$$

$$\ln U'(W) = -\gamma \ln W + c \qquad (A4.14)$$

Raising (A4.14) to the power of e gives:

$$U'(W) = e^c W^{-\gamma} \qquad (A4.15)$$

Integrating (A4.15) gives two solutions, the first for γ not equal to one and the second for γ equal to one:

$$U(W) = a\frac{W^{1-\gamma}}{1-\gamma} + b$$

$$U(W) = a \ln(W) + b \qquad (A4.16)$$

A.5   MEAN VARIANCE ANALYSIS

In the discussion of risk adjustment in the utility section it was established that this is approximately a function of variance of wealth alone if the wealth outcomes are approximately normally distributed. It can be shown theoretically that if the distribution is normally distributed then risk and any risk adjustment is a function of variance alone. Mean variance analysis is thus exact for an asset return PDF that is normally distributed. When a PDF is not normally distributed, mean variance analysis is only exact if the investor is a mean variance investor, or one who views variance as risk anyway.

A.5.1   Correlation

Francis Galton (1822–1911) introduced correlation and covariance, one of the key concepts necessary for mean variance analysis. Covariance reflects the degree to which different assets are correlated with each other. The covariance shown over n observations between asset j and asset k is defined by the following formula:

$$\sigma_{jk} = \sum_{i=1}^{n} \frac{(j_i - \mu_j)(k_i - \mu_k)}{n} \qquad (\text{A5.1})$$

Clearly the covariance of an asset with itself is just its variance. The correlation between j and k is closely related to the covariance and equals:

$$\rho = \frac{\sigma_{jk}}{\sigma_j \sigma_k} \qquad (\text{A5.2})$$

A.5.2   Matrix algebra

A simplifying methodology used in mean variance analysis is vector and matrix algebra. By arranging asset returns and weights in vectors and covariances in matrices, these allow the analyst to handle portfolios containing more than one asset. Each cell in the vector array refers to one asset's return or portfolio weight while each cell in the matrix array refers to the covariance between two assets. We shall call the return vector $\mathbf{R}$, the weighting vector $\mathbf{X}$, and the covariance matrix Ω. Mean (A1.11) expected portfolio return is the product of the return vector and the weighting vector $\mathbf{R.X}$, while portfolio variance (A1.12) is $\mathbf{X'\Omega X}$ where the prime denotes that the vector is transposed. The covariance (A5.1) between portfolios $\mathbf{X}$ and $\mathbf{Y}$ is $\mathbf{X'\Omega Y}$.

A.5.3   Utility maximisation

For an investor with constant relative risk aversion, everything has to be expressed relative to wealth. Expression (A5.3) defines his utility:

$$\mathbf{X.R} + (1 - \mathbf{X.J})F - \mathbf{X'\Omega X}\gamma/2 \qquad (\text{A5.3})$$

$\mathbf{J}$ is a vector of ones so that $\mathbf{X.J}$ represents the weight in risky assets. The first term is his expected return on risky assets, the second term is the return on that portion of the portfolio he invests in risk-free assets for a return of F and the third term is his risk-adjustment factor. Expression (A5.3) is an example of a function of a vector variable $\mathbf{X}$. This category of function can be differentiated using a fourth property of calculus, which is that functions of vector variables can be differentiated with respect to these vector variables in a manner analogous to the more familiar differentiation of functions of scalar variables. Thus, the $\mathbf{X}$ that maximises (A5.3) is the $\mathbf{X}$ that satisfies:

$$\mathbf{R} - \mathbf{J}F - \Omega\mathbf{X}\gamma = 0 \tag{A5.4}$$

Provided the covariance matrix can be inverted, the solution is given by (A5.5) where the double prime refers to an inversion:

$$\mathbf{X} = \Omega''(\mathbf{R} - \mathbf{J}F)/\gamma \tag{A5.5}$$

The optimal portfolio weight, as a fraction of wealth, in each risky asset therefore depends on all the expected excess returns, the inverted covariance matrix and the inverse of gamma.

A.5.4 Maximising the mean variance ratio

The mean variance approach uses Lagrangian* multipliers to derive the $\mathbf{X}$ that maximises the return for a given level of variance. This form of the solution is:

$$\mathbf{X} = \Omega''(\mathbf{R} - \mathbf{J}F)C \tag{A5.6}$$

where C is a constant. The advantage of this approach is that you only need to know that the investor is a mean variance investor; you do not need to know what his risk preferences are. The disadvantage is that because you do not know what his preferences are, you only know what his risky asset portfolio is and not whether he combines it with cash or borrowings.

A.5.5 Optimal investment in risky assets

Consider a risky asset with return R, variance σ^2 and risk-free rate R_0. Then from (A5.5), the proportion of wealth in the risky asset is:

$$w = \frac{(R - R_0)}{\gamma\sigma^2} \tag{A5.7}$$

All wealth is invested in the risky asset when:

$$\gamma = \frac{(R - R_0)}{\sigma^2} \tag{A5.8}$$

A.5.6 Two asset optimisation

Consider a portfolio with a weight in equities B and a weight in bonds M that is net of duration-adjusted liabilities. The covariance matrix is:

$$\Omega = \begin{pmatrix} \sigma_b^2 & \sigma_{bm} \\ \sigma_{bm} & \sigma_m^2 \end{pmatrix} \tag{A5.9}$$

The return vector is:

$$\begin{pmatrix} R_b \\ R_m \end{pmatrix} \tag{A5.10}$$

---

* Named after Joseph Louis Lagrange, 1736–1813.

Then from (A5.5) and (A5.6) the weighting vector between B and M is:

$$X = \begin{pmatrix} w_b \\ w_m \end{pmatrix} = \left(\frac{C}{\sigma_b^2 \sigma_m^2 - \sigma_{bm}^2} \right) \begin{pmatrix} (R_b - R_0)\sigma_m^2 - (R_m - R_0)\sigma_{bm} \\ (R_m - R_0)\sigma_b^2 - (R_b - R_0)\sigma_{bm} \end{pmatrix} \quad (A5.11)$$

where C is either such that $X.J = W$ (A5.6), or the reciprocal of γ (A5.5). Equation (A5.11) also proves how leveraged optimal weights are to small changes in returns, variances or covariances. For example, the partial differential of the optimal weight in the matching asset with respect to the return on the matching asset is given by the following expression:

$$\frac{\delta w_m}{\delta R_m} = \frac{C\sigma_b^2}{\sigma_b^2 \sigma_m^2 - \sigma_{bm}^2} = \frac{C}{\sigma_m^2 (1 - \rho_{bm}^2)} \quad (A5.12)$$

Equation (A5.12) shows that the more highly correlated B and M are, the more the optimal weight in M changes for a given change in expected return.

A.5.7   Liability matching condition

From (A5.11), the weighting in M is 0, so the weight in bonds exactly matches the duration-adjusted weight in liabilities, when the following is satisfied:

$$(R_m - R_0)\sigma_b^2 = (R_b - R_0)\sigma_{bm} \quad (A5.13)$$

From the definition of correlation coefficient this can be re-expressed as:[4]

$$\rho_{bm} = \frac{\left(\dfrac{R_m - R_0}{\sigma_m} \right)}{\left(\dfrac{R_b - R_0}{\sigma_b} \right)} = \frac{S_m}{S_b} \quad (A5.14)$$

where S is the Sharpe ratio, or ratio of asset class excess return to standard deviation of excess return. Consider a situation where the asset portfolio has a dollar present value of liabilities L, which are identical to matching assets or bonds M in yield and duration. If the dollar weights of the asset portfolio are b in equities and m in bonds then the weights of the net worth are b in equities and $m - L$ in bonds. But these are solutions to (A5.11) so the condition for m to equal L is that the ratio of the Sharpe ratio of bonds to the Sharpe ratio of equities equals the correlation coefficient between bonds and equities.

A.5.8   Portfolio eligibility

If the matching asset condition is met so that the weight of bonds in net worth is zero, the condition for any other asset A to enter the risky asset portfolio is:

$$\frac{S_a}{S_b} \geq \rho_{ab} \quad (A5.15)$$

Consider what happens when a small weight n of an asset A is introduced to a risky asset portfolio consisting of cash and an optimal weight w in risky asset B. Condition (A5.15) is satisfied and the investment in A is funded by selling B.

From (A5.7), the original certainty equivalent is equal to:

$$(1 - w)R_0 + wR_b - \frac{\gamma w^2 \sigma_b^2}{2} \tag{A5.16}$$

The new certainty equivalent is equal to:

$$(1 - w)R_0 + (w - n)R_b + nR_a - \frac{\gamma}{2}\left(w^2\sigma_b^2 + 2nw\left(\sigma_{ab} - \sigma_b^2\right) - n^2\left(\sigma_b^2 + \sigma_a^2 - 2\sigma_{ab}\right)\right) \tag{A5.17}$$

The rate at which certainty equivalent is being gained by shifting from B to A is arrived at by subtracting (A5.16) from (A5.17), dropping terms in n^2 as n is small and dividing by n. This is equal to:

$$(R_a - R_b) - \gamma w\left(\sigma_{ab} - \sigma_b^2\right) = [R_a - R_0 - \gamma w \sigma_{ab}] - \left[R_b - R_0 - \gamma w \sigma_b^2\right] \tag{A5.18}$$

When the excess return of A relative to B is independent of B, the covariance between A and B equals the variance of B and, from the left-hand side of (A5.18), incremental certainty equivalent for a small investment in A equals excess return. As w is an optimal weight, from (A5.7), (A5.18) can be rearranged as:

$$\alpha_{ab} = (R_a - R_0) - \frac{\sigma_{ab}}{\sigma_b^2}(R_b - R_0) \tag{A5.19}$$

Equation (A5.19) defines alpha (α) or the risk-adjusted excess return of A over B. Positive α wins a place for A in the risky asset portfolio for when $\alpha = 0$, (A5.19) shows that the correlation between A and B equals the ratio between their Sharpe ratios. The ratio of the covariance between A and B to the variance of B is known as beta (β). Alpha and beta get their names because regressing the excess return on A against the excess return on B gives a straight line with intercept, or first regression coefficient, α and slope, or second regression coefficient, β.

Let us define B as the market portfolio so that α and β are relative to the market. Rearranging (A5.19) as an expression for the return on asset A, we get:

$$R_a = R_0 + \beta(R_b - R_0) + \alpha \tag{A5.20}$$

The Efficient Market Hypothesis described in Chapter 6 postulates that all α's are zero. From (A5.20), it therefore also postulates that the return on an asset equals the risk-free rate plus the market excess return multiplied by β. This is known as the Capital Asset Pricing Model,[5] which is thus dependent on the EMH. One test of how closely the EMH and the CAPM reflect reality is to plot historical asset returns against historical β for different assets. The more the slope reflects market excess return and the more closely the points of the plot line up, the more accurate the CAPM prediction. Empirical studies that show β having little or no relationship with return[6] can thus be interpreted as evidence that inefficiencies exist.

A.5.9   Information ratio

Consider a product A, which has a benchmark Q. The information ratio is the average return on A less the average return on Q divided by the standard deviation of the return on A less the return on Q. For this to equal skill, past skill has to be a good estimator of future skill and the following equality has to hold, where T is the true independent active overlay, so that skill equals the return on T divided by its standard deviation:

$$S_a = \frac{R_t}{\sigma_t} = \frac{R_a - R_q}{\sqrt{\sigma_a^2 + \sigma_q^2 - 2\sigma_{qa}}} \tag{A5.21}$$

This implies that the numerator is such that:

$$R_a = R_q + R_t \Rightarrow R_t = R_a - R_q \tag{A5.22}$$

In other words, the active product equals the overlay plus the benchmark. It also implies that the denominator is such that:

$$\sigma_a^2 = \sigma_q^2 + \sigma_t^2, \quad \sigma_q^2 = \sigma_{qa} \Rightarrow \sigma_t = \sqrt{\sigma_a^2 + \sigma_q^2 - 2\sigma_{qa}} \tag{A5.23}$$

In other words, the active overlay is independent of the benchmark.

The product Sharpe ratio only equals skill if the product excess return over cash equals risk-adjusted excess return. From (A5.18), this happens when the product excess return is independent of policy so that:

$$R_a = R_0 + R_t, \quad \sigma_a = \sigma_t \Rightarrow S_a = \frac{R_a - R_0}{\sigma_a} \tag{A5.24}$$

Suppose now that the benchmark used is wrong and that the true benchmark, or A less T, where T is the true active overlay, is really Q plus N, where N is an overlay with return of zero but finite variance. As T is independent, its covariance with N is zero and the information ratio measured using Q as the benchmark is:

$$\frac{R_t}{\sqrt{\sigma_t^2 + \sigma_n^2}} \tag{A5.25}$$

A.6   INDUSTRY ECONOMICS

As established later in (A6.30), the only component of overlay return that is valuable to an investor is the independent component as the dependent component is assumed to be already optimally present in his portfolio. In the analysis that leads to results (A6.1)–(A6.26) and (A6.36)–(A6.43), the return and active risk that determine skill are therefore the independent return and its standard deviation.

A.6.1   Demand for freestanding overlays

Consider y investors, for whom the only risky investments available are n skilfully managed and mutually independent freestanding active overlays. Any investor wants to maximise his return less his risk adjustment:

$$\mathbf{X.R} - \mathbf{X}'\mathbf{\Omega X}\gamma/2 \tag{A6.1}$$

where $\mathbf{X}$, $\mathbf{R}$,$\mathbf{\Omega}$, γ are his weighting vector, the overlay return vector, the overlay covariance matrix and his risk aversion. Differentiating and setting equal to zero, then solving for $\mathbf{X}$, we get:

$$\mathbf{\Omega''R}/\gamma \tag{A6.2}$$

These two expressions are analogous to (A5.3) and (A5.5). Now consider investor J's weight in overlay I. As the overlays are independent, all the covariances are zero and the covariance matrix is just a diagonal of all the variances of the overlays. The inverse of such a matrix is also a diagonal matrix, but now of the reciprocals of the variances. His money weight in I is the ith weight in (A6.2) multiplied by his wealth W_j:

$$w_{ji} = \frac{W_j R_i}{\gamma_j \sigma_i^2} \tag{A6.3}$$

Thus the total money weight of all the investors in overlay I equals:

$$\sum_{j=1}^{y} w_j = \frac{R_i}{\sigma_i^2} \left[\sum_{j=1}^{y} \frac{W_j}{\gamma_j} \right] \tag{A6.4}$$

As a money weight in a self-financing overlay is a slightly odd concept, we can multiply (A6.4) by σ_i to give the size of I's overlay, or the total active risk demanded by the y investors:

$$S_i \sum_{j=1}^{y} \frac{W_j}{\gamma_j} \tag{A6.5}$$

As freestanding active overlays require supporting capital, it is probably more realistic to introduce budget constraints for investors. This alters the summation components of (A6.4) and (A6.5) but leaves (A6.4) proportional to active return divided by active variance and (A6.5) proportional to skill.

A.6.2   Demand for products with style

The derivation is slightly more complicated for investors for whom style is a consideration, but a very similar relationship emerges. Consider an investor with a policy P made up of predetermined weights of n styles. He has identified m skilfully managed products with independent active overlays, which he has sorted by style. He needs to know how much of each product to acquire while keeping to an unchanged policy. The unchanged policy requirement means that the total weight of active products acquired within each style category I has to be less than (if index products are used) or equal to the weight assigned to I within P. Say there are k skilfully managed products within style I. Then:

$$\sum_{j=1}^{k} w_j \leq w_i, \qquad \sum_{i=1}^{n} w_i = W, \qquad \sum_{i=1}^{n} k_i = m \tag{A6.6}$$

where W is the investor's total wealth. The incremental certainty equivalent he achieves from active management is given by the expression below where w refers to a money weight while the returns and standard deviations are those of the independent components of the active overlay returns, expressed as percentages:

$$\sum_{j=1}^{m} w_j R_j - \frac{\gamma}{2} \sum_{j=1}^{m} w_j^2 \sigma_j^2, \qquad \sum_{j=1}^{m} w_j \leq W \tag{A6.7}$$

But because we are only looking at the independent components of the active overlays, (A6.7) can be divided up by style. Furthermore, because the weights for each style are fixed and the active excess returns are independent, if he maximises the ratio of active excess return to active variance within each style, he also maximises the ratio of active excess return to active variance for his portfolio as a whole. The inverse of the covariance matrix of the products within the style is a diagonal matrix as before. Thus for style I, the k active product weights are optimised when the weight in product j is:

$$w_j = K \frac{R_j}{\sigma_j^2}, \qquad K = \frac{w_i}{\displaystyle\sum_{j=1}^{k} \frac{R_j}{\sigma_j^2}} \qquad (A6.8)$$

From (A6.8), we can see that the optimal active risk an investor should expose himself to from actively managed independent overlay j is proportional to the skill with which j is being managed:

$$w_j \sigma_j = K \frac{R_j}{\sigma_j} = K S_j \qquad (A6.9)$$

Next consider a universe of y mean variance investors, all seeking to fit the same m skilfully managed products into their policies. For style I, each investor will have a weight assigned in his policy. This weight could be zero. Each investor will acquire the k skilfully managed products with style I with weights determined by (A6.8). Adding up the weights in style I of all y investors gives a total Q_i. When w_{il} is the weight in I of investor L, this is given by:

$$Q_i = \sum_{l=1}^{y} w_{il} \qquad (A6.10)$$

The demand for product j from our y investors is then given by:

$$\frac{R_j}{\sigma_j^2} \left(\frac{Q_i}{\displaystyle\sum_{j=1}^{k} \frac{R_j}{\sigma_j^2}} \right) \qquad (A6.11)$$

A.6.3   Revenue maximising fee

For an overlay with return R and standard deviation σ, if the fee f is a set proportion of the return R, the net return on the overlay is $R - f$. To simplify matters, assume that σ is unaffected by the fee.* The revenue equals the fee multiplied by the demand function. If skill drives demand, the revenue equals:

$$\frac{f(R - f)K}{\sigma^2} \qquad (A6.12)$$

where the constant K is the bracketed expression in either (A6.4) or (A6.11). Differentiating (A6.12) with respect to f and setting to zero we get:

$$\text{Revenue maximising fee equals } R/2 \qquad (A6.13)$$

---

* This approximation is exact for flat fees and reasonable for asymmetrical performance fees. It is clearly wrong for symmetrical performance fees.

Substituting (A6.12) back into (A6.11) or (A6.4) we get maximum revenue to manager from product as:

$$\frac{K}{4}\left(\frac{R}{\sigma}\right)^2 = \frac{K S^2}{4} \tag{A6.14}$$

Because the fee equals half the gross return, this also equals the net, or after fee, profit to its investors from the product.

A.6.4 Combining overlays

Consider what happens when a group of n independent overlays are used for the same product. From (A6.4) and (A6.11), the maximum skill they can achieve is when overlay j has a weight proportional to its excess return divided by its variance. Assume the constant of proportionality is A. The return on the product is:

$$R = \sum_{j=1}^{n} w_j R_j = A \sum_{j=1}^{n} \frac{R_j^2}{\sigma_j^2} \tag{A6.15}$$

The standard deviation of the product is:

$$\sigma^2 = W\Omega W' = A^2 \sum_{j=1}^{n} \frac{R_j^2}{\sigma_j^2} \Rightarrow \sigma = A \sqrt{\sum_{j=1}^{n} \frac{R_j^2}{\sigma_j^2}} \tag{A6.16}$$

The maximum skill that can be achieved by combining the overlays is then (A6.15) divided by (A6.16), or:

$$S = \sqrt{\sum_{j=1}^{n} \frac{R_j^2}{\sigma_j^2}} \tag{A6.17}$$

The maximum revenue that can be achieved is proportional to S^2 from (A6.14). From (A6.17), S^2 is equal to:

$$S^2 = \sum_{j=1}^{n} S_j^2 \tag{A6.18}$$

From (A6.18) and (A6.14), it is clear that the maximum revenue possible from combining overlays in a product is equal to the maximum revenues achievable by marketing the overlays separately. The weighted average standard deviation of all these overlays is:

$$\sum_{j=1}^{n} w_j \sigma_j = A \sum_{j=1}^{n} \frac{R_j}{\sigma_j} = A \sum_{j=1}^{n} S_j \tag{A6.19}$$

Comparing (A6.19) and (A6.16) establishes that the weighted average standard deviation of the overlays exceeds the standard deviation of the combined overlays. $\hspace{2cm}$ (A6.20)

A.6.5   Information costs

Let us assume that there is a cost of information e, which is a fixed proportion of the return on the overlay. The cost of this information is either charged to the product or to the manager. In the first case, from (A6.12), the manager's revenue is:

$$\frac{f(R - e - f)K}{\sigma^2} \tag{A6.21}$$

Differentiating (A6.21) with respect to f and setting equal to zero gives a revenue-maximising fee of:

$$(R - e)/2 \tag{A6.22}$$

In the second case, the manager's revenue is:

$$\frac{f(R - f)K}{\sigma^2} - \frac{e(R - f)K}{\sigma^2} \tag{A6.23}$$

Subtracting (A6.21) from (A6.23) gives the difference in revenues between charging the manager and charging the product. It is equal to:

$$\frac{eK(2f - R)}{\sigma^2} \tag{A6.24}$$

Differentiating (A6.23) with respect to f and setting equal to zero gives a revenue-maximising fee of:

$$(R + e)/2 \tag{A6.25}$$

In either case, the maximum revenue net of information costs for the manager is:

$$\frac{K(R - e)^2}{4\sigma^2} \tag{A6.26}$$

So with optimal fee setting the manager is indifferent between the different methods of charging for information.

A.6.6   Relaxing the independence assumption

Consider an investor, with wealth normalised to one, who has a risk aversion of γ and a weight w in a portfolio P of both index funds and active overlays. He invests a small amount n in active overlay A. His variance becomes:

$$w^2\sigma_p^2 + 2wn\sigma_{ap} + n\sigma_a^2 \tag{A6.27}$$

The incremental certainty equivalent from investing in this way is therefore:

$$n(R_a - R_0) - \frac{\gamma}{2}\left(2wn\sigma_{ap} + n^2\sigma_a^2\right) \tag{A6.28}$$

Differentiating (A6.28) with respect to n and setting it equal to zero gives (A6.29), which defines the n that maximises certainty equivalent. It is easy to show, by substituting (A5.7) into (A6.29) and comparing with (A5.19), that the numerator of this fraction is α, or the component of the return on A that is independent of the return on P:

$$n_{\max} = \frac{(R_a - R_0 - \gamma w\sigma_{ap})}{\gamma\sigma_a^2} = \frac{\alpha_{ap}}{\gamma\sigma_a^2} \tag{A6.29}$$

Substituting back into (A6.28) gives an expression for maximum certainty equivalent:

$$CE_{max} = \frac{\alpha_{ap}^2}{2\gamma\sigma_a^2} \tag{A6.30}$$

When the return of A is independent of the return of P, (A6.29) reduces to (A5.23) and (A6.30) reduces to (A5.24). Thus the only component of the return of A that has economic significance for the investor is the independent component. For if α is zero, from (A6.29) and (A6.30), the optimal weight and maximum incremental certainty equivalent from investing in A are also both zero.

A.6.7   Self-investing

As his active overlay is independent of any other investments he may have, an investment professional is seeking a weight x as a fraction of his wealth, which maximises the risk-adjusted return he gets from it:

$$xR - x^2\sigma^2\frac{\gamma}{2} \tag{A6.31}$$

Differentiating (A6.31) with respect to x and setting equal to zero gives a maximum weight, which can be expressed in money terms by multiplying by his wealth W:

$$x_{max} = \frac{WR}{\gamma\sigma^2} \tag{A6.32}$$

Substituting (A6.32) back into (A6.31), he finds his risk-adjusted profit from investing on his own account to be:

$$\frac{WS^2}{2\gamma} \tag{A6.33}$$

A.6.8   Running a hedge fund

Equation (A6.14) gives the maximum incremental certainty equivalent for an investment professional from having outside investors alongside him in his active overlay. Adding this to (A6.33) gives an expression for his expected risk adjusted profit from investing in and running a hedge fund:

$$S^2\left(\frac{K}{4} + \frac{W}{2\gamma}\right) \tag{A6.34}$$

As pricing is optimal (A6.13), his profit from outside investors equals their profit from the product (A6.14). As profit from a product divided by return equals weight in the product, the total weight outside investors have in the product is proportional to (A6.14) divided by the return they receive, which is half the return the investment professional gets. The weight the investment professional has in the product is (A6.32). The ratio of the weight of the product he owns himself to the weight of the product owned by outside investors is therefore:

$$\frac{2W}{\gamma K} \tag{A6.35}$$

A.6.9   Hedge fund style

An investment professional who only invests in his own product has an incentive to include an overlay B, of equities financed by borrowing. Because his active overlay V is uncorrelated with B, his optimal weights in V and B as a proportion of his wealth are, from (A6.32), such that the product skill, or Sharpe ratio if it has a cash benchmark, is:

$$\frac{R_v}{\sigma_v^2 \gamma}, \quad \frac{R_b}{\sigma_b^2 \gamma} \Rightarrow$$

$$S_p = S_v \sqrt{1 + \left(\frac{S_b}{S_v}\right)^2} \tag{A6.36}$$

$$S_p \approx S_v \left(1 + \frac{1}{2}\left(\frac{S_b}{S_v}\right)^2\right)$$

(A6.36) is a special form of (A6.17), where there are two overlays combined with optimal weights. The correlation between a product with these optimal weights and B is ρ:

$$\rho^2 = \frac{(w_b \sigma_b)^2}{(w_b \sigma_b)^2 + (w_v \sigma_v)^2}$$

$$\rho = \frac{S_b}{\gamma \sqrt{\left(\frac{S_b^2}{\gamma^2} + \frac{S_v^2}{\gamma^2}\right)}} = \frac{1}{\sqrt{1 + \frac{S_v^2}{S_b^2}}} \tag{A6.37}$$

A.6.10   Trading limits

How the sub-overlays are managed is also important. If the organiser sets the right weights,* the profits from each trader's sub-overlay will be proportional to the square of the trader's skill and thus be a legitimate measure of his share of the value added. This is because the profit equals the return times the weight, which is proportional to:

$$R_i \frac{R_i}{\gamma \sigma_i^2} = \frac{S_i^2}{\gamma} \tag{A6.38}$$

Getting the wrong weights therefore means both that the product shows sub-optimal performance and that traders' pay will be distorted.

Consider two independent traders with standard deviations σ but with expected returns such that one is twice the other's expected return of R. With optimal limit setting, the more skilled trader will have limits equal to twice the limits of the less skilled trader:

$$w_1 = k\frac{R}{\sigma^2}, \quad w_2 = k\frac{2R}{\sigma^2} \tag{A6.39}$$

The squared Sharpe ratio of the product will be five times the squared Sharpe ratio of the less skilled trader:

$$S_p = \frac{w_1 R_1 + w_2 R_2}{\sqrt{w_1^2 \sigma^2 + w_2^2 \sigma^2}} = \sqrt{5\frac{R^2}{\sigma^2}} \tag{A6.40}$$

---

* As this is an overlay, the weights are essentially position limits.

The more skilled trader will be four times as profitable as the less skilled trader and receive a bonus four times as large:

$$w_1 R_1 = k \frac{R^2}{\sigma^2}, \qquad w_2 R_2 = 4k \frac{R^2}{\sigma^2} \qquad \text{(A6.41)}$$

But now consider what happens when the limits are transposed so that the less skilled trader has twice the limits of the more skilled trader:

$$w_2 = k \frac{R}{\sigma^2}, \qquad w_1 = k \frac{2R}{\sigma^2} \qquad \text{(A6.42)}$$

The squared Sharpe ratio of the product will now be four times the Sharpe ratio of the less skilled trader:

$$S_p = \frac{w_1 R_1 + w_2 R_2}{\sqrt{w_1^2 \sigma^2 + w_2^2 \sigma^2}} = \sqrt{4 \frac{R^2}{\sigma^2}} \qquad \text{(A6.43)}$$

But both traders will be equally profitable and will receive equal bonuses. Thus the misallocation results in the product attracting 80% of the assets it should attract while the more skilled trader gets half the bonus he should get and the less skilled trader gets twice the bonus he should get. The potential for this kind of conflict is particularly great when the less skilled trader also sets the limits.

A.6.11   Trader experience

Consider an investment professional whose skill and differential of skill are the following functions* of years experience, t:

$$S_v = \frac{R_v}{\sigma_v} = 1.8t^{\frac{1}{2}} - 0.3t - 1.5$$

$$\frac{dS_v}{dt} = 0.9t^{-\frac{1}{2}} - 0.3 \qquad \text{(A6.44)}$$

Setting the differential of skill with respect to time to zero tells us that with this skill function, skill peaks after nine years at 1.2. The formula for the average skill demonstrated between time a and time b can be derived by integrating the skill function with respect to time. Setting b equal to zero gives the career average:

$$\text{Average} = \frac{\int_b^a S_v dt}{\int_b^a dt} = \left| 1.2t^{\frac{3}{2}} - 0.15t^2 - 1.5t \right|_b^a / (a - b) \qquad \text{(A6.45)}$$

A.6.12   Tenure and investor confidence

A trader only has to have half his historical average skill for future periods for confidence in his skill to continue to grow. To see why this is so, let us calculate the proportion p of the average return m over a time period t that the return between t and $t + 1$ has to be so that

---

* The function is chosen both to have the right kind of shape and to be easy to manipulate. Real skill functions are likely to be much more complicated.

the confidence interval at t equals the confidence interval at $t + 1$. As t is large, let us assume that the historical standard deviation at time t is approximately equal to the historical standard deviation at time $t + 1$:

$$m\sqrt{t} \approx \frac{(mt + pm)\sqrt{t + 1}}{t + 1}$$

$$1 + \frac{p}{t} \approx \left(1 + \frac{1}{t}\right)^{\frac{1}{2}} \tag{A6.46}$$

$$p \approx \frac{1}{2}$$

ENDNOTES

1. Bernstein, p. 140.
2. W.A. Spurr and C.P. Bonini, *Statistical Analysis For Business Decisions*. Homewood, IL: Irwin, 1973.
3. Formulae for skewness, kurtosis and variances of same are taken from: J.Y. Campbell, A.W. Lo and A.C. McKinlay, *The Econometrics of Financial Markets*. Princeton: Princeton University Press, 1997.
4. A version of this expression appears in E.J. Elton, M.J. Gruber, M. Padberg, "Simple criteria for optimal portfolio selection", *Journal of Finance*, December 1976.
5. First put forward in W.F, Sharpe, "Capital Asset Prices: a theory of market equilibrium under conditions of risk;', *Journal of Finance*, vol. 19, 1964.
6. See, for example, Malkiel, pp. 231, 232.

Index